Merging Traffic

Merging Traffic

The Consolidation of the
International Automobile Industry

John A. C. Conybeare

ROWMAN & LITTLEFIELD PUBLISHERS, INC.
Lanham • Boulder • New York • Toronto • Oxford

ROWMAN & LITTLEFIELD PUBLISHERS, INC.

Published in the United States of America
by Rowman & Littlefield Publishers, Inc.
A wholly owned subsidiary of The Rowman & Littlefield Publishing Group
4501 Forbes Boulevard, Suite 200, Lanham, Maryland 20706
www.rowmanlittlefield.com

PO Box 317, Oxford OX2 9RU, United Kingdom

British Library Cataloguing in Publication Information Available

Library of Congress Cataloging-in-Publication Data
Conybeare, John A. C.
    Merging traffic : the consolidation of the international automobile industry / John
A. C. Conybeare.
        p.   cm.
Includes bibliographical references and index.
    ISBN 0-7425-2828-6 (Cloth : alk. paper) — ISBN 0-7425-2829-4 (Paper : alk.
paper)
    1. Automobile industry and trade—Mergers. 2. Globalization. I. Title.
    HD9710 .A2C65 2004
    338.8'3629222—dc21

                                                                                    2003007758

Printed in the United States of America

♾™ The paper used in this publication meets the minimum requirements of
American National Standard for Information Sciences—Permanence of Paper for
Printed Library Materials, ANSI/NISO Z39.48-1992.

For Daniel, Nancy, and Rachel

Contents

	List of Tables	ix
	Preface	xi
Chapter 1	Introduction: One Hundred Years of Consolidation	1
Chapter 2	Cost-Cutting Imperatives	23
Chapter 3	The Quest for New Products and New Markets	51
Chapter 4	The Lure of Market Power	79
Chapter 5	Sovereign States and Corporate Governance	107
Chapter 6	Conclusions: Economics, Politics, and Strategy	133
	Notes	143
	Bibliography	169
	Index	175
	About the Author	179

Tables

1.1   Major Motor Vehicle Producers in 1977 and 2001   18

1.2   Automobile Groups and Market Shares in 2001   19

2.1   Scale and Productivity in European Auto Plants in 1999   27

2.2   Percentage of Total Components Costs Outsourced   29

2.3   Labor Productivity in the International Auto Industry in 1989   43

2.4   Labor Productivity in the Auto Industries of the United States, Japan, and Germany in 1990   43

2.5   Labor Productivity at North American Assembly Plants in 2001   44

3.1   Income, Urbanization, and Auto Ownership   66

3.2   World Auto Sales (1,000s) in 1995 and 2000   66

5.1   Profitability of Auto Companies, 1991–1999   130

Preface

The origins of this book are twofold. I have spent the past few decades exploring various aspects of the politics of international economic relations, including interstate trade wars, domestic lobbying over trade issues, and prescriptive rules for regulating international externalities, such as environmental spillovers across national boundaries. These projects have, reinforced by the high level of general and scholarly interest in multinational corporations during recent decades, inevitably led me into areas of international industrial organization. The political importance of the automobile industry to so many countries makes the topic fertile ground for cross-disciplinary exploration. The relevance of the auto industry to my core scholarly interests was reinforced by a more personal interest in cars and decades of steadily consuming the motoring magazines of the countries in which I have lived, culminating in what I suppose to be a classic middle-aged form of acting out, the purchase of a well-used Porsche 911.

The more immediate impetus to examining the consolidation of the auto industry during the past few decades was a feeling of puzzlement from reading the popular accounts of auto mergers in business news sources, including such magazines as *BusinessWeek*, *The Economist*, and the *Wall Street Journal*. Mergers, acquisitions, and alliances were almost invariably hailed, at least initially, as examples of brilliant corporate strategy carried out by visionary leaders. Yet the reasons offered by business journalists, industry consultants, and even some academic observers were curiously unsatisfying. Some, such as the assertion that the possession of cash reserves leads to acquisitions, were obviously non sequiturs. Some, such as the argument that global excess capacity necessitated mergers, seem to have embedded in them many implicit assumptions. Others, such as the claim that auto mergers were being driven by the need to acquire economies of scale, could be found to be empirically doubtful after only a very little cursory research. Hence, my aim has been to set out, categorize, and examine the various causal factors offered as reasons for industrial concentration in the industry.

The methods used here have been primarily a careful reading of secondary sources, data collections, consultants' reports, case studies, and the contemporary automotive and financial press. I make no claim to be employing original statistical tests or modeling techniques, though I do hope I have assembled some useful and interesting data to buttress some of the main arguments. This is primarily a wide-ranging qualitative study of the politics, economics, and corporate strategy of an industry.

I am a political scientist by training, though I do have some modest competence in microeconomics and international trade. My only claim to intellectual comparative advantage with respect to this topic is a long immersion in the various debates of that nebulous field called "international political economy" and a moderate faith that researchers new to a particular subfield might sometimes attain insights that those more deeply steeped in it may not. It is also my belief that corporate expansion is often a very explicitly political form of behavior, even if only in the sense that it might be motivated by reasons inconsistent with the conventionally assumed goal of profit maximization. Finally, this is, after all, an age in which everyone has an opinion on the merits or otherwise of "globalization." In addition to providing an instructive example of multinational corporate consolidation, an examination of the auto industry offers insights into some of the larger issues of international political economy and particularly the contentious debates over the political, social, and economic effects of globalization.

I would particularly like to thank Glenn Mercer of McKinsey & Company for suggestions on the entire manuscript and for supplying me with information unobtainable elsewhere. Graeme Maxton of Autopolis offered helpful comments on the first chapter and several valuable analytic comments.

CHAPTER ONE

Introduction:
One Hundred Years of Consolidation

A specter haunts the world's auto industry: the specter of a rapidly declining number of firms. In the early decades of the twentieth century, there were nearly 200 car manufacturers in Britain, almost 100 in the United States, several dozen in France, and about ten in Germany. Five individual firms—Toyota, Volkswagen (VW), General Motors (GM), Ford, and PSA (Peugeot-Citroën)—now account for more than 50 percent of automobile production in this global oligopoly market.[1] The six largest groups or alliances of auto producers account for more than 80 percent of global production. For the first time in modern history, we may observe the global consolidation of a major world industry that is of great political and economic importance to many countries. Auto executives offer consolidation as a tactic of survival and profit, governments try to assess the effects on their multiplicity of goals, many trade unions are vehemently opposed to what they see as a threat to their bargaining power, and the consumer wonders why the interior of his new Jaguar looks like that of a Ford Taurus.

The wave of auto mergers during the past several decades has affected the industrial structures and public policies of the major economic powers (the Daimler-Chrysler merger and the Renault-Nissan alliance), smaller developed countries (the alliance of GM and Fiat), newly industrializing countries (the sale of Daewoo to GM), and even the still-poor developing countries (India's planned sale of its national auto firm, Maruti). Stakes in the outcomes are high. Governments want economic growth, employment, tax revenue, and sometimes competitive markets; they almost always aspire, if at all

1

possible, to steer the potential profits from this global industry to their own producers. Their reactions to the merger trend range from determined protection of their national brands to meekly offering inducements to foreign auto firms to save their ailing companies from oblivion. Firms want higher profits, sales, and market shares, the latter perhaps leading managers to attempt to maximize the absolute or relative size of their firms. Voters want jobs and cars that are cheap, fashionable, reliable, and useful. This work is an attempt to explain why rapid industrial concentration has occurred. Explaining this development will also shed light on the prescriptive question asked by government regulators, consumers, and auto company shareholders: Is industrial concentration desirable and, if so, desirable for whom?

Studying the international auto industry is a multidisciplinary task. It spans the fields of political science (politics being the art of getting people to do things they would not otherwise do), economics (efficiency in the production and allocation of resources), and corporate strategy (how firms organize themselves for competitive success). The explanations for the consolidation of this major global industry range across all three fields. What will make this effort different from conventional economic studies of an industry or a business school case study of corporate strategy is that it will draw from a larger pool of social science theories. The usual explanations for mergers, acquisitions, and alliances assume profit maximization to be the goal of managerial behavior. These are explanations that focus on, for example, economies of scale as a reason for firms to combine. The analysis will also consider less conventional explanations, including external political intervention and aspects of corporate governance. Some part of the consolidation of the auto industry might be explained as something more akin to empire building, either for nonrational reasons (an "objectless disposition to expand," as Schumpeter put it in his classic study of imperialism)[2] or because expansion serves private interests (such as power, prestige, and salary) at the expense of the corporation as a whole.

Why Focus on the Auto Industry?

The most obvious reasons are that it is large, global, and present in a wide range of upper-, middle-, and low-income countries. It is still, despite the rhetoric we hear about a shift to services in "postindustrial" economies, one of the world's largest single industries. Production is distributed widely around the globe. Automobiles constitute the largest part of motor vehicle production. In 2001, the Asia–Oceania area produced 17.9 million vehicles (74.9 percent of which, or 13.4 million units, were automobiles); the European Union (EU), 17.2 million vehicles (86.6 percent, or 14.9 million, being cars); the North American Free Trade Area (United States, Canada, and Mexico), 15.8 million (7.4 million autos, 46.8 percent of the total); eastern Europe, 2.9 million (2.5 million cars); and Africa, 0.4 million (0.3 million cars).[3]

The auto industry exemplifies many of the debates that have swirled around the topic of multinational corporations for the decades since the 1960s, when French journalist Jacques Servan-Schreiber painted a bleak picture for Europeans of American multinationals taking over Europe, and a Harvard Business School professor, Raymond Vernon, could title his book *Sovereignty at Bay* and explain how states were increasingly unable to regulate these footloose corporate entities.[4] Mercifully, the debate has come a long way since these simple characterizations depicting multinationals as modern Jurassic monsters trampling on defenseless nations.[5] Yet many of the themes remain and are constantly being revived and repackaged for popular consumption, albeit with new labels such as "globalization" and, most recently, the transnational and postindustrial "empire."[6] The antiglobalization movement sees auto companies as prime examples of entities that exploit workers in both the home and host countries (by moving or threatening to move production overseas and by paying lower wages in the host than in the home country), damage the global environment by moving to locales with more lenient pollution rules, and undermine democracy and violate national sovereignty. Beyond these views of multinationals as transnational sovereignties challenging the power of nation-states, there also remain the traditional political and ideological views of these corporations. Marxists still see international auto companies as means by which the rich capitalist core dominates and exploits the periphery. Neomercantilists, who regard themselves as political "realists," view auto companies as pawns in the interstate game of power politics.[7] Advocates of free markets still regard them as a benign phenomenon by which capital moves around the world seeking the highest rate of return and, in the process, raising aggregate world income, though not necessarily the income of every country in the world.

Working downward from these paradigmatic generalities, there are many more concrete issues that can be examined. The major topics of analysis with respect to multinational corporations may be illustrated with reference to the auto industry: portfolio versus direct investment, the desirability (or otherwise) of multinational investment from the perspective of the home and host countries, the regulation by governments of foreign investment, and firm-level questions about the optimal strategy and structure for the corporation. Consolidation has proceeded by way of both portfolio investment (noncontrolling share ownership, such as GM's purchase of 20 percent of Fiat) and direct investment (a controlling interest, such as Ford's buyout of Volvo). The global expansion of the auto industry invariably attracts the attention of governments that purport to be seeking to maximize the national interest, whether it is the British government offering inducements for BMW to maintain production at Rover's British factories in 1999 or the Chinese government limiting the ability of foreign companies to buy up or crowd out their own infant auto industry once China joins the World Trade Organization (WTO). The industry itself debates the appropriate global strategy. Should a firm expand by way of merger (Daimler and Chrysler), acquisition (Ford's purchase of Land Rover), or alliances (mutual minority equity holdings between GM and Fiat)? These issues will all arise in the course of examining the reasons for global consolidation in this industry.

Why Care about Auto Mergers?

Industrial concentration entails a reduction in the number of firms possessing a large share of the world market. The auto industry is extraordinarily large and may account for up to 7 percent of the national incomes of the developed industrial countries. Contrary to popular myth, the industry is not shrinking, and in the United States it contributed the same proportion to national income in 2000 as it did in 1987.[8] The size of the industry, both globally and in proportion to the individual economies of even the largest industrial nations, gives it the capacity to affect markets for labor and capital, governments' macroeconomic and industrial goals, consumer welfare, and a nation's international position or comparative advantage in trade. Increasing concentration makes these issues even more important, as it enhances the ability of both the oligopolistic market and individual firms, domestic and foreign, to have a significant independent influence on the creation, distribution, and growth of a nation's wealth. The combination of providing a significant proportion of national income and having this share being accounted for by a decreasing number of firms makes for a politically potent mix.

Examples are numerous. BMW's purchase and later abandonment of Rover, the remains of Britain's once-proud auto giant and patronizingly referred to by BMW managers as "the English patient," had the potential to bring down cabinet ministers. Collusive market restraints by European automakers recently reached crisis dimensions in the European Union, forcing a major and politically divisive policy decision to rescind the auto industry's partial exemption from competition rules (the so-called Block Exemption). American state governments actively compete to attract foreign auto plants.

Governor Bob Taft of Ohio visited South Korea in 2001 in an unsuccessful attempt to persuade Hyundai to build its first U.S. assembly plant in the state, a prize that ultimately went to Alabama.[9] The government of South Korea spent several years desperately trying to balance its desire to find a buyer for bankrupt Daewoo with the hostility of trade unions to a foreign takeover. The threats of Japanese car manufacturers to remove production from Britain, absent a move by Britain to join the EU currency (the euro), has the power to influence that debate far more than most other industries.

Forms of Consolidation

A merger is normally an arrangement between the managements of two or more firms in which the assets of all firms are combined under the name of one firm (and the others cease to exist) or a new firm is created and all the constituent firms cease to exist. The merger between Daimler and Chrysler, for example, created a new corporation, Daimler-Chrysler. An acquisition entails purchasing all or part of another firm, either by arrangement with the management of the target firm or by making an offer to buy directly to the shareholders. When BMW divested itself of Rover, it sold part of the company, Land Rover, to Ford. Falling short of acquisition would be the purchase of a large enough portion of the target firm's share capital to control the management (such as Renault controlling Nissan or Ford controlling Mazda). Ownership of more than one-third of the equity in a corporation normally yields enough control to choose the senior management and direct corporate policy.

There are many other forms of corporate cooperation or alliance short of merger and acquisition. Firms may engage in limited forms of cooperation for specific purposes. In July 2001, for example, Peugeot (PSA) and Toyota announced plans to jointly build a small-car platform. Companies may exchange noncontrolling share ownership, as have GM and Fiat. GM is well known to favor alliances over acquisitions. GM's chief executive officer (CEO) Rick Wagoner, calls alliances a "faster and more capital efficient way to grow."[10] An alliance requires less financial commitment but allows less control over the partner and often leads to a full takeover or merger. GM moved to acquire 100 percent ownership over Saab after ten years of continuing losses following the purchase of 50 percent of Saab's equity.

All these variations share one feature: relinquishing autonomy or control in exchange for resources (such as cash reserves, products, technology, or an established presence in particular markets) that the firm believes would be more costly to acquire in the absence of collaboration. There must be some value added from the arrangement, and the sum of the parts less the transaction costs of consolidation must be worth more than the parts separately.[11] Throughout this book, I will use the term "merger" loosely to refer to all forms of collaboration, though at many points it will be necessary to clarify the nature the association.

The U.S. economy has experienced well-known waves of mergers, from the horizontal monopolization mergers of the early 1900s to the conglomerate mergers of the 1960s and the hostile takeovers of large firms in the 1980s.[12] What made the 1990s distinctive was the exponential increase in the number and value of cross-border mergers and acquisitions, rising in value during the last five years of the decade from $200 billion to $800 billion.[13] Paradoxically, about half these mergers destroy rather than enhance shareholder value.[14] This raises the obvious question of why so many mergers are occurring when they fail, roughly half the time, to add value to the firms engaging in the merger. The answer lies in examining the reasons for the mergers in the first place. In the case of the auto industry, it will be argued that some of the reasons offered for mergers do not bear up well to close scrutiny. If mergers fail to add value to the firms, it may be for reasons related to incentives that have little to do with shareholder value, being deep-seated psychological drives and interests that are not consistent with the well-being of the corporation.

Concentration in National Auto Markets

The history of the world auto industry, from its origins in the late nineteenth century, has been told in many places.[15] For present purposes, the following discussion is limited to setting out the seemingly inexorable process of consolidation in an industry that had more than 300 firms at the beginning of the twentieth century and now has fewer than a dozen firms of global importance.

Most firms remained securely planted within their domestic markets until after World War II, with a few exceptions. British automakers took advantage of their preferential access to the Commonwealth, following the Ottawa Conference of 1932, to become the dominant suppliers to the small markets of Australia, New Zealand, and South Africa. Ford began assembling Model Ts in Britain in 1909 and started local production in 1911, with a capacity of 15,000 vehicles per year. Ford and GM both rapidly expanded European production facilities during the 1920s and operations elsewhere in the world (such as Australia) that assembled autos from knocked-down kits. By 1938, production or assembly outside the United States accounted for 23.2 and 19.6

percent of the total outputs of Ford and GM, respectively.[16] Ford's biggest foreign operations were in Britain, while GM focused on Germany, producing under the Opel name. High levels of tariff protection, particularly during the interwar period of the Depression, generated most of this activity by making the importation of fully assembled vehicles prohibitively expensive.

After 1945, national markets consolidated rapidly. In the United States, the auto industry became one of the most concentrated sectors of the economy. Between 1909 and 1920, 169 firms entered the industry. Most failed quickly, though in 1918 there were still eighty-eight vehicle producers.[17] By the 1960s, the number of large U.S. producers had been reduced to three. Smaller producers, such as Packard, Studebaker, and (in the 1980s) American Motors, disappeared. Third-ranked Chrysler struggled to survive by selling off its foreign assets and ultimately seeking a government loan of $1.5 billion in 1980. Since 1950, GM's share of the U.S. market has fluctuated between 40 and 50 percent and Ford's share between 20 and 30 percent.

The number of British auto companies rose from around fifty in 1900 to a peak of almost 200 in 1913, falling steadily thereafter. At the end of World War II, the market still sustained over thirty different companies. Entropy quickly set in, and by 1968, the sector had collapsed into one ailing, government-subsidized, multibrand conglomerate: British Leyland. This holding company comprised some of the greatest names in British motoring history, including Austin, Morris, Wollesley, Riley, Triumph, Rover, MG, and Jaguar. Suffering poor labor relations, indifferent management, low productivity, underinvestment, and an obsolescent capital stock, British Leyland continued the decline of its constituent parts. By 1975, it was unable to compete in the larger market of the European Community following British entry in 1973 and was once again financially bailed out and effectively nationalized by the Labor government as a result of a report by the Ryder Commission.[18] During the period of many privatizations initiated by the Conservative Thatcher government, British Leyland was renamed the Rover Corporation in 1986 and sold to British Aerospace in 1988, minus the few assets that were attractive acquisitions to foreign auto companies. Jaguar was privatized in 1984 and bought by Ford in 1989. Honda bought 20 percent of Rover in 1990, and BMW bought the British Aerospace share in 1994. During its fourteen years of government ownership, British Leyland had absorbed a further $5.4 billion in taxpayers' funds.[19]

This left a small number of specialist producers, some of which also were absorbed by foreign firms (such as Aston Martin to Ford and Lotus to the Malaysian company Proton); a few independent firms thriving in tiny niche markets (such as Morgan, a maker of wood-framed sports cars that retain their 1930s styling); and a few exotic sports car makers living at the margins of profitability, surviving only by making extensive use of mass-produced components (such as TVR, Ginetta, and Marcos). High-volume auto production is vanishing from the British economy. Ford and GM closed their largest British auto plants at Dagenham and Luton, respectively, early in 2002. Nissan and Peugeot are scaling back or threatening to close their respective plants at Sunderland (Nissan) and Ryton (Peugeot), partly because of the high value of the British pound with respect to the euro.[20]

The number of German volume producers has never been large, mostly because of the cartelistic industrial structure of Germany and the prevalence of bank financing that discriminates against small firms.[21] In 1931, Auto Union was formed from the amalgamation of DKW (a pioneer in the development of front-wheel-drive technology), Audi, Wanderer, and Horch. Daimler purchased Auto Union in 1958, selling the brand name and a new factory to VW in 1964. Auto Union purchased NSU in 1969, providing VW with water-cooled technology for its next generation of autos. VW occasionally collaborates with Porsche.[22] A few larger conglomerate firms with a small presence in the auto market (such as Messerschmidt) gave up and focused on their core business. The number of large German manufacturers had shrunk to two by the 1970s: Daimler and Volkswagen. Volkswagen's largest shareholder, the state of Lower Saxony, with 18.9 percent of its shares, both protects the company from takeover and ensures its lower profitability as an employment and welfare agency for the state. German law (currently being questioned as a violation of rules guaranteeing the free movement of capital within the European Union) limits the number of votes that any shareholder may possess to 20 percent of the total, effectively making sure that Lower Saxony cannot be outvoted by, for example, another firm attempting to take over Volkswagen.[23] Daimler's largest shareholders, the Deutsche Bank (holding a 12 percent equity share) and the government-owned Kuwaiti Investment Authority (7 percent), may provide a similar function, protecting the company from a hostile takeover.

BMW has remained a successful medium-size producer of over one million vehicles per year, more profitable than most, with a 4.9 percent net profit margin in 2001 but vulnerable to takeover. In recent years, both Ford and VW have been reported as exploring the possibility of buying BMW.[24] It is protected primarily by the large proportion of its shares (48.1 percent) owned by the Quandt family.[25] Porsche (50 percent owned by the Porsche and Piëch families) survives on an annual production of about 50,000 niche-market sports cars, constantly vulnerable to the discretionary incomes and tastes of that market. Yet from near bankruptcy in the early 1990s, it has maintained itself as one of the world's most consistently profitable producers (selling its vehicles at 45 percent over cost), belying the notion that size is necessary for success.[26]

Volume automobile production began in France in 1898, the United States following as the next entrant in 1900. As in other auto-producing nations, the beginnings of the industry spawned a number of manufacturers, including such long-forgotten names as Darracq, Berliet, De Dion, and Delahaye. The three firms that had dominated the French market since the 1920s have been reduced to two, Renault and Peugeot-Citroën (PSA). Up to the 1990s, they were vigorously protected from foreign competition by the French government. Each had swallowed the remains of smaller French producers, PSA acquiring the brands Talbot, Simca, and Panhard, and Renault taking Alpine and Matra. Like BMW, PSA is very much a family firm. The Peugeot family held 37.44 percent of the voting rights in the company in 2002 and plans to increase its ownership to over 50 percent.[27]

Fiat was an early market entrant, founded in 1895 by the grandfather of the current chairman, Giovanni Agnelli. Fiat eventually became a vast conglomerate, autos being its most publicly visible manufacturing activity and constituting about 42 percent of the Fiat group's revenue in 2002. It was for many years Europe's largest auto company. A number of postwar Italian firms, including such illustrious names as Ferrari, Maserati, and Lancia and some minor names such as Abarth, Autobianchi, and Innocenti, all had become part of Fiat Auto by the end of the 1970s. The largest acquisition was Alfa Romeo, purchased in 1987 for $1 billion (and $1 billion debt assumption) from the Agency for Industrial Reconstruction (IRI), a state-owned corporation that had taken over Alfa Romeo in 1933. The IRI had been about to sell the automaker to Ford when Fiat stepped in and, with encouragement from the Italian government, bought Alfa Romeo with a lower bid. Sports car maker Lamborghini survived longer since the company also made farm machinery and could subsidize the losses on automaking until it too went to Volkswagen. By the end of the century, Fiat itself was struggling to survive, and the holding company seriously (but very reluctantly) considered leaving the auto business.

Japan escaped this pattern of diversity followed by concentration because the industry was already highly oligopolistic and government-managed from the beginning, a general characteristic of the cartelistic Japanese industrial structure. In 1931, Japanese auto production was less than 500 units, while Ford and GM assembled 30,000 vehicles for the Japanese market. The Auto Manufacturing Law of 1936 excluded all foreign manufacturers, setting the conditions for an oligopoly market of domestic producers. As in Germany, institutional and political factors favoring industrial concentration—primarily banking and industrial cartels approved by governments—made for an absence of the many small firms seen in Britain and in early twentieth-century America. The Japanese government preferred to have a concentrated auto sector and in the early 1950s even encouraged further consolidation in the belief that each manufacturer should specialize in a certain size of vehicle, a move successfully resisted by Japanese auto companies.[28] For several decades following World War II, both European and Japanese governments encouraged industrial consolidation in the belief that large firm size was a requisite for global competitive success. However, Japanese firms are said to be averse to expanding through acquisition because they would normally wish to replace the existing management with their own, a move that would tend to reduce the gain from paying the going concern value for an existing enterprise,[29] hence a preference for expansion through internal growth. A rare exception to the lack of acquisitions in Japan was Toyota's purchase of 51 percent of the small Daihatsu company, primarily a maker of commercial vehicles.

In the early 1950s, Nissan was the largest Japanese producer, followed by Toyota and Honda. By the 1970s, Toyota had displaced Nissan, with Honda, Mazda and Mitsubishi battling for third place. Tie-ups with foreign companies were slow in coming. Ford turned down Toyota's offer of an alliance in 1950.[30] Japanese auto firms have not been major players in the international takeover scramble of the 1990s. This is partly for the domestic reasons cited earlier, partly because some (such as Nissan) were themselves weak and had not the resources for international investment, and partly because the strong Japanese companies (notably Toyota and Honda) prefer to limit themselves to joint ventures for specific projects. Honda had since the 1970s sold both engines and knocked-down kits to British Leyland and ultimately did take a small equity interest in Rover until the latter was purchased by BMW in 1994. In the 1980s, Toyota began selling kits to GM to be assembled at a GM plant in Fremont, California. In July 2001, Toyota and PSA announced plans for a 50/50 joint venture in eastern Europe with an annual production of 300,000 small cars. When Japanese auto firms do take an equity interest in foreign companies, it is normally a result of an already established strong relationship, such as Honda and Rover, and Nissan's announcement in March 2002 that it is purchasing a 13.5 percent interest in its French partner, Renault.

A similar industrial culture exists in South Korea, where three large firms (Hyundai, Daewoo, and Samsung) briefly flourished in the 1980s and 1990s before being absorbed by larger foreign firms. Daewoo Motor had originally been established in 1970 as a 50/50 joint venture between GM and the Daewoo Group, with GM relinquishing its share in 1972 for $170 million. South Korea seems to be an advanced case of what may become more common as the trade and investment rules of the WTO spread to the developing countries of the world. A labor-abundant country lacking comparative advantage in producing autos, Korea used protection from imports to force feed the industry. As developing countries succumb to pressure to remove protection, these auto companies become vulnerable and may come to rely on foreign partners. As Korea makes the transition to capital abundance, if it has not already done so, it will have a greater ability to sustain an efficient auto industry.

Outside the developed world and the newly industrialized countries such as Korea, auto companies have been mostly creatures of state enterprise, heavily subsidized and protected. The Indian market, for example, has been dominated by Hindustan and Maruti. Global free trade might well eliminate these companies, at least those not closely allied with global firms. The Chinese auto industry has developed through joint ventures between state producers and foreign partners. Chinese membership of WTO provides a special transition period for the auto industry, as most of these ventures are unlikely to be viable under free trade. Whatever effort foreign producers are making to ally with domestic Chinese auto firms is premised on the assumption that the Chinese government will continue to protect its domestic market despite WTO rules that encourage developing-country members to open up their markets to competition.

Consolidation and Globalization

The process of international consolidation is clearly a phenomenon of the last few decades of the twentieth century. There had been a few international acquisitions during the interwar period. GM acquired the British company Vauxhall in 1925 and Germany's Opel in 1929, while Ford preferred to establish its own manufacturing plants outside the United States. Ford had assembly plants for knocked-down kits in Europe prior to 1914 and in Japan in 1925.[31] There was a considerable amount of direct foreign investment in the auto industry during the interwar period, but not through mergers, acquisitions, or alliances. Auto companies established foreign manufacturing or assembly plants primarily to jump over high tariff walls and to comply with the insistence of many governments on high levels of local production content in vehicles sold in that country.[32]

It was not until the 1960s that international mergers became common. Parts of the declining British auto industry were sold off to foreign companies.

Chrysler, for example, acquired one-third of Rootes in 1964 and a majority stake in 1967, when a Labor government faced the prospect of nationalizing, selling, or letting Rootes go bankrupt. Chrysler had also bought a minority share of the French car maker Simca in 1958 and acquired full control after buying Fiat's share of Simca in 1963.[33] Fiat and Citroën briefly collaborated from 1970 to 1973, Fiat buying a stake in Citroën with a view to eventual takeover. The latter move was vetoed by the French government, and Fiat's share sold back to the Michelin family, one of Citroën's larger shareholders.[34] Renault had acquired 46 percent of American Motors by 1980 for $500 million but sold it to Chrysler in 1987 and much later purchased a controlling interest in the large but debt-laden Nissan in 1999 for $5.4 billion and acquired Samsung in 2000. Chrysler acquired 15 percent of Mitsubishi in 1973 after its plan to acquire 35 percent was stymied both by its own financial weakness and by the opposition of the Japanese government.[35] The terms of its financial rescue by the U.S. government in the early 1980s (the Loan Guarantee Act) later forced Chrysler to sell its stake in Mitsubishi.[36]

By the 1980s, consolidation was accelerating and becoming almost exclusively international. Ford and GM both embarked on ambitious global expansion plans, beginning during the late 1970s. In 1971, Henry Ford II visited Japan in an unsuccessful attempt to persuade Japanese Prime Minister Sato and Mazda executives to allow Ford to buy 20 percent of Mazda, and Ford had to settle for technical cooperation,[37] though it eventually gained control of Mazda through an equity share that rose from 25 percent in 1979 to 33.4 percent by 1996.[38] Ford acquired several small but well-known European companies, notably Jaguar for $2.6 billion in 1989 and Volvo's passenger car division for $6.5 billion in 1999.

GM bought 50 percent of Saab in 1989 and a full 100 percent in 2000. During the 1990s, GM bought interests in the Japanese companies Isuzu (34 percent in 1971), Suzuki, and Subaru (the last mentioned in 2000). Also in 2000, GM negotiated a cross-shareholding alliance with Fiat (20 percent of Fiat for 5 percent of GM). Most recently, GM agreed to buy Daewoo's Korean assets over the long-standing and strenuous objections of Daewoo's militant trade unions, and Daewoo vehicles will now be sold under the GM badge. Ford's bid of $7 billion for Daewoo had been accepted in 1999, but Ford subsequently withdrew its bid when the extent of Daewoo's $17 billion debt became clear. In April 2002, GM agreed to pay $257 million for 67 percent of a new corporation, GM-Daewoo Auto and Technology Company. GM's partner Suzuki plans to take a 15 percent interest (from GM's share), and Daewoo's creditors are to contribute 33 percent, or $197 million, of the new company's capital. GM's partners, Fiat and Shanghai Automotive Industry Corporation, may also purchase interests in Daewoo.[39] The new firm will include Daewoo's two modern plants in Korea but not necessarily its older plant at Pupyong, where most of the labor opposition to the merger had originated. Also included would be a plant in Vietnam and nine foreign sales units, excluding Daewoo's U.S. marketing and sales operations. One factor that delayed the acquisition had been GM's refusal to guarantee the jobs of 10,000 assembly-line workers.[40]

In addition to the Daewoo sale, the past decade has produced several other highly politicized international cases, all extensively covered by the media and all involving the fate of major national producers. In 1994, BMW purchased Rover (the successor to British Leyland) for $1.2 billion from British Aerospace. Honda, which had been selling engines to Rover for over a decade, had offered to raise its minority stake to 47.5 percent but was unwilling to take all of Rover. By 2000, BMW had poured over $3.4 billion into Rover, yet the latter still lost $1.2 billion in 1999, and in April 2000, BMW sold Rover to the British Phoenix consortium for the nominal sum of $15, though it kept the Mini name and sold Land Rover to Ford for $3 billion. Since BMW also agreed to lend Phoenix over $700 million, to be repaid if and when Phoenix sold the now renamed MG Rover Group, BMW ended up actually paying Phoenix to take Rover off its hands.[41] Bitter accusations of bad faith were directed at BMW from both British trade unions and government ministers, since the sale entailed the near closure of a large car plant at Longbridge in the depressed English Midlands. The British minister of transportation was especially incensed because he had offered BMW a subsidy to keep production of a new Rover model at Longbridge.[42]

Central to its strategy of moving away from air-cooled-engine technology, VW developed the new Golf model in the early 1970s. It invested directly in U.S. production with a plant in Westmoreland, Pennsylvania, that began production in 1978, renaming the car the Rabbit for the U.S. market. Volkswagen stopped U.S. production 1989 after nearly disastrous quality control problems and lack of cost competitiveness in the face of Japanese competition.[43] North American production was relocated to Mexico, and Volkswagen refocused its attention on Europe, buying Spanish producer SEAT in 1986 and Czech manufacturer Skoda in 1990.

Perhaps influenced by Volkswagen's failure at further penetrating of the U.S. mass market by moving from exporting to unilateral direct investment without a local partner, Daimler merged with Chrysler in 1998, a deal worth $40.5 billion. Daimler-Chrysler then purchased interests in Mitsubishi[44] and Hyundai in 2000. Mounting losses at Chrysler accelerated Daimler's assertion of control over the merged entity and, by the end of

2000, the replacement of the American CEO with a Mercedes executive. The rapid deterioration of Daimler-Chrysler's financial fortunes in 1999 and 2000 has stimulated some spirited debate over both the reasons for the merger and the distribution of benefits therefrom. Some Daimler-Chrysler shareholders have sued, and the tenure of CEO Jürgen Schrempp has appeared to be in jeopardy, though the company's largest shareholders, the Kuwaiti Investment Bank and the Deutsche Bank, continued (during 2001 and 2002) to publicly express confidence in Daimler-Chrysler's global strategy. It was indicative of the tremulous state of Daimler-Chrysler that early in 2001 it was reported to be consulting with Deutsche Bank on preparing to defend itself against a takeover by Toyota.[45]

The most recent crisis has been the case of Fiat, a saga that increasingly resembles the long and painful demise of British Leyland, both firms being plagued with poor-quality products that fewer and fewer motorists wished to buy, industrial relations problems that hampered restructuring, and national governments that pressed them to take on the role of public welfare agencies. One of the first automakers in the world and long a major European producer and exporter, Fiat Auto has progressively lost its market share, dogged by its confinement to the subcompact market (and inability to compete with Japanese producers in that segment once protection was removed from its core domestic Italian market in the early 1990s), adherence to an outdated "world car" product strategy, a reputation for inferior-quality products, technological obsolescence, excessive diversity of platforms (fifteen in 2002), dependence on the Italian market, and pressure from the Italian government to serve various political objectives, including the absorption of smaller, failing Italian auto companies and avoiding layoffs at Fiat Auto. Its European market share fell from 14 percent in 1990 to 7 percent in 2002.

The fate of Fiat is partly dependent on the preferences of the Agnelli family, which owns 30.5 percent of Fiat. GM acquired 20 percent of Fiat's auto business and an option to buy the remainder should the Agnelli family consent, though Fiat's chairman (a senior member of the Agnelli family) has publicly long opposed Fiat's exercising this option to sell. The alliance was completed by Fiat buying 5.1 percent of GM shares. The Libyan Arab Foreign Investment Company has joined GM as shareholder in Fiat, having purchased 2 percent in March 2002.[46] Its agreement with Fiat includes a provision allowing GM to purchase the remaining Fiat shares over a five-year period starting in 2004. GM was apparently trying to forestall a Daimler-Chrysler bid for Fiat, the latter following failed talks between BMW and Fiat. Technically, Fiat acquired a "put" option to force GM to buy the rest of Fiat starting in 2004 as long as there had been no changes in the control of Fiat Auto. Fiat's deteriorating financial condition and asset sales led many financial analysts to suggest that Fiat would be increasingly likely to exercise this option regardless of the desire of the Agnelli family to remain in the auto business. Yet it is indicative of Fiat's dedication to holding on to Fiat Auto that in 2002 it sold 34 percent of Ferrari (which itself owns 100 percent of Maserati), one of the few profitable areas of its automotive activity, to a consortium led by the Italian investment bank Mediobanca.[47]

At the beginning of 2003, Fiat Auto was staking its survival on bank loans of nearly $3 billion, management changes, the sale of its stake in GM (to Merrill Lynch) and divestments of some auto manufacturing (Ferrari), auto components subsidiaries (Magneti Marelli, Fiat's major parts supplier), and other auto-related businesses (Fiat's consumer financing arm, Fidis). The Fiat group reported losses of $4.6 billion for 2002, of which $1.5 billion was attributed to Fiat Auto. Some creditors and investors (notably Mediobanco) were reportedly seeking to push Fiat into bankruptcy so as to be able to acquire its remaining profitable assets. The Italian government, eager to offer aid to Fiat, is blocked by EU subsidy rules, though it may invest state funds as long as it is on the same terms as private investors.[48] Early in December 2002, Fiat began the process of shedding one-fifth of its workforce by laying off 5,600 workers, resulting in strikes and demonstrations at Fiat sites around Italy. Several other rescue plans were being discussed at the end of 2002 and early in 2003. Under a plan presented to the Fiat board in December 2002, Alfa Romeo would be moved to the Ferrari-Maserati group and a significant stake in this group sold to Volkswagen.[49] With the Ferrari–Maserati–Alfa Romeo group sold to a creditor (Mediobanca) and Volkswagen, Fiat would be left with the least profitable parts of Fiat's auto business. An alternative was offered by Italian financial entrepreneur Roberto Colaninno: He would arrange $8 billion of new capital, release GM from its purchase obligations, and replace the Agnelli family as Fiat's principal shareholder.[50]

GM wrote down its $2.4 billion investment in Fiat to $220 million in 2002 and is reportedly looking for ways to escape from its obligation to purchase the rest, though it may well wish to continue lesser forms of collaboration in components purchasing, power trains, and small-car engineering. Suggestions that Fiat might merge with GM's Opel subsidiary evoked horrified denials from Opel executives, already chafing under directives to cooperate with Fiat on joint auto projects. A government stake in Fiat might constitute a change in control sufficient to release GM from its purchase obligations. If Alfa Romeo is separated from Fiat and sold off to the Mediobanca/Volkswagen group, GM would be released from its obligation to buy the rest of Fiat Auto. It would then be left to the Italian government to decide whether to let Fiat Auto disappear or to invest taxpayer money into a failing enterprise to mollify militant Fiat workers.

Toyota, Honda, and Peugeot (PSA) have stayed aloof from most of this merger activity. Unlike some other manufacturers, Toyota has been using its cash reserves to buy back its own shares rather than go on a global acquisition spree. During 2002, Toyota began to buy back 4.6 percent of its own shares for $4.7 billion.[51] Toyota is well established as a full-line manufacturer with a presence in all major global markets and perhaps sees no need for liaisons. The management of Toyota is said to believe that "mergers and acquisitions are the last resort of companies that no longer have full confidence in their core business."[52] Both Honda and Peugeot are relatively healthy companies with secure market niches. Honda's business plan for 2003–2006, titled "Spirited Independence," reaffirmed Honda's strategy of avoiding mergers.[53] Peugeot's chairman has publicly rejected a merger strategy, saying, "We are not looking for economies of scale."[54] Peugeot's apparent disbelief in the existence of economies-of-scale benefits from merger, a subject taken up in the next chapter, is noteworthy.

As of the beginning of 2003, the structure of global ownership is as follows: GM owns 20 percent of Fiat, 21 percent of Fuji (maker of Subaru), 49 percent of Isuzu,[55] 100 percent of Saab, and 10 percent of Suzuki, which itself owns 54 percent of the Indian automaker Maruti (and has permission to purchase another 25 percent from the Indian government). Ford owns 33.4 percent of Mazda and 100 percent of Jaguar, Aston Martin, Volvo, and Land Rover. Daimler-Chrysler owned 37 percent of Mitsubishi (with an option to buy majority ownership in 2003) and 10 percent of Hyundai until 2002, when the stakes were increased to 43 percent and 50 percent, respectively.[56] Hyundai had itself purchased 51 percent of the smaller Korean manufacturer Kia in 1999, and Mitsubishi owns 13 percent of Hyundai and 16 percent of the Malaysian company Proton (owner of 81 percent of the British sports car maker Lotus). VW bought 35 percent of the Czech manufacturer Skoda in 1990 (increased to 70 percent in 1995 and 100 percent in 2000), 99 percent of Audi, and 100 percent of Rolls Royce, Bentley (historically, the sister company to Rolls Royce), Lamborghini, Bugatti, and SEAT (a Spanish producer, formerly owned by Fiat, of which VW acquired 51 percent in 1986 and 100 percent in 1990). By prior agreement, the Rolls Royce name was transferred to BMW at the beginning of 2003.[57] After a brief ownership of American Motors in the 1980s and a near merger with Volvo in 1994, Renault's foreign holdings are 44.4 percent of Nissan (and 22.5 percent of Nissan Diesel),[58] 70 percent of Samsung, and 93 percent of Romanian automaker

Dacia, though it has owned since the 1970s the defunct British marques Hillman, Sunbeam, and Singer (purchased from Chrysler as the latter divested itself of its European holdings during its chronic financial crises of the 1970s). Nissan now owns 13.5 percent of Renault.

Table 1.1 shows production and world market share data for the largest vehicle manufacturers in 1977 and 2001. Ranked by global market share of production in 2001, the largest automobile manufacturers are Toyota (12.3 percent), Volkswagen (12.0 percent), GM (11.4 percent), Ford (9.1 percent, including Volvo), PSA (6.6 percent), and Honda (6.4 percent). A cursory examination of the average net profit margins of these companies for the three-year period 1999–2001 reveals no obvious relationship between size and profitability: Honda (4.3 percent profit), Toyota (4.1 percent), Daimler-Chrysler (2.9 percent), PSA (2.8 percent), Volkswagen (2.3 percent), Ford (2.2 percent), and GM (2.1 percent).[59] During the same period, Porsche had profit margins of 5.9 percent on a volume of 50,000 cars per year. Perhaps these mergers have not yielded some of the most often cited benefits of amalgamation (such as economies of scale) and may have been driven partly by political and other motives not necessarily consonant with the interests of shareholders. Nor has consolidation obviously helped raise market share, if that is a goal. Ford, Mazda, and Volvo, for example, had a larger combined market share in 1977, when they were separate companies, as did Daimler and Chrysler.

Focusing more specifically on auto-sector groups, table 1.2 shows the shape of things to come. When the data for firms with strong ties, through merger, alliance, or cross shareholdings, are combined into groups, the intensity of concentration in the auto industry becomes clear. The market leadership of the GM group, with over 20 percent of world sales, is striking.[60] The four largest groups produced 60 percent of the world's autos.

There are several ways to measure concentration. The most accurate is the Herfindahl index, computed by summing the squared market shares of all the firms in the industry, yielding an index that ranges from zero (no concentration) to unity (one firm supplies the entire market). Here we have an apparent paradox: The degree of concentration has actually declined since 1977. Using the data for individual firms from table 1.1, the Herfindahl index for the motor vehicle industry as a whole was 0.179 in 1977 and 0.155 in 2001, consistent with the market shares held by the top four firms being 58.4 percent in 1977 and 45.3 percent in 2001. The reason for the decline is that the market shares of some the major European and American brands have fallen and the output of Asian automakers has increased during this period. However, when vehicle production is grouped

Table 1.1. Major Motor Vehicle Producers in 1977 and 2001

Manufacturer	1977 Output (1,000s)	Share (%)	2001 Output (1,000s)	Share (%)	2001 Auto Output (1,000s)	Share (%)
GM/Opel	8,442	20.6	7,583	13.5	4,663	11.4
Ford	5,981	23.4	6,676	11.9	3,699	9.1
Toyota	3,097	7.6	6,055	10.8	5,021	12.3
VW Group	2,220	5.4	5,109	9.1	4,881	12.0
Daimler-Chrysler	—	—	4,364	7.8	2,393	5.9
Daimler	662	1.6	—	—	—	—
Chrysler	2,791	6.8	—	—	—	—
American	213	0.8	—	—	—	—
PSA	1,613	3.9	3,102	5.5	2,710	6.6
Honda	665	1.6	2,674	4.8	2,609	6.4
Nissan	2,595	6.3	2,559	4.5	1,967	4.8
Hyundai/Kia	110[a]	0.3	2,518	4.5	2,088	6.1
Fiat	2,268	5.5	2,409	4.3	1,929	4.7
Renault	1,793	4.4	2,375	4.2	2,070	5.1
Mitsubishi	776	1.9	1,648	2.9	1,242	3.0
Suzuki	239	0.6	1,541	2.7	1,162	2.8
Mazda	800	2.0	957	1.7	780	1.9
BMW	290	0.7	947	1.7	947	2.3
AvtoVAZ	n/a	n/a	786	1.4	786	1.9
Subaru	334[a]	0.8	569	1.0	479	1.2
Daewoo	n/a	n/a	504	0.9	470	1.2
Isuzu	425[a]	1.0	454	0.8	101	0.3
Rover	770	1.9	163	0.3	163	0.4
Volvo	245	0.6	155	0.3	0[b]	0
Other	4,538	11.1	3,177	5.6	692	1.7
Total	40,947	100	56,325	100	40,852	100

[a]Data for 1979 from G. Maxcy, *The Multinational Automobile Industry* (New York: St. Martin's, 1981), 194.
[b]Volvo auto production included with Ford.
Sources: International Organization of Motor Vehicle Manufacturers, *OICA Statistics 2001*, www.oica.net; Motor Vehicle Manufacturers Association, *World Motor Vehicle Data, 1979* (Detroit: Motor Vehicle Manufacturers Association, 1980); Maxcy, *The Multinational Automobile Industry*, 194.

into the categories shown in table 1.2, the Herfindahl index (counting the groups as single firms) rises to 0.202, a 13 percent increase over the ungrouped data for 1977 and a 30 percent increase over the ungrouped index for 2001. Although the market share of some of the older brand names (such as Ford, Fiat, and Leyland/Rover) has declined since the 1970s, when the companies are grouped into their contemporary global alliances, the extent of consolidation is clear. It is only a slight exaggeration to say that concentration in the world motor vehicle sector has increased by almost one-third during the past quarter of a century.

Table 1.2. Automobile Groups and Market Shares in 2001

	Auto Output (1,000s)	Market Share (%)
GM/Fiat/Suzuki/Isuzu/Subaru/Daewoo	8,804	21.6
Daimler/Chrysler/Mitsubishi/Hyundai	5,723	14.0
Toyota/Daihatsu	5,021	12.3
VW/Audi/Skoda/SEAT	4,881	12.0
Ford/Mazda/Volvo	4,479	11.0
Renault/Nissan/Samsung/Dacia	4,037	10.0

Source: Table 1.1.

Why Merge? The Key Issues

In a feature article on auto mergers, apocalyptically titled "Who Will Survive?" *BusinessWeek* identified four reasons for the mergers: excess capacity, technology, cash stockpiles, and culture (that is, declining nationalism).[61] It is symptomatic of the need for more analysis that these reasons are largely unpersuasive. Merger does not by itself remove excess capacity, and no firm would merge with another simply to shut down the production of one of them. Possession of technology does not vary greatly across the major firms and in any case can often be purchased without the loss of autonomy entailed in organizational integration. Cash reserves are volatile (Chrysler's large reserves disappeared rapidly after the merger with Daimler) and might be better used on other activities, such as research and development, paying off debt, or repurchasing a company's own shares. If it is true that political or cultural nationalism is on the wane, this may make mergers easier if governments and public opinion are less inclined to disapprove, but this factor does not by itself provide corporations with a reason to merge.

This book examines the major reasons for industrial consolidation insofar as they apply to the auto industry and in doing so will also suggest answers to some of the prescriptive questions that inevitably arise out of any process of globalization. Are there winners and losers in the global consolidation of this industry? Should governments encourage, discourage the reduction in the number of world auto firms, or practice benign neglect?

Chapter 2 examines arguments that mergers may reduce the cost of production through such benefits as economies of scale, cost sharing, capacity reduction, and utilizing the different comparative cost advantages of the participating firms or their geographic production locations. Cost sharing is clearly important to the auto companies. Though sensible in theory, some cost arguments do not always apply well to mergers in the auto industry. Most auto plants, for example, already have economies of scale at the existing size. Chapter 3 continues the theme of comparative advantage. Auto firms may see merger as means to obtain unique products or technologies that they do not have or that they at least might acquire more cheaply than by developing them independently. Though there is much evidence of this factor being invoked by auto executives, it has not been clearly decisive in the most celebrated auto mergers. In some instances, merger has proven to be an extraordinarily expensive way to acquire particular products or technologies. Chapter 3 also examines one aspect of globalization, namely, that mergers may be driven by the desire to secure easy access to new markets where the firm has little presence, notably in large, less developed countries, such as Russia, Brazil, and China. Most large auto companies already possess an impressive global reach. A sanguine assessment of the auto companies' prospects in these markets suggests not only that opportunities are very limited (and hence perhaps not worth a merger), but also that merger with other global vehicle manufacturers (rather than politically directed joint ventures with local firms) is usually unnecessary to secure entry.

Chapter 4 moves beyond intrafirm economics and examines a classic set of power motives for merger: altering the structure of markets to the advantage of the merging firms by reducing competition in the markets for autos or the resources used in their construction. Oligopolistic collusion in product pricing and dividing markets (perhaps ultimately leading to monopolization) is a risky strategy, given the vigilance of antitrust authorities in most developed countries and especially given their attention to cross-border mergers.[62] Merged firms may also be in a more powerful bargaining position with respect to labor and components suppliers, though benefits with respect to the latter may be illusory, as the components industry itself is rapidly consolidating. The bargaining power of labor is clearly suffering as a result of auto industry mergers, though concentration in the supplier industries may countervail the enhanced market power of the auto assemblers.

Chapter 5 considers less traditional factors that are more explicitly political in nature. These variables are classified as endogenous or exogenous to the corporation. Governments may offer incentives to merge for subsidies, to jump over protectionist barriers to trade, or to comply with foreign investment restrictions. The placing of such inducements in the path of automakers is motivated more by political objectives, such as sectoral economic growth, employment, or income redistribution toward consumers (and, less directly, vote maximization), than by any desire to effect an efficient allocation of national resources. Unfortunately for auto firms, they seem to realize too late that governments have their own agendas that rarely include the profitability of the foreign firm that is being encouraged to take over a domestic firm. Such mergers may prove to be Faustian bargains.

Political reasons to merge may also be endogenous, or internal to the corporate governance of firms. Mergers in the auto industry are an example of the much larger phenomenon of organizational expansion. Some political scientists argue that empires tend to overexpand and collapse, as some organizational theorists argue that organizations go through a similar life cycle of expansion and decline.[63] More generally, businesses and other organizations may be driven to expand in size without regard to the stated or generally assumed objectives of the institution. The reasons for this relate to individual motives encompassing both latent psychological drives and personal gain, both at the expense of the welfare of the organization as a whole. These motives are not necessarily examples of the fashionable phrase "irrational exuberance." An irrational action is one that does not achieve the objective of the actor. Organizational overexpansion may be nonrational, driven by deep-seated and possibly unconscious values or power motives that are believed to be promoted by ever larger size. Alternatively, maximizing the size of an organization, public or private, is often quite rational for individual managers since size is associated with salary, perks, power, and prestige.

Attributing relative weights to these various explanations, traditional or otherwise, for the global consolidation in the industry may also help us answer some of the more prescriptive questions that arise in debates about this and other aspects of "globalization." Are there winners and losers in this process? Shareholders and trade unions certainly seem to think so. Is it a suitable object for public policy, or is it best left alone by governments? Could the mergers lead to predatory behavior? Governments have to date encouraged or at least not opposed global mergers in the auto industry.

CHAPTER TWO

Cost-Cutting Imperatives

Major international auto mergers are invariably accompanied by enthusiastic predictions of enormous cost savings. Consider the following forecast made at the time of the merger between Daimler and Chrysler:

> Chrysler spent $30 billion a year on direct materials . . . while Daimler's expenditure fell just short of $13 billion. If you put these two together and cut costs a modest 1 percent, the combined companies would be able to save $430 million in the first year alone. . . . They would save $150–180 million by starting to produce Mercedes' popular M-class in a Chrysler factory. They would sell 20,000 Chrysler trucks through the Daimler distribution network in Latin America and other parts of the world, saving $55 million. Tens of millions could be trimmed from production costs by putting Daimler's diesel engines into Chrysler's off-road vehicles. . . . The engineers came up with savings of $1.4 billion in total short term savings. . . . Longer term, they calculated, the two companies would be able to shave $3 billion a year from their combined costs.[1]

This example appears to be referring mainly to the potential for savings through spreading fixed costs across the products of the two companies. There is a multiplicity of ways in which mergers might enable the constituent firms to save production costs. It is therefore a good starting point for examining the causes of these mergers. Can merger help reduce the cost of manufacturing the corporation's existing product mix? This chapter analyzes arguments suggesting that the act of merger itself presents cost-saving possibilities that could not be attained by the firms in isolation from each other.

Only "real" cost savings will be considered here, being savings derived from actually reducing the cost of production and distribution. "Pecuniary" savings, derived from redistributing revenues by, for example, forcing suppliers to lower prices is considered in chapter 4. Four categories of sources of real cost savings are examined: economies of scale (the lowering of average unit costs of production through the greater annual output of a larger firm), sharing the expenses of research and development (R&D), closing redundant capacity, and production complementarities (lowering costs by utilizing the principles of comparative advantage, where two or more firms have different areas of expertise or have facilities located in geographic areas with factor cost advantages).

Economies of Scale

The potential cost savings from a large volume of production are frequently cited as a rationale for horizontal mergers. Paradoxically, insofar as plant- or product-specific economies of scale do occur as a result of merger, they are a sign of market failure—the inability of existing firms to attain efficient operation. Economies of scale occur when the average cost of producing a unit of a good (in this case, the unit being a motor vehicle) declines as the volume of production increases. Minimum efficient economies of scale (MES) is the smallest level of production at which minimum average unit costs are attained. A major source of economies of scale is the spreading of fixed or overhead costs (such as a certain minimum size of factory buildings, number of machines, or level of staffing that is independent of the level of production) over a larger volume of output. Spreading fixed costs across a large volume of output cannot be the only aspect of economies of scale since, if it were, there would be no limit to cost savings through large-scale production. Volume production may also facilitate, both within and between firms, cost reductions through specialization and learning, or the accumulation of experience and skill by workers and management. All these sources of economies of scale eventually reach limits; learning curves flatten out, specialization may at some point become dysfunctional,[2] and overhead costs per unit are reduced to insignificance. Depending on market conditions for inputs, scale economies may also be pecuniary, being procurement cost savings through volume purchasing of raw materials and other inputs or factors (see chapter 4). There is also the possibility of diseconomies of scale because of organizational inflexibility, communication costs, or technological constraints.

An authoritative work on the global auto industry by two management consultants asserts that economies of scale are the key to being globally competitive in this industry, "the ultimate source of competitive advantage," but provide no empirical evidence on the output at which such economies occur or the extent to which existing producers have attained economies of scale. Yet the theme is constantly echoed in the reports of consulting firms.[3] The PricewaterhouseCoopers report *The Second Automotive Century* proclaimed that "economies of scale will continue to dominate the thinking of executives searching for greater returns to investors."[4] This quest for economies of scale is frequently cited as a reason for firms to merge, the belief being that since the output of two firms combined is greater than that of each firm alone, economies of scale will be forthcoming. General Motors (GM) has defended its investment in Fiat by suggesting that Fiat give GM economies of scale in Europe,[5] though given GM's existing large production volume in Europe (929,000 vehicles in Germany alone in 2001), such a statement seems rather disingenuous.

Scale economies are traditionally found at the plant level. What matters is output per plant, not total firm output. Some older studies misleadingly cite MES estimates that are unusually high. Dunnett, for example, cites MES in the 1970s as being between one and two million vehicles per year.[6] Yet his data are for firms, not plants, aggregating the outputs of different models and multiple plants. Multiplant economies of scale may exist if the manufacturer could save transportation costs by producing the same vehicle at different locations. There is little evidence of multiplant economies of scale either in the auto industry or in the manufacturing industry generally.[7] American auto manufacturers prefer to concentrate production of each model at a single plant.[8] Chrysler claims to save several thousand dollars of costs by concentrating production of its PT Cruiser model at a single plant in Mexico.[9]

Simply merging with another firm does not by itself yield plant-level economies of scale. In order for merger to produce economies-of-scale gains, the merger would have to entail shifting production from plants unable to attain economies of scale to those able to operate at the necessary greater output level, either because the existing plant is unable to attain the higher production level or because some plants are operating below capacity and consolidating production in fewer plants will produce scale benefits. Peugeot and Fiat share a light commercial vehicle factory, presumably for this purpose, though they do so without the need for any formal alliance or merger.[10] If existing plants in the merged entity are operating at capacity and still producing below MES, they will have to be replaced with new production facilities.[11] GM subsidiary Saab recently announced the building of a new plant capable of raising annual output from 132,000 units per year in 2000 to between 230,000 and 250,000 units by 2008.[12] Saab's product development and manufacturing operations are to be combined with those of GM's larger subsidiary, Opel. GM believes that Saab has never been a profitable investment because of low output and lack of scale economies on volumes less than 200,000 vehicles per year. However, it is a moot point whether one could call this a benefit of merger since if the replacement of smaller plant were profitable and capital markets efficient, Saab should have been able to raise the capital to do so without having to be taken over by GM.

Estimates of MES vary widely, but most (albeit rather dated) studies agree that it is reached with final assembly plants that produce more than 250,000 vehicles per year.[13] Most auto plants, even those of smaller and medium-size companies (such as Honda and BMW), produce in excess of this level. The listing in table 2.1 of the thirty-two largest European auto plants in 1999 shows that only six of them produced fewer than 250,000 units per year.[14] Note that these data do not appear to be distorted by any particular geographic or firm-specific pattern: Almost all producers, everywhere in Europe, reach MES at the plant assembly level.

The major vehicle manufacturers have had these scale economies from the early decades of the twentieth century. Chrysler's plant at Hamtramck, Michigan, produced 400,000 vehicles per year in 1910, and its plant in Poissy, France, produced 450,000 in 1939. Volkswagen's Wolfsburg, Germany, plant produced one million vehicles annually in 1938, and Ford's Dagenham plant in England produced 350,000 in 1938.[15] One reason why MG Rover struggles to survive after being purchased from BMW is that its production at Longbridge, England, has stagnated at 180,000 autos per year, contributing to the company's large losses (£254,000 in 2000 and £165,000 in 2001).[16]

Furthermore, the MES estimates of 250,000 were performed in the 1970s and 1980s; current economies of scale are likely to occur at a much lower output. In 2002, BMW opened a new green-field plant in Leipzig, Germany, to produce an annual output of 156,000 "3" series BMW sedans,[17] a production volume that must be yielding economies of scale for BMW. New auto plants in China have been estimated to require annual production of 150,000 units to attain MES.[18] There are several reasons why economies of scale may be attained at lower levels than in the past. New production hardware and computer-aided design technology have reduced the fixed costs that are a major component of economies of scale.[19]

Robotic technology and the reduction in the number of basic vehicle platforms (Volkswagen currently uses only four)[20] allow producers to use the same assembly line for different models, so that MES may be spread across several types of vehicles, a technique pioneered by Volkswagen in the early

Table 2.1. Scale and Productivity in European Auto Plants in 1999

Maker	Plant	Country	Vehicle Production (1,000s)	Vehicles per Employee
Nissan	Sunderland	United Kingdom	271	94
Toyota	Burnaston	United Kingdom	179	81
Renault	Flins	France	403	80
Ford	Saarlouis	Germany	370	77
Ford	Valencia	Spain	342	73
Renault	Valladolid	Spain	275	71
GM	Eisenach	Germany	152	70
Fiat	Melfi	Italy	375	70
GM	Zaragoza	Spain	410	69
Renault	Palencia	Spain	252	69
Renault	Douai	France	362	68
SEAT	Martorel	Spain	481	66
Suzuki	Magyar	Hungary	68	64
Honda	Swindon	United Kingdom	114	64
GM	Antwerp	Belgium	323	63
Renault	Maubeuge	France	229	63
PSA	Aulnay	France	370	62
PSA	Mulhouse	France	401	61
VW	Pamplina	Spain	221	60
Fiat	Mirafiori	Italy	389	58
PSA	Vigo	Spain	350	52
VW	Wolfsburg	Germany	753	50
GM	Luton	United Kingdom	145	47
Ford	Dagenham	United Kingdom	191	46
Fiat	Cassino	Italy	219	44
PSA	Poissy	France	209	43
Renault	Sandouville	France	227	40
PSA	Rennes	France	267	39
Daimler	Rastatt	Germany	193	38
Skoda	M. Boleslav	Czech Republic	261	32
PSA	Sochaux	France	251	31
VW	Emden	Germany	247	29

Source: www.autonewseurope.com/bol/bolproductivity.htm (accessed March 20, 2001).

1980s.[21] GM has one basic midsize platform used in the Opel Vectra, Chevrolet Malibu, Pontiac Grand Am, and Saab 9-3.[22] Each of Honda's four North American plants can produce any Honda model because of the use of programmable robots, standardized production techniques, and "one size fits all" conveyor belts. Toyota has a "global body line" system whereby each assembly line in its North American plants can produce eight different models. This yields economies of scope—the ability to make different products within the same plant.[23] Modular construction offers the opportunity to use the same modules in a range of different vehicles, spreading scale economies across different models, further enhancing economies of scope. Volkswagen-Audi has been particularly effective in both modular construction and the sharing of these modules across the product line. Daimler-Chrysler is now producing the Mercedes sport-utility vehicle (SUV) and the Jeep Cherokee on the same assembly lines in an Austrian plant.[24]

Auto manufacturers are increasingly outsourcing components, with implications for many aspects of auto manufacturing, including both economies of scale and market bargaining power, the latter theme being taken up in chapter 4. Some aggregate data on the proportion of value outsourced by major manufacturers and the increases over two decades are reproduced in table 2.2. Automakers increased outsourcing from around 50 percent to between 60 and 80 percent of their costs during the last two decades of the twentieth century. Outsourcing does not necessarily imply an arm's-length transaction, since suppliers may be closely affiliated with the brand-name owner.[25] This trend is accelerated by the move to modular construction, which often entails the outsourcing of large integrated units of components (such as entire dashboard assemblies). The value of the automotive modular assembly sector was estimated at $42.7 billion in 2000 and is expected to grow to $111 billion by 2010.[26]

American automakers have been inhibited in their ability to move toward modularity. The United Auto Workers (UAW) union thwarted GM's attempt to introduce modular construction to its small-car plant at Lordstown, Ohio, in 1999, concerned about job losses. Nissan, whose workers have twice rejected the UAW (in 1989 and 2001), faced no such problems introducing modularity to its Smyrna, Tennessee, plant. Outside the United States, modular construction faces fewer labor obstacles. The Volkswagen factory in Resende, Brazil, is considered to be a model for the future: 75 percent of the employees work for module suppliers. GM's Blue Macaw plant, also in Brazil, was built in 1998 to reduce vehicle costs by up to one-third and, like Volkswagen, has suppliers not only provide the modules but sometimes assemble them on the vehicles.

Though scale economies in auto assembly may be attained at volumes of 250,000 or even less, many components require much larger volumes in order to achieve MES. One study by McKinsey & Company suggested that component procurement for three million vehicles yields cost savings of 8 percent on component purchasing.[27] To the extent that assemblers can outsource these components, they have no need to produce vehicles at such a high volume in order to reduce component costs. As more of the value of a

Table 2.2. Percentage of Total Components Costs Outsourced

Manufacturer	1985	1986	1989	1990	1995	1996	1997
BMW	n/a	50	56	n/a	n/a	64–67	65–70
Rover	n/a	n/a	43	n/a	n/a	n/a	60
Ford Europe	n/a	25	n/a	n/a	n/a	40	60
Ford Germany	n/a	n/a	52	n/a	n/a	n/a	n/a
Ford North America	50	n/a	n/a	55	60	61	50
Ford United Kingdom	n/a	n/a	68	n/a	n/a	n/a	n/a
Volvo	n/a	n/a	n/a	n/a	n/a	65	70
GM Europe	n/a	n/a	n/a	n/a	n/a	67	60
GM North America	40	n/a	n/a	45	50	55	n/a
Fiat	45	n/a	55	n/a	65–70	70	65
Opel	n/a	n/a	49	n/a	n/a	n/a	n/a
Vauxhall	n/a	n/a	75	n/a	n/a	n/a	n/a
Mercedes-Benz	n/a	n/a	35	46	n/a	60–62	60
Mercedes-Benz North America	n/a	n/a	n/a	n/a	n/a	n/a	80
Chrysler	60	n/a	n/a	65	70	64	75
PSA	n/a	n/a	50	n/a	65–70	67	65
Renault	n/a	n/a	55–60	n/a	65–70	60–70	70
VW	n/a	n/a	53–55	n/a	n/a	57	60
Audi	n/a	n/a	51–53	n/a	n/a	n/a	75
SEAT	n/a	n/a	75	n/a	n/a	n/a	70
Skoda	n/a	n/a	n/a	n/a	n/a	n/a	75

Source: Personal communication from Glenn Mercer (McKinsey & Company) of information collected from various sources.

car is outsourced to component makers, the locus of economies of scale shifts away from the brand-name assembler to the supplier. As manufacturers sell off their parts-making subsidiaries (for example, Ford and GM spun off their major parts makers, Visteon and Delphi, in 1999 and 2000, respectively) and cooperate in making Internet markets for parts (such as Covisint, created in 2000),[28] the scale imperative in auto assembly plants further diminishes and shifts economies of scale to suppliers who service many auto companies. This has allowed the manufacturers themselves to move to smaller plant sizes that merely assemble externally supplied, prefabricated parts or entire modules. These plants are not only smaller than the traditional assembly plant but also leaner, flexible, and easy to assemble and disassemble as the manufacturer moves from one concept or model to another. These new plants have been described as being like a tent that can be easily thrown up and later taken down. Engineering services are also being outsourced. Audi now outsources more than 50 percent of its engineering work, compared to less than half before 1995.[29]

Cars are becoming more like personal computers, an industry in which the manufacturer makes very little of the product and simply assembles (or supervises the assembly of) components purchased from volume suppliers of parts. The "unbundling" of automobile manufacturing and assembly has removed many of the traditional sources of economies of scale for automakers. Consider the example of the Ford plant in Cologne, Germany, producing the Fiesta subcompact. The surrounding supplier park of independent contractors designs, develops, and produces most of the subsystems that collectively constitute the car. Much of the equipment within the factory is owned and operated by outside suppliers who work on the "pay on production" principle. Ford takes responsibility for the completed product, but it increasingly does little more than oversee the process.[30]

Outsourcing also enables low-volume vehicle manufacturers, with little hope of ever attaining significant economies of scale on their own, to do so without a large increase in production. Despite its profitability, Porsche's annual sales during the past decade have stayed in the region of 50,000 vehicles. After struggling with near bankruptcy in the early 1990s, Porsche has achieved enviable success. One reason for this may be that, starting with the 1994 model of its 911 series of sports cars (designated the 993), Porsche began to outsource a large portion of the car's components. Reaping the benefits of supplier economies of scale enabled it to both lower prices and maintain very high profit margins. Porsche purists complain that the fabled high quality of Porsche autos has steadily fallen as a result, though that opinion is not sufficiently widespread to have hurt sales.

Engines and transmissions typically have a higher MES, estimates from the 1970s and 1980s suggesting about 500,000 and possibly as high as one million units per year.[31] As in the case of auto assembly, the level of power train production volume at which MES is attained has most likely fallen. Beginning in 2005, Chrysler is to supply 600,000 four-cylinder engines annually to itself and to the U.S. assembly plants of Mitsubishi and Hyundai.[32] It is reasonable to assume that Chrysler must be reaching MES at that volume. There are obvious scale benefits in Ford's decision to have Land Rover and Volvo begin using standard Ford parts,[33] and Ford hopes that this practice will help it build up Land Rover's share of the American SUV market. Beyond low-volume brands like Land Rover, economies of scale in such major components as engines and transmissions are unlikely to provide a powerful motive for merger for companies that already have large production volumes. Engines are shared by many models built in different plants by the same manufacturer, making it relatively easy for even smaller companies to attain MES in engine production well within the production boundaries of their own firm. Even Porsche derives some economies of scale in engine production by using (since 1999) the same basic liquid-cooled engine in its two models, the 996 (successor to the 911) and the Boxster. In the early 1990s, Porsche was using different variations on both liquid- and air-cooled engines in a variety of models. Standardizing engines and outsourcing components have helped Porsche survive and prosper.

Finally, it should be noted that any automaker can guarantee itself power train economies of scale by outsourcing engines and transmissions without the need to merger with another automaker. Thus, while companies like Land Rover and Volvo may attain greater economies of scale by using Ford engines and other parts, it is not unimaginable that they could have used the parts from any large global manufacturer without the need for merger. Several very small British automakers (such as Marcos, TVR, and Morgan) have survived and even thrived by using power trains from high-volume manufacturers such as Ford. There is clearly some sort of market or managerial failure that in some cases requires a merger to occur before a company can find economies of scale.

If merger yields cost savings for large auto companies in this area, they are unlikely to be economies of scale but rather a mixture of savings in other areas: development costs, reducing organizational duplication, specialization, and increasing capacity utilization. Ford's relationship with Mazda, established in the early 1970s, gave it Mazda engines for the Ford Escort, just as British Leyland's relationship with Honda in the 1980s gave it Honda engines for the Sterling model. Ford Europe continues to use Mazda engines and transmissions.[34] Peugeot and Citroën cars share the same engines, gearboxes, and brakes. Yet all these companies undoubtedly already had economies of scale in engine and drive train production. What they must have been saving was R&D and tooling costs. The same is true for most contemporary collaborations in engine production that have resulted from merger or alliances. Fiat and GM have announced their intent to use common platforms and have a jointly owned operation to make engines and transmissions for European and Latin American markets. They claim to expect to jointly save two billion euros by 2005.[35] Chrysler plans to make some use of Mercedes engines by 2004,[36] notably in the new Chrysler Crossfire.

Beneficial as such sharing arrangements may be in sharing development costs or perhaps even attaining economies of scale, they do not obviously require merger. There is an increasing amount of sharing of engines and transmissions between companies that have no formal organizational links. Nissan and Mitsubishi, each associated with the rival Renault and Daimler groups, plan to procure automatic transmissions and continuously variable transmissions from the same company, Jatco, which will sell to many auto companies.[37] Ford and Peugeot have a joint venture to produce 1.6 million diesel engines annually by 2005 without any formal organizational integration.[38] BMW is to buy 10,000 to 20,000 diesel engines per year from Toyota for its new BMW Mini model and is to jointly develop a new family of small engines with Peugeot.[39] Honda provides engines for GM's Saturn, and Isuzu provides Honda with turbo-diesel engines for the Honda Civic.[40] Whether the benefits of such exchanges derive from economies of scale, cost sharing, capacity utilization, or the comparative advantages of specialization, it is clear that merger is not required in order to obtain the gains.

Distribution and sales, traditionally about 25 percent of the cost of an auto, is also a diminishing source of economies of scale. In the 1950s, U.S. dealerships typically stocked only one brand, as is still the case in many other countries. Small manufacturers could hardly afford the high fixed cost of a large network of dealers that may have provided some incentive to merge with a larger company. American Motors would have experienced this problem prior to its takeover by Chrysler in 1987. During the past few decades, independent dealers have begun to sell multiple brands, and the fixed costs to an individual manufacturer of a specific number of outlets served by mega-dealerships are spread widely, helping all automakers (especially small ones) attain economies of scale.[41] This becomes particularly important as dealers have to invest in increasingly specialized repair and diagnostic equipment. The Lynch group in Chicago, for example, is a dealership selling Ford, GM, Chrysler, Porsche, and Volkswagen.[42] A small company like Porsche, with annual sales of less than 60,000, no longer has to sacrifice market coverage in order to avoid the crippling expense of spreading the fixed cost of a large number of dealerships across a small volume of sales. Moves by manufacturers to sell directly to the public through the Internet should further reduce the need for large fixed investments in sales organizations, though dealers in at least one state (Texas) have successfully opposed direct sales by manufacturers.

Economies of scale in advertising, which may occur through the cumulative effects of saturating a market, may discriminate against smaller auto companies, providing an incentive to merge with a larger partner. Yet this effect may also be of diminishing importance as dealers become less tied to particular makes and multibrand auto supermarkets give similar sales promotional advantages to all brands.

Apart from specific functional areas of auto production and marketing, there is the more general question of organizational economies of scale. The classic Weberian view of bureaucracy is that large size enhances efficiency by allowing greater division of labor, specialization, hierarchical supervision, and the avoidance of duplication of functions.[43] When organizations combine their functional divisions, the implication is that there must be organizational economies of scale, presumably spreading fixed costs. Adding to these considerations are the more contemporary arguments about how organizational expansion, merger, and multinationalization reduce transaction costs. The classic justification for merging previously separate organizations, particularly if they are located in different countries, is to reduce transaction costs (that is, the costs of gathering information, bargaining, and enforcing contracts) through bringing the entire process under one corporate roof.[44]

On the other side, there are the familiar arguments about organizational diseconomies of scale (such as informational bottlenecks, fragmentation of decision making, inflexibility, and an inability to respond to changing market environments, to name a few). GM is often the subject of such negative generalizations on the dysfunctional organizational implications of large size. The classic Weberian perspective has been increasingly questioned by modern organization theorists who suggest, among other things, that flatter, decentralized organizational structures might be better able to respond to changing business environments. The overall question of whether mergers result in organizational economies or diseconomies is unlikely to be resolved by any systematic empirical test. In the case of the auto industry, it might be more fruitful to simply ask to what extent auto mergers have been accompanied by organizational integration and how important such integration may have been in motivating the consolidation.

Auto companies, particularly those with a long history of international operations, have multidivisional rather than functional structures. Instead of a simple pyramidal structure divided into functional activities such as production, finance and marketing, they have decentralized themselves along product and geographic lines, yielding a flatter structure with organizational peaks focused on product lines, brand names, or geographic market areas.[45] Perhaps because of this recognition of the need to maintain multidivisional structures, the mergers that have occurred during the past decade have not always been accompanied by any major efforts to combine organizations and reduce duplication. Ford has been careful to keep its European acquisitions (Land Rover, Aston Martin, and Jaguar) away from its core Ford organization, particularly with regard to sales and marketing. These brands are housed under a separate division, Ford's Premier Automotive Group, led by former BMW executive Wolfgang Reitzle from the unit's inception until May 2002. Similarly, Daimler's merger with Chrysler has not resulted in organizational integration.[46]

Efforts at organizational integration may be seen in limited areas, primarily in sales and marketing, where fixed costs may be spread across brands that are "compatible." Renault and Nissan appear to have gone the farthest in this respect, perhaps because they are aiming at the same market segment. Nissan's European sales and marketing operations are to be moved to Renault's headquarters in Paris. By 2005, the 2,000 Renault dealerships in Europe and the 1,700 Nissan dealerships are to be combined into 800 integrated sales outlets.[47] Chrysler is consolidating its Dodge, Chrysler, and Jeep dealers, though it could have done that without Daimler's guidance.[48] Another area where integration may be helpful is in back-office functions that are common to different divisional distinctions. Daimler-Chrysler, for example, hopes to have a common system of information technology and salary payments for Mercedes, Chrysler, and Mitsubishi.[49]

While organizational integration may yield both cost savings from reducing duplication and organizational economies of scale, it is unlikely to be a major factor motivating a merger. The amount of postmerger integration has been small. Insofar as mergers have occurred between firms aiming at different market segments, such integration might well be damaging. One would not expect, for example, Mercedes-Benz autos to be sold from the same dealership that sells Chrysler vehicles. Daimler does not want Mercedes to be organizationally integrated with Chrysler for reasons of brand-image contamination. Nor would one expect to see Aston Martins and Jaguars in a showroom with Ford minivans. GM announced that it would be integrating European dealerships for its two upmarket brands, Cadillac and Saab, and a month later dropped the plan, most likely out of doubts about the complementarity of the two brands.[50] Even in cases where the merged firms aim at a similar market niche, integration may have negative consequences. Selling Nissans and Renaults side by side may hurt the sales of one or the other. Companies that sell a large range of vehicles on a small range of platforms may invite unfavorable comparisons. In recent years, Volkswagen has struggled with, and failed to solve, the problem that customers seeing an Audi A4 or A6 next to a Volkswagen Passat may take note of the fact that all three are structurally very similar though with widely varying prices.

Since the economies-of-scale argument is such a popular rationale for explaining auto mergers, it is worth concluding by citing the summary opinion of one scholarly expert on the subject:

Plant-specific and product-specific scale economies can and do result from mergers. But for a significant fraction of the cases in which they do, it is because competition has failed to stimulate efficient plant investment, specialization or closure choices. Mergers are a second best solution, given the failure of competition. It follows obversely that the more effectively competition is working, the less essential mergers are as a source of scale economies.[51]

Research and Development

Model changes and tooling costs used to be a major source of preproduction expenses, requiring large production runs for the firm to be competitive in pricing. The development costs of the Ford Taurus and the Mercury Sable variation, introduced in 1985, were $1.9 billion.[52] This has been particularly true for U.S. firms that made extensive annual model changes. Yet again, some of the same factors that have reduced the minimum output necessary for economies of scale, such as computer-aided design, have also cut development costs. Sharing engines and platforms and the outsourcing of engineering development and components have also reduced the importance of tooling costs. The steady reduction in the time lag between product conception and production reflects these savings. The Pontiac Aztec (newly introduced in 2001) took only twenty-six months to develop and is built at a Mexican plant that was designed in eight weeks.[53] Even American manufacturers no longer make the kinds of annual model changes that reduce the production run across which these costs may be spread. Basic platforms and structural components have a longer life span, and innovations are much more likely to entail technological and qualitative improvements that do not require significant new tooling costs.

Perhaps the most important benefit of size is the capacity to absorb R&D costs. These are sunk costs that must be incurred prior to production, independently of the fixed and variable costs of actually producing the item, the latter being subject to possible economies of scale. Highly engineered autos, such as Porsches and Ferraris, are expensive not only because of small production runs and lack of economies of scale (to the extent that they forgo the benefits of outsourcing) but also because of high development costs necessary to make a superior product. Insofar as R&D requires a large investment of unrecoverable or sunk costs, bigger companies have an advantage that could drive smaller companies into mergers in order to avoid being rendered technologically obsolete. Some of the most famous names in European motoring, such as Aston Martin, Saab, and Alfa Romeo, had fallen noticeably behind in their automotive technology by the early 1970s, and this contributed both to their demise as independent entities and to their current use of parts from high-volume partners. Current models of Aston Martin, for example, use engines that are variations on the Ford Taurus power plant. Saabs and Opels are now built on generic GM platforms.

Yet there are also companies that have (at least in the past) done very well delivering advanced technology to the market despite their small size. Lotus, Porsche, and BMW are salient examples.[54] The results of R&D, like other components, can be purchased and might not by themselves necessitate incorporation into a larger entity. Furthermore, many forms of technology do not necessitate large setup costs. Porsche derives 15 percent of its sales revenue from selling technology and design work to other, mostly larger, manufacturers, such as Volkswagen. Over one-third of the employees at Porsche's Weissach Development Center work on projects outsourced by other auto manufacturers.[55]

The Daimler-Chrysler, Mitsubishi, and Hyundai group may provide the best example of how companies hope that merger will yield savings in R&D. It plans to develop a four-cylinder engine, originally a Hyundai design, and develop it into a "world engine" that can easily be tailored to specific markets. The group claims that development costs will be reduced by one-third. Mercedes vehicles will not use the engine; Chrysler, Mitsubishi, and Hyundai will each contribute $384 million to the development costs.[56] Daimler and Chrysler also plan to use a "common electrical architecture" that will share the same electronic control module.[57] Nissan and Renault plan to start using common platforms, as may Fiat and GM-owned Opel[58]— moves that should yield similar benefits in sharing the preproduction sunk costs of R&D. In March 2002, Renault and Nissan began production of the high-volume-production Micra subcompact, the front half of the vehicle made by Renault and the rear half by Nissan, though each firm will still use its own engine in its own variation of the Micra.[59] Ford's Premier Automotive Group (comprising the brands Volvo, Jaguar, Land Rover, and Aston Martin) will eventually use common engines and electrical architecture and will share many components from Ford's European parts bin.[60]

Similar cost-sharing benefits may exist where new technologies for future generations of autos are being developed. To what extent have mergers been motivated by the need to share these costs or to acquire these new technologies? There is no doubt that large amounts of resources are being put into developing alternatives to the gasoline-powered internal combustion engine, including gasoline/electric hybrids currently on the market (like Honda's Insight and Toyota's Prius),[61] natural gas, and fuel cell technology that uses hydrogen to produce electricity without the need for battery power. It is unclear to what extent the development of alternative power has or ought to cause mergers. Nissan and Renault have a $656 million project on hybrids, but Nissan had the technology before merger.[62]

Much of the R&D on new methods of vehicle propulsion and other technologies is being done through joint research projects that do not require merger or integration beyond the project itself. Toyota is collaborating with both Nissan and Ford to share development costs of gasoline/electric hybrid vehicles.[63] Toyota is also cooperating with Peugeot to develop new technology to reduce carbon dioxide emissions.[64] GM and Toyota began cooperating in 2001 (and were joined in 2002 by Volkswagen) to develop in-vehicle telematics (communications and entertainment systems).[65] GM and Ford plan to jointly develop a new six-speed fuel-saving transmission.[66] Paradoxically, the same companies that one might think would lack the resources to engage in such research are actually very active. Honda not only produced one of the first electric hybrids but also is active in research to reduce emission, including a venture with a California company (Catalytic Solutions) to use less of the costly catalyst palladium.[67] BMW, a company frequently cited in the financial press as vulnerable to takeover because of its small size, is active in many areas of R&D, including computerized control systems ("X-by-wire") and hydrogen fuels.[68] Finally, even large companies may outsource R&D, not only enhancing the savings from two or more companies procuring R&D from the same developer but also making it possible for smaller companies to acquire R&D that they might otherwise be too small to fund themselves. It is noteworthy that Daimler-Chrysler and Ford have transferred parts of their research on fuel cell–powered electric vehicles to a Canadian company, Ballard Power Systems.[69]

Thus, while there are clearly savings to be made in sharing the costs of R&D, reaping these benefits does not seem to necessitate mergers and should not be expected to do so given the ability of companies to cooperate to acquire technology from others and the ability of even small companies to remain at the forefront of some new technologies. Paraphrasing an earlier citation of F. M. Scherer (pp. 34–35), merger to acquire R&D is a sign of market failure since an efficient market would be able to "unbundle" R&D from the rest of the automobile production process and make it available to a market beyond the large firm.

Reducing Redundant Capacity

Virtually every contemporary analysis of the plight of the global auto industry refers to the problem of massive excess capacity, estimated at nearly 25 million units in 2000 and forecast to fall only slightly, to 20 million units, by 2006.[70] Capacity utilization in 2000 varied considerably across groups, Volkswagen having the highest utilization (92 percent), followed by Renault (91 percent), PSA (76 percent), GM (74 percent), Ford (60 percent), and Fiat (54 percent).[71] Merger might be a device to increase capacity utilization and the latter is often cited in the popular business literature as a motive for merger in the auto industry. The simplest conjecture would be that two firms producing a homogeneous product in two plants with underutilized capacity could merge, shut down one of the plants, and operate the remaining one at full capacity. This scenario is unlikely to be relevant to the auto industry under most circumstances. Since different auto companies do not produce homogeneous products, shutting down capacity in one firm would not necessarily allow the other partner to increase capacity utilization unless the merged entity could produce the vehicles of both firms in the same plant, a production tactic that is sometimes employed (such as by Ford and Mazda subcompacts in Spain and Daimler and Chrysler SUVs in Austria). As speculation built up during 2002 about whether GM would be forced to take over Fiat, Opel's chairman publicly pointed out that Opel had no use for Fiat's underutilized plants.[72]

Given that most auto companies have multiple plants and should be able to close down the ones with the most unused capacity, the more pertinent question is why a merger is necessary to close down unprofitable capacity. Perhaps it is a variation on the "failing firm" explanation of mergers, in which a healthy firm absorbs a failing one, believing that it can make better use of the assets. Yet again, the argument assumes some sort of market failure or at least internal managerial failure.[73] More generally, one would imagine that a firm would prefer a healthy merger partner to a sick one. Empirically, this seems to be the case. Target firms have better-than-average performance prior to takeover.[74]

As a practical matter, separate firms ought to be able to reduce capacity just as well as one merged firm, and this is much in evidence in the auto industry. Renault has been reducing capacity since 1998.[75] By the middle of 2001, Ford was engaging in a massive restructuring of its European operations, closing plants in Britain, Portugal, and the Netherlands and using excess capacity in Ford plants to produce Mazdas and Volvos.[76] Daewoo announced a 14 percent cut in its overseas workforce while still an independent company.[77] Such actions are common among the major automakers at the start of the millennium and do not necessarily require new management or mergers.

However, casual empiricism suggests that in most cases merger is followed by plant closings. Shortly after acquiring American Motors (AMC) from Renault in 1987, Chrysler shut down AMC's large plant in Kenosha, Wisconsin, reducing the AMC workforce by one-third. AMC returned to profit soon after. Why could AMC's former owner, Renault, not have returned its subsidiary to profitability by doing the same thing? Perhaps the answer lies in union relations. Completely dependent on AMC in its U.S. market, Renault had little bargaining power over the hostile local union at its Kenosha plant. Chrysler could simply solve the problem by shutting down Kenosha and moving the production of AMC vehicles elsewhere. If this is the case, we should note that it is not merger by itself that is allowing capacity to be reduced but, rather, different managers utilizing intracorporate capital mobility.

During the first three years of the new millennium, most recently acquired auto firms have announced capacity reductions. Mazda is to shut 40 percent of its U.S. dealerships.[78] Isuzu is to cut 26 percent of its workforce, following GM's acquisition of 49 percent of the small Japanese producer.[79] Fiat and GM began cutting employment in jointly owned engine plants in Italy in 2002.[80] GM plans to reduce Saab's workforce by 17 percent in 2003.[81] In September 2001, Mitsubishi announced a global restructuring plan that would entail reducing its workforce by 14 percent and its productive capacity by 20 percent and also cutting the number of models offered.[82] While this action was clearly related to Daimler becoming Mitsubishi's largest shareholder (34 percent), we are still left with the question of why Mitsubishi could not restructure itself without external intervention. Part of the answer may be the (albeit disappearing) system of lifetime employment in Japanese management and labor relations practices and perhaps also the more general intangible phenomenon of managerial inertia.

Labor unions are certainly one part of the puzzle. British unions were outraged at BMW's plan to cut output at Rover's main Longbridge plant during the 1990s and even more incensed by its decision to sell Rover. The strength and militancy of British unions may well be a good reason why British firms have to be taken over by firms not intimidated by British unions before restructuring can take place. Two years after buying Land Rover from BMW, Ford announced its intention to cut employment and production.[83] The most famous contemporary case is Chrysler. After replacing Chrysler's American chief executive officer (CEO), the new German manager of Chrysler, Dieter Zetsche, having obtained the cooperation of the UAW, announced the layoff of 26,000 employees. Yet one is still left wondering why the old Chrysler management could not have done this. Perhaps the greater capacity for international capital mobility gives Daimler-Chrysler more bargaining power with respect to the UAW than Chrysler had by itself.

Whatever the reasons why the existing managers could not reduce capacity in these target firms, it is hard to see capacity reduction as a reason to merge, except in the case of a duopoly market in which an acquirer can shut down its only rival.[84] The managers of a target firm would not seek to merge because they do not have the willingness to cut capacity and would prefer that someone else do it, even if only because their own tenure as managers would be called into question (What company needs managers who cannot make hard choices?). The acquiring firm does not acquire the target so that it can reduce capacity. Cutting capacity may be something the acquiring firm has to do to restore the target to profitability, but it is not a reason to merge. On the contrary, a firm that is unprofitable in part because of excess capacity that the existing management is unwilling or unable to reduce makes the firm (everything else being equal) less rather than more desirable. Redundant capacity is a cost of merger rather than a benefit. The only circumstance under which excess capacity would be a motivating reason for one firm to seek to take over or merge with another would be if the management of the initiator believes both that capacity reduction is a necessary condition for profitability and that it has the power, knowledge, or expertise to do what the existing management cannot or will not do.

Taking note of the international nature of auto mergers may also have some explanatory value. One argument for why the U.S. Congress delegated authority for negotiating foreign trade to the executive in the early 1930s was that it wanted to insulate itself from protectionist pressures from constituents. Fiscally injudicious governments, like that of Argentina, may actually welcome stern admonitions and threats of withholding aid by the International Monetary Fund, as the International Monetary Fund obliges them to take measures that would otherwise be politically difficult to undertake unilaterally. If the government of South Korea is wary of the political or electoral consequences of angering Daewoo's trade unions, it might welcome the opportunity to delegate the revival of Daewoo to a foreign corporation like GM, which does not face the same constraints and presumably could also be blamed for future layoffs by an electorally sensitive government. As noted earlier, a new German management at Chrysler might well have more bargaining power with respect to the UAW than the previous American management, even if only because of the geographic mobility of the merged entity. This issue is revisited in chapter 4 in discussion of mergers for market power.

Complementarity and Comparative Advantage

Nations trade because of comparative advantage. Differences in production costs make it relatively cheaper for a nation to specialize in particular goods. The rising volume of exports of Japanese cars to the United States by the early 1980s was based on marginal cost differences of $1,500 to $2,500 per vehicle.[85] GM's chairman, Roger Smith, was reportedly horrified when told that the proposed GM "S" car of the 1980s would cost $2,874 more than a comparable Isuzu and promptly killed the "S" car project, leading ultimately to a joint production venture with Toyota.[86] Though some believe that the locational decisions of auto companies have little to do with principles of comparative advantage, mainly because of the prevalence of state intervention, it may be worth considering the possibility that a merger between two auto companies may occur for the same reasons that nations trade, each bringing a comparative advantage to the exchange.[87]

The two major "classical" explanations of trade focus on productivity and on the abundance of factors of production (that is, inputs or resources). The early nineteenth-century English economist David Ricardo suggested that nations trade because of differences in productivity, particularly labor productivity. If the ratio of labor hours it takes to produce a pound of bread relative to a gallon of wine is lower in England than in Portugal, England has a comparative advantage in bread and Portugal in wine. Each will specialize in what it does best, and trade will occur. For the same reason, auto companies might merge because each has relatively higher productivity in particular areas of the industry. The ultimate source of the productivity advantage may be unique to the firm, to the auto companies of a particular country, or to a particular geographic area.

An alternative theory of trade suggested by two Swedish economists, Eli Hecksher and Bertil Gotthard Ohlin, focused on the fact that countries vary in their endowments of resources. A country that has an abundance of labor relative to capital will have relatively cheaper labor than a country with a higher ratio of capital to labor. An auto company seeking cheaper labor may wish to acquire a company located in a country with an abundance of labor. The United States is a capital-abundant country, capital is cheap, and the United States has a comparative advantage in capital-intensive goods. Merger with a U.S. company may provide a firm from a country having a less abundant capital endowment with access to cheaper capital for those aspects of auto production that are capital intensive.

More contemporary trade theories might also be helpful in explicating auto mergers. Much international trade occurs in nonhomogeneous, differentiated products between countries that have similar technology and similar factor endowments (such as the United States, Japan, and western Europe) and is less well explained by the classical theories. The Linder theory of trade suggests that countries specialize in a variation of a good that is in high demand at home and export to countries that share that demand. The United States producing large autos and Italy specializing in small autos may be an example. Establishing a significant presence in a foreign market might require or be aided by merger with a firm that produces the type of vehicle preferred in that market. For expository simplicity, the present discussion is limited to exploring the relationship between auto mergers and the two classical theories of international trade.[88]

The empirical issue is to what extent the mergers that have happened may be attributed to these varieties of comparative advantage incentives. Consider first the productivity argument. Japanese auto firms have had substantially higher productivity than U.S. or European firms at least since the 1960s, and this can be attributed to a variety of factors. The most general term applied to the Japanese productivity advantage is "lean production," a production management system that "transfers the maximum number of tasks and responsibilities to those workers actually adding value to the car on the line, and it has in place a system for detecting defects that quickly traces every problem, once discovered, to its ultimate cause."[89] Lean production in practice includes a wide variety of tactics: flexible work assignments, team production, worker participation in managerial decisions, minimal inventories ("just in time" procurement of supplies), and continuous incremental improvements (*kaizen*).[90] By the early 1980s, labor productivity in Japanese auto plants was 36 percent greater than in U.S. plants.[91] Table 2.3 displays geographic differences in labor productivity in the auto industry in 1989. The superiority of Japanese plants in Japan is striking, taking 16.8 hours to produce a vehicle. The corresponding numbers for U.S. plants in North America and European plants in Europe were 24.9 and 35.5 hours, respectively.[92] Japanese plants had more than twice the labor productivity of European plants. A different measure of labor productivity, value added per hour worked, yielded the same ranking. Table 2.4 compares value added in the auto industry in Japan, the United States, and Germany.

Such dramatic productivity differences might make Japanese companies attractive targets for takeover. Yet apart from Ford's acquisition of an increasing share of Mazda starting in 1986 (but following a decade of collaboration), the large-scale acquisition of control over Japanese auto companies (namely, Nissan and Mitsubishi) did not come until the end of the century. By this time, however, Japanese production techniques had been diffusing throughout the industry. This suggests that these productivity advantages were not unique to the firms being domiciled in Japan or to anything inherent in the nature of the Japanese economy, and hence the productivity differences should not have been the proximate causes of the mergers.

Contemporary international data comparable to the 1989 study cited in table 2.3 are not available, but there are many indications that European and American firms are catching up to Japanese productivity levels. Euro-

Table 2.3. Labor Productivity in the International Auto Industry in 1989

	Best	Weighted Average	Worst
Japanese-owned plants in Japan	13.2	16.8	25.9
Japanese-owned plants in North America	18.8	20.9	25.5
U.S.-owned plants in North America	18.6	24.9	30.7
U.S.- and Japanese-owned plants in Europe	22.8	35.3	57.6
European-owned plants in Europe	22.8	35.5	55.7
Plants in Mexico, Brazil, Taiwan, and Korea	25.7	41.0	78.7

Note: The data measure labor hours per vehicle.
Source: J. Womack, D. Jones, and D. Roos, *The Machine That Changed the World* (New York: Simon & Schuster, 1990), 85.

pean plants are improving productivity through robotics, automation, and the adoption of Japanese management techniques, including lean production.[93] The data in table 2.1 suggest that some European plants are competitive with European-located Japanese plants in productivity. The consulting firm Harbour and Associates surveyed U.S. plant productivity in 2000 and found that although U.S. firms still lag behind Japanese transplants, they were rapidly catching up. The number of labor hours necessary to produce a vehicle in 1999 in North America were 17.4 hours for Nissan, 19.9 for Honda, 21.6 for Toyota, 25.7 for Ford, and 26.8 for GM. Differences in rates of growth are noteworthy: GM efficiency increased by 9.4 percent. Ford's efficiency declined by 2.8 percent. Honda, Toyota, and Nissan increased labor

Table 2.4. Labor Productivity in the Auto Industries of the United States, Japan, and Germany in 1990

	Auto Assembly	Auto Parts
Germany vs. United States United States = 100	66	76
Japan vs. United States United States = 100	116	124
Japan vs. Germany Germany = 100	176	163

Source: William Lewis, Hans Gersbach, Tom Jansen, and Koji Sakate, "The Secret to Competitiveness—Competition," *McKinsey Quarterly* 4 (1993): 29–43.

productivity by 1.7, 0.7, and 7.3 percent, respectively.[94] These data suggest that Japanese firms in North America still have a clear productivity advantage over U.S. firms but that in Europe the gap has been disappearing. Further evidence on the diffusion of productivity and that the gap may well have closed, at least in the United States, is provided by the 2002 Harbour report, extracts from which are reproduced in table 2.5. Labor productivity in U.S. vehicle plants is unrelated to manufacturer nationality.

However, while productivity in U.S. and European plants may be catching up with local Japanese plants in those regions, the most productive auto plants are still those of Japanese companies in Japan. According to a World Markets Research Centre study released in July 2002, the nine most productive auto factories in the world are in Japan, and the tenth is in Korea. The most efficient auto plant in the world is Mitsubishi's Mitsushima plant in Japan, where each worker produces 180 cars per year. The most efficient European plant is operated by Nissan in Sunderland (also the most efficient European plant in 1999; see table 2.1), producing 95 autos per worker per year. In the United States, Honda's Marysville, Ohio, plant ranks first, with 96 cars per worker each year.[95]

It certainly is possible to find examples of mergers where one firm benefits from another's productivity. Renault reported in 2000 that it expects to save $200 million over three years by adopting Nissan's lean production practices.[96] Daimler hopes to benefit from Chrysler's expertise in mass marketing

Table 2.5. Labor Productivity at North American Assembly Plants in 2001

Company	Location	Vehicles	Hours per Vehicle
GM	Oshawa #1	Monte Carlo, Impala	16.79
Nissan	Smyrna	Altima	17.30
Ford	Atlanta	Taurus, Sable	17.78
Ford	Chicago	Sable, Taurus	18.31
Nissan	Smyrna	Frontier	18.36
GM	Oshawa #2	Century, Lumina, Regal	18.47
Nissan	Smyrna	Xterra	18.63
Honda	East Liberty	Civic	19.20
Toyota	Cambridge North	Corolla	19.83
Honda	Marysville	Accord, Acura CL/TL	20.28

Source: www.autonews.com (accessed June 13, 2002).

and low-cost production and Chrysler from Daimler's engineering expertise. Chrysler will, for example, adopt the Mercedes "quality gate" system in which a project may not go forward to the next stage until all issues (such as marketing, quality, and manufacturing) are resolved.[97] The question that remains is whether such efficiency-enhancing managerial techniques really demand merger in order to be utilized. The techniques of lean production, for example, are by now widely known to all manufacturers. GM was able to learn much about lean production through its New United Motors Manufacturing Incorporated (NUMMI) joint venture with Toyota, begun in 1984.[98]

Comparative advantage may also derive from access to cheaper inputs or factors of production. Might this explain some mergers? The United States is a capital-abundant country, and access to cheap capital might motivate the acquisition of a U.S. auto company by a firm from a high-capital-cost country. Yet the major acquisition we have here is Daimler acquiring Chrysler, and Germany is also a capital-abundant country. Similarly, Japan is no more a capital-abundant country than France or Germany, so that the acquisition of Japanese firms by Renault (Nissan) and Daimler (Mitsubishi) do not obviously fit this explanation.

Perhaps labor abundance may explain some mergers. Korea has been, at least until very recently, a labor-abundant country and foreign companies have acquired all Korean firms. But is it cheap labor they seek or access to the protected Korean market and a production base close to China? Since auto production is generally considered to be a capital-intensive activity, the acquisition of auto companies in labor-abundant countries by firms from capital-abundant countries is unlikely to be fully explained by factor cost incentives. Furthermore, what developing countries offer in terms of low labor costs may be offset by much lower labor productivity. The data in table 2.3 show labor productivity in developing countries (in 1989) to be considerably lower than in Japan, the United States, and Europe. Finally, auto firms seeking the benefits of lower labor costs need not merge in order to benefit from these costs, unless compelled to do so by host governments. Volkswagen did not need to merge in order to take advantage of lower labor costs in Brazil in the 1950s; rather, it simply invested directly in Brazilian assembly plants. American firms do not need to merge to produce in Mexico, as they can do so through their own subsidiaries. Porsche assembles half the annual production of its Boxster model in Finland, partly because of lower labor costs. If low labor costs are the motivating factor, U.S. and European firms could do better than seeking partners in Korea, which has, by East Asian standards, relatively high-cost labor. Collaborative ventures with local firms in developing countries, including merger and acquisition, are more likely the result of political constraints than of any market incentives. China is an obvious example; foreign firms have been forced into coproduction alliances with local firms by the foreign investment and trade policies of the Chinese governments. Absent such interference, they would be more likely to export to China from more capital-abundant countries, given the relatively high cost of automobile production in China.[99]

Labor-abundant countries will in general have a comparative disadvantage in producing autos. The fact that international auto companies do produce in highly labor-abundant economies, such as China, is simply evidence of the strength of trade barriers against imports. Companies that do produce autos in China find their production costs much higher than in more capital-abundant economies. Some parts of the auto industry may well be able to use labor-intensive technology, and manufacturers can to some extent vary the factor intensity of production to accommodate the relative abundance of labor in some locations, but it is unlikely that the fundamental cost disadvantage of labor-abundant economies could be entirely overcome.

Yet labor costs may well play a role in certain mergers. Volkswagen attributes its success at rebuilding Czech producer Skoda in part to lower wages in Czechoslovakia. Yet again, if low wages were Volkswagen's objective, other eastern European countries could offer lower labor costs than Czechoslovakia. The primary attraction of Skoda was a product range suitable for mass marketing in developing countries, particularly Latin America, China, India, and Russia.[100] Czechoslovakia is also, unlike Third World countries, well endowed with human capital.

Portfolio Considerations

There is another form of complementarity that involves reducing risks rather than costs. It is well known that investors may reduce risk by constructing a portfolio of investments whose fortunes do not fluctuate in unison. If the rates of return in two assets are less than perfectly positively correlated (that is, they do not move in the same directions by the same proportions), the investor who divides his portfolio equally between the two will see a rate of return that is the simple average of the two but a risk (variation over time in the rate of return on the portfolio) that is less than the simple average of the two because the fluctuations in rates of return will tend to at least partially cancel out each other. If the rates of return of the two stocks are perfectly (positively) correlated, there will no risk reduction gains from diversification.

Auto firms might derive portfolio gains from merger under two conjectures. One would be if they have products that occupy different segments of the market and their revenues do not have a high positive covariation over time. If, for example, sales of Volvos rise when sales of Ford Tauruses go down, Ford will have derived portfolio risk reduction from its acquisition of Volvo. Unfortunately, there is little evidence that sales of autos in different market segments are not highly, positively correlated. Demand for Chrysler autos rises and falls with the demand for Mercedes because both are responding to the same macroeconomic conditions, though luxury autos may be somewhat less vulnerable to income fluctuations (that is, they have a lower income elasticity of demand).

The other beneficial portfolio situation would exist if two companies occupy different geographic market spaces in which demand fluctuates independently. Insofar as global macroeconomic cycles are negatively correlated across countries (for example, if Japan booms when Europe is in a depression), a European–Japanese merger could generate risk reduction gains. Such gains are increasingly unlikely to be found. The benefits of geographic diversification in the stock market have diminished considerably during the past ten years. The correlation between American and foreign share prices has increased from 0.4 in the mid-1990s to 0.8 in 2000.[101] This makes it increasingly implausible that a merged firm could gain risk reduction through geographic diversification because the increasingly high correlation of stock market and macroeconomic cycles across countries also means that the demand for autos is likely to be similarly correlated.

Proponents of the Daimler-Chrysler merger made much of the argument that Daimler is strong in Latin America and Africa, where Chrysler has little presence, and Chrysler could provide Daimler with the earnings stability of the American market independently of Daimler's global fortunes. Though this might appear to be a portfolio risk reduction argument, it is probably not. Global international economic interdependence is going to make an auto company's fortunes fluctuate simultaneously in all its markets. If there is merit in this geographic argument, it is that such mergers may allow each partner lower cost entry into sales opportunities in markets where it previously had little presence, though one might still ask why a merger is necessary for a firm to establish a presence in a new market. This is a theme that is taken up in chapter 3.

Cost Cutting: The Evidence

The cost-cutting rationale for merger is that it creates opportunities for savings that were not available to the individual firms separately prior to the merger. A study of mergers in general has suggested that merged firms are less effective at cutting costs than nonmerging firms.[102] But what of the auto industry specifically? Is there evidence that mergers have helped firms cut costs through scale economies, cost sharing, capacity reduction, capacity reduction, or comparative advantage?

Casual observation of recent mergers would suggest that such gains are not as quickly forthcoming as the proponents of merger would have hoped. The cost-cutting efforts we have seen subsequent to recent mergers, such as Renault and Nissan and Daimler-Chrysler, have not obviously been a mutual benefit made possible by merger as the theory would have it. Rather, they have been cases of relatively healthy firms acquiring firms that were financially ailing, in at least one case (Chrysler) to an extent not understood, or perhaps even exacerbated, by the acquiring firm. The latter then had to impose drastic cost-cutting measures on its acquisition in order to reduce the financial burden of the acquisition. This is hardly consistent with the hypothetical example of two firms that merge to take advantage of cost-cutting opportunities that may be created by the merger.

Renault manager Carlos Goshn (nicknamed "le cost cutter") performed the remarkable task of turning Nissan from a loss-making to a profit-making enterprise, partly by cost-cutting measures. Nissan posted a profit of $2.7 billion for the year ending March 2001. Since moving to Nissan in 1999, Goshn has cut materials costs by 20 percent, closed capacity (raising capacity utilization from 50 percent to 74 percent), cut 10 percent of the workforce, and reduced Nissan's debt from $10.9 billion to $7.7 billion.[103] Yet how much of this should necessarily be attributed to the merger itself? Goshn (or a similarly competent management consultant) could have been hired by Nissan to take exactly the same kinds of measures. The only way that the cost reduction at Nissan can be attributed directly to the merger would be if one could show that it somehow would have been impossible for Nissan to take these same measures in the absence of merger and external control. While this might indeed be the case, no systematic analysis of the Nissan–Renault relationship has attempted to make such a case, though anecdotal evidence of such situations abounds. Consider the remarks of Daimler executive Rolf Eckrodt, dispatched to Tokyo to run Mitsubishi and ultimately to replace Japanese CEO Takashi Sonobe:

> I had no choice. . . . And unfortunately I did not have enough time to be diplomatic. You see, clocks tick to a different rhythm here in Japan. Top management typically does not understand what good cars are about and is not really interested in product either. Sadly, the same applies to second tier executives. Their only motivation is to make that final step up the ladder, and they act ac-

cordingly. But middle management is truly promising. . . . I am going to promote forward thinkers, because they will have to run this company when our job is done.[104]

Daimler is optimistic that it can do the same thing with Chrysler. In January 2001, the new Chrysler CEO, Dieter Zetsche, announced plans to close six Chrysler plants and reduce the workforce by 26,000 employees in the expectation of restoring Chrysler to profitability by 2002. Yet again, one cannot consider this a desirable situation, a cost-cutting opportunity created by merger. On the contrary, it is an attempt to recover Daimler's fortunes from the disastrous effect of merging with a company that was financially self-destructing.

Much of the financial press coverage of these two auto mergers has focused on the efforts of the acquiring firm to cut costs. Both Zetsche and Goshn were charged with reducing the costs of Chrysler and Nissan, respectively. In both cases, the cost cutting involved internal measures (such as reducing personnel, cutting production capacity, and changing product lines) and attempts to force lower procurement costs onto suppliers. These obviously are not examples of cost saving made possible through merger. Rather, they are examples of healthy firms acquiring ailing firms and intervening to stem the losses the acquired firm imposes on the partner. These sorts of changes could have been made unilaterally, at least in principle, by the acquired firm itself without the need for merger, though one could argue that new management was necessary for such measures to be organizationally feasible within the management of the firm (Nissan? Chrysler?) or politically feasible to external constituencies, such as governments or labor unions (Daewoo? Fiat? Rover?).

Ford has had a similar experience with Mazda. After placing an American manager in charge of Mazda, Ford has spent much of the past decade attempting to restore Mazda's financial fortunes, but with mixed results. In the year ending March 2001, Mazda made a loss of $1.29 billion.[105] Once again, instead of a cost-cutting opportunity, Ford acquired an unprofitable organization that has been a financial drain on the parent. Whether Ford can restore Mazda's market fortunes remains to be seen, but this is again not an example of a cost-cutting opportunity created by merger but rather an example of cost cutting necessitated by an otherwise financially disappointing merger.

GM has had no better luck. Its recent acquisitions and alliances have involved companies making substantial losses (Saab, Isuzu, and Fiat), prompting one auto analyst to remark that "GM has allied itself with some of the worst car companies in the world."[106] GM's main European subsidiary, Opel, lost $1 billion in 2000–2001. Saab lost $515 million in 2002, and GM's European operations as whole lost more than $900 million in 2002. During 2001, Fiat began a massive restructuring plan involving plant closures in an attempt to stem mounting losses that climbed to nearly $1 billion by the end of 2002. The weak record so far has not stopped companies from making rosy predictions about cost saving through merger. Fiat and GM claim to have saved 500 million euros in 2001 from joint purchasing and shared platforms.[107] Yet Daimler and Chrysler were equally euphoric in their postmerger announcements.

Conclusion

Conventional industrial organization analyses offer a variety of reasons for how a merger may enable the combined firms to lower costs.[108] In reality, such a feat is extraordinarily difficult. The most often cited attraction, economies of scale, has been greatly diminished in the contemporary auto industry. What scale economies remain can be acquired even by small companies through outsourcing. Some reasons, like capacity reduction, are in principle possible but unlikely to be a serious (or at least logical) inducement to merge, except in the rather distorted sense that merger may entail new management prepared to do things that previous management was not. Complementarities akin to the comparative advantage of nations are usually attainable without all the extra baggage of a merger. Sharing the sunk, preproduction costs of R&D and tooling does stand out as a still-powerful incentive to combine forces. Yet when examined closely, it is apparent that much R&D is available to small auto companies that purchase it from outside the firm, a tactic employed by even the largest automakers in the area of alternative fuel systems. Finally, the empirical record of recent cases suggests that, far from enabling mutual gains from cost cutting, recent mergers have simply saddled healthy firms with distressed firms in need of aid and new management, though such a judgment may be premature. Whether the major auto companies can attain from their acquisitions the long-run cost savings that they have failed to achieve in the short run remains to be seen.

CHAPTER THREE

The Quest for New
Products and New Markets

The president of General Motors' (GM's) European operations has suggested that GM has two objectives beyond sustaining economies of scale: building a "global sales footprint" and pursuing a "multi-brand" strategy.[1] Firms may merge or ally to acquire products or enter markets more quickly or efficiently than would be the case if they had to do so unilaterally. The leaders of some auto companies appear to believe that they must break away from the market niches in which they were initially successful and span the entire range of automobile size and functional variations, producing subcompacts to full-size vehicles and sports cars to all-terrain vehicles. These aspirations sometimes focus on specific items, such as a type of vehicle or technology, and sometimes on a more general faith in the existence of "synergies" between merged firms. Some even attempt to move beyond the auto sector into related sectors, a theme taken up in chapter 4. There is a similar imperative that drives companies to want to penetrate all possible geographic markets, globally diversifying their portfolios. Most auto manufacturers are highly optimistic about future auto sales in populous developing countries, and ensuring a presence in these markets has figured in some prominent merger negotiations. Globalization also brings them into strategic interactions both with host governments that have their own objectives and with the rules of international trade regimes that can make major alterations to their investment incentives.

Putting aside for now the issue of why auto firms have such goals (rational profit maximization? intrafirm organizational politics?), this chapter takes up the question of to what extent existing mergers have been driven by this quest for new products, markets, and, more generally, synergies that firms cannot achieve in isolation. Part of the answer to these questions will take the form of asking whether the acquiring firm could have produced the same results in the absence of merger. If a new product or market could have been acquired either by in-house development or by purchasing from another firm in an arm's-length transaction, the plausibility, or at least the rationality, of product or market expansion as a motive for merger is less persuasive. A related way of exploring the argument is to ask whether acquiring a particular product or entering a specific market would prove to be beneficial to the company. This latter form of evidence may be illuminating but does not necessarily shed light on motives for mergers. Firm X may acquire firm Y, thinking that Y's products or its access to particular markets will be profitable, but firm X may be mistaken.

Evidence that a belief is mistaken does not, of course, disprove the possibility that the belief was a motive for action. In the nineteenth century, European countries thought that their newly acquired colonies would be profitable, but for the most part they were wrong. Yet it is still reasonable to suggest that profit was a motive for imperial expansion. Countries and corporations can make mistakes just like individuals, though they are also collectivities of individuals, and as such are subject to a wider array of motivations. Countries and corporations, unlike individuals who internalize the sum of all the cost and benefits of an action, can also embark on strategies that are harmful to the organization as a whole but beneficial to well-placed individuals or groups within the collectivity, a theme taken up in chapter 5. A merger may serve the interest of a manager or group of executives at the expense of the corporation as a whole, an accusation frequently leveled at the management of Daimler by groups of dissident shareholders.

Merger as a Source of New Products

Have mergers provided auto companies with new products that have significantly enhanced their offerings to customers and in a way that is more profitable than developing those same products internally and unilaterally? Superficially, this would certainly appear to be the case, an impression encouraged by the manufacturers. The auto industry has long since moved away from the simple market taxonomy of cheap small cars and expensive large ones for the appropriate income category into a highly differentiated pattern of segmentation based more on vehicle function (for example, a small, sporty, high-power station wagon, such as the Audi S4 Avant).[2] The much wider contemporary array of product categories may provide a greater incentive to broaden a firm's product range through alliances. The strategy is fraught with dangers for companies such as Mercedes-Benz, whose success has been historically based in particular niches defined by price and type of vehicle.

One of the most successful examples of this motivation is Volkswagen's (VW's) acquisition of Auto Union in 1964. Despite the extraordinary success of the Beetle, VW was clearly trapped by its dependence on one model, a single air-cooled-engine design (in several variations) and rear-wheel-drive technology. What Auto Union and its revived Audi nameplate brought to VW was liquid-cooled-engine technology and front-wheel drive, which together revived VW's fortunes as production of the obsolete Beetle was sloughed off to developing countries. VW's current product line, the Golf, Jetta, and Passat models, all stem from its acquisition of Auto Union. Former VW Chairman Ferdinand Piëch frequently criticized Audi as having been a very expensive acquisition, even suggesting that it would have been cheaper to develop the technology within VW.[3] Nevertheless, opportunity cost aside, it is clear that the Audi acquisition did bring the technology to VW. When Porsche chose to abandon air-cooled engines, it did follow the path of in-house development of liquid-cooled engines, though it nearly went bankrupt in the process. Nor was the transition to liquid-cooled engines easy for VW. The Beetle's successor, the Golf (Rabbit in the United States) was so severely plagued with problems of quality, reliability, and transitional technology—partly because of VW's new U.S. manufacturing plant in Westmoreland, Pennsylvania—that VW came close to abandoning the U.S. market in the late 1980s.[4]

VW's recent acquisitions of Bentley, Bugatti, and Lamborghini have less obvious benefits other than the prestige of their "boutique" name brands. VW purchased Lamborghini for $111 million in 1998 to acquire a presence in the rarefied world of exotic supercars. Lamborghini expects to sell only 400 copies annually (at $275,000 each) of its first new creation in over a decade, the Murciélago.[5] Neither Bentley nor Lamborghini has technologies needed by VW. None of these brands makes money for VW. Bentley needs to sell at least 10,000 cars per year to make a profit; it currently sells fewer than 1,500. Rolls Royce (whose brand name was transferred to BMW in 2003 by prior agreement) lost VW $150 million in 2001. These low-volume specialty marques soak up a considerable amount of VW's engineering effort, and it is hard to imagine that the "goodwill" of brand image could be worth what it costs VW.[6]

American companies have historically seen acquisitions as a means to acquire small cars for the U.S. market. Chrysler bought the French manufacturer

Simca in 1958 primarily to have a small car to compete with VW's Beetle in the U.S. market, though the effort was unfruitful. Ford's alliance with Mazda in the 1970s, evolving into full control by the 1990s, provided Ford both specific products (notably Mazda's engines and front-wheel-drive technology utilized in the popular Ford Escort) and the opportunity to learn Japanese production techniques, especially the multifaceted aspects of lean production. Mazda also provided Ford with access to the Wankel rotary engine, for which Mazda had purchased a license from the German company NSU in 1961. Although Mazda has struggled to increase its market share and has been financially troubled during the 1990s, the relationship did help Ford establish a presence in the subcompact front-wheel-drive market and helped rescue Ford from its own disastrous efforts in the subcompact market, notably the infamous Ford Pinto, which suffered from a problem with the fuel tank.

Ford's recent acquisitions have been in the luxury end of the market: Volvo, Jaguar, Aston Martin, and Land Rover. It has grouped them into an organizationally separate unit, the Premier Automotive Group (PAG), along with its domestic Lincoln brand. Ford's hope is that this newly acquired luxury brands group will, despite meager sales of fewer than one million in 2001, enhance profitability through the higher profit margin of luxury vehicles and standardization of parts across these luxury marques. By 2005, Ford expects PAG to provide one-third of its global pretax profits despite the unit's collective losses of nearly $1 billion in 2002.[7] All these specialty brands have been financially troubled companies, and whether they can collectively make a significant and profitable contribution to Ford's product portfolio remains to be seen. Ford came very close to closing Jaguar in 1991 because of large losses, and it is arguable whether it might have been cheaper to develop its own luxury brand. Jaguar did not make a profit for Ford until 1999 and lost $500 million in 2002. Much of Ford's confidence appears to be focused on tailoring Jaguar to a mass market, which it has done by rebadging and rebodying more basic Ford products. The newest "X type" Jaguar is, to the uncharitable, merely a modified Ford Contour (in Europe, the Ford Mondeo).[8] There is considerable speculation in the automotive press as to whether Ford is debasing the Jaguar brand name for short-term profits.[9] Aston Martins use a variation on the Ford Taurus engine and share many other Ford components. As these luxury brands make more and more use of the Ford parts bin, it may become increasingly questionable whether Ford has actually acquired any new products at all. Did Ford merely pay a very high price to acquire the mystique and image of famous nameplates to apply to Ford products?[10]

GM's acquisition of Saab is more of the same. A once-chic Swedish automaker, Saab fell on hard times because its products began to lag far behind the market in technological content and consumer appeal. Saab was too big to be a specialty brand and too small to be a volume manufacturer. The company continued to languish under GM management, leading GM to briefly consider merging Saab with Cadillac's European organization, a linkage that would have hardly been likely to appeal to Saab's median owner. In a dozen years of ownership, GM has sunk over $1.5 billion into Saab and received back a profit in only two of those years. Once again, the Saab acquisition begins to look much like Ford's acquisition of Jaguar—purchasing a name that may raise the image of the host company and possibly offer the opportunity to sell more mundane vehicles under an upmarket name. Finding itself the owner of a brand too expensive to compete in the mainstream market but lacking the appeal of other premium brands (such as Audi and BMW), GM is being pushed toward the same strategy as Ford and may resort to simply re-badging mass-market vehicles with the Saab name, as Ford has done with Jaguar.

Opel and Fiat are two of Europe's worst-performing auto companies. GM's alliance with Fiat has been justified as providing the American company with genuinely new products, principally the range of subcompact autos that are Fiat's market niche in Europe and in the rest of the world. Fiat also brings to GM a range of luxury marques analogous to Ford's strategy (Alfa Romeo, Ferrari, and Maserati). GM has some prior experience at the Ford tactic of rebadging luxury autos, with its ill-fated attempt to sell a Cadillac–Maserati in the 1980s. To the extent that Fiat provides GM with new products, it will occur through collaboration with GM's European subsidiary, Opel, a company that has long produced GM's European models, especially in the compact and subcompact range. Hence the question again arises: With the exception of its small-volume luxury marques, does Fiat bring any genuinely new products to GM, products that it could not develop by itself or under its German subsidiary Opel? As Fiat sinks under the weight of its mounting financial woes, the relationship is of doubtful value to GM. GM's purchase of Daewoo provides an alternative source of small-car production, based on a previously successful alliance that had been dissolved in 1992. Between 1987 and 1993, GM imported from Daewoo 236,000 Korean-built versions of the Opel Kadett, sold in the United States as the Pontiac Lemans. With the 2002 acquisition in place, GM began shipping Daewoo autos to Mexico for sale in the North American market under the GM name. In the European market, Daewoo will displace the cheapest Opels.

Insofar as companies like Ford and GM are merely buying nameplates rather than genuinely new products or technologies, they create further problems for themselves by inviting consumers to compare the prices of their different name brands that attempt to conceal nearly identical products.[11] This problem is not uniquely a result of merger and acquisition. VW has had a significant issue in this regard as a result of having only four basic platforms and thus a product line that displays to the consumer autos that are very similar yet with high variation in price.

Daimler merged with (or, in retrospect, acquired) Chrysler partly because of a perceived need to extend itself into mass-market vehicles, including the expanding sport-utility vehicle (SUV) and minivan markets. The main difficulty with this rationale is that Daimler was perfectly capable of extending its own Mercedes brand into these markets and indeed did so during the 1990s. It developed the subcompact "Smart" car, its own four-wheel-drive SUV (the Mercedes-Benz ML320), the "Baby Benz" A- and C-class sedans, and the behemoth Unimog, the last mentioned to compete with GM's military-derived Hummer. The ML320, manufactured at Daimler's Tuscaloosa, Alabama, plant, has been remarkably successful, sales expanding from 65,000 in 1998 to 80,000 in 1999.[12] Daimler's rescue of the financially ailing Chrysler actually forced it to cut back expansion of production of its Smart car program, sales of which had increased by 60 percent in 2000.[13] As the dust settles from this emotionally charged merger several years after the event, it is unclear that Daimler has actually acquired any new vehicles or technologies. Chrysler is to produce a new vehicle named the Crossfire with a Mercedes engine—a meager result, especially so when such exchanges can easily occur without merger.

BMW purchased Rover in 1994 for much the same purpose: to break out of its semiluxury sports sedan niche into the mass market.[14] A lesser motive was to acquire Land Rover's all-wheel-drive (AWD) technology, though BMW developed its own AWD and now successfully markets its X5 AWD SUV. BMW was already selling its own cheaper mass-market model (the BMW 318), and Chairman Joachim Milberg later admitted that BMW had no need for Land Rover's AWD technology.[15] Land Rover was later sold to Ford, which also did not need the AWD technology but apparently thought it could use the brand name. Having paid $1.2 billion for Rover, BMW invested $3.4 billion in it and sold the remains in 1999 for about $15, though it had separately sold Land Rover to Ford for $2.8 billion. What BMW held back from the Rover sale was the newly marketed Mini, a modern version of the famous front-wheel-drive subcompact from the 1960s. BMW has been reported to have made so many design changes to the Rover concept that it will be many years before the vehicle becomes profitable.[16] The vehicle that emerged was very much a BMW with little in common with its Rover origins except for the brand name. BMW is also facing the costs of absorbing Rolls Royce from VW in 2003, an acquisition made even more problematic by

Rolls Royce's losses of over $200 million in 1999.[17] As BMW moves it own product line up into superluxury territory with the new BMW 7 series, it is questionable what it has to gain from absorbing a British luxury brand that is losing money.

The general record of auto firms merging in the quest for new products has been mostly unhappy and unnecessary since they developed or could have developed those same products themselves. Some newly acquired products appear to be little more than exercises in rebadging. Even in the absence of self-development, auto firms do not need to merge in order to acquire new products or technologies. Toyota's policy is to supplement its product line not through merger but more simply by arm's-length collaboration with other makers. Toyota sells both Ford and VW-Audi products through its Japanese dealers.[18] Toyota is to collaborate with Peugeot-Citroën (PSA) in the production of a cheap subcompact designed for the European market, particularly that of eastern Europe. Expected to begin production in 2005, the factory in the Czech Republic will produce 300,000 vehicles annually, to be sold under all three brand names.[19] VW plans to purchase telematics equipment from Toyota, which in turn has a telematics alliance with GM.[20]

Apart from a desire to acquire specific products or technologies, merger may be motivated by a more general belief that a company may benefit from another's human capital, that being expertise or experience in particular activities. One survey of auto projects found that Japanese auto companies excelled at rapid product development and build quality and that European firms had the advantage in design quality.[21] Most cooperative ventures in the 1970s and 1980s (such as Toyota and GM, Mazda and Ford, and Honda and Rover) were motivated by the desire of Western auto companies to acquire Japanese expertise in engineering, manufacturing techniques, and production management and the desire of Japanese companies to learn Western ideas about brand management, design, and financial controls. The most famous was GM's joint venture with Toyota in 1984, NUMMI, in which an old GM plant in Fremont, California, was used to display Japanese manufacturing and management techniques in an American context.[22] Yet we should note that the collaboration did not lead to a GM–Toyota merger. More recently, Ford has discussed various forms of cooperation with Toyota, the latter tapping into Ford's expertise in financial services and Ford benefiting from Toyota's work on low-emission vehicles.[23]

What Chrysler learned about lean production from Mitsubishi later helped make it attractive to Daimler, while Chrysler hoped to benefit from Daimler's engineering skills. For example, Mercedes learned from Chrysler how to speed the transition from manufacturing old products to new ones, while Chrysler learned how to treat convertible tops so that both hardtops and convertibles could move down the same assembly line.[24] Daimler-Chrysler's more recent link to Mitsubishi and Hyundai is hoped to provide expertise in small cars. GM's relationship with Suzuki gave it access to the latter's expertise in making small cars, and with Subaru came access to a superior AWD technology.[25]

The luxury brands that Ford has grouped under its PAG are intended to be "centers of excellence" in building Ford's expertise in particular areas of design. Volvo is to be the "safety center," Jaguar the leader in "sporty driving dynamics," Land Rover to lead in AWD development, and Aston Martin a test bed for high technology and lightweight materials.[26] GM has a similar "Premier Alliance" strategy designed to pool the expertise from Saab, Opel, Lancia, Fiat, Cadillac, and Alfa Romeo, the purpose being to enable GM to successfully market "premium niche vehicles" having a "flexible vehicle architecture that allows auto makers to more quickly respond to changing consumer tastes."[27] Laudable as such goals may be, it is still questionable as to whether acquiring expensive and ailing luxury auto companies is the best way to acquire such expertise.

Chrysler and BMW have provided an alternative exemplar of how to acquire expertise without exchange of equity. In 1996, Chrysler and BMW embarked on a joint project to produce a small auto engine in Brazil for the BMW Mini and the Chrysler Neon.[28] The aim of the collaboration was to enable BMW to learn low-cost design and manufacturing from Chrysler and for the latter to learn how to produce durable and reliable engines for the European market. Each side owned 50 percent of the joint venture and had veto power over important decisions and the right to terminate the agreement at one year's notice. As the first engines were being produced in early 2001, Chrysler announced that it was reviewing the commitment because of a reduction in the production of Neon cars (and perhaps also because of Daimler–BMW rivalry), and the venture has since ended.[29] Nevertheless, the project stands out as an instructive example of how firms may benefit from the expertise of each other without partial or full merger. BMW has since turned to Toyota to provide diesel engines for the Mini.

In Search of Synergies
The previously discussed factors are all tangible benefits—additions to a firm's product or technological capabilities as a result of collaboration. There may also be intangible benefits, usually referred to by the mysterious name "synergy." One of the few attempts to measure synergy is that of Sirower,[30]

who deals with the elusiveness of the concept by defining it simply as all forms of value added as a result of corporate consolidation. If the value of the whole exceeds the values of the parts that had previously been priced separately by the market, synergy has occurred. While this definition makes measurement relatively simple, it includes all forms of value added when a merger takes place. All gains from merger are subsumed under the term "synergy." If, for example, a merger enables economies of scale to be achieved, Sirower defines that gain as synergy. Rather than consolidate everything under the term "synergy," it may be more illuminating to use the traditional terms to refer to familiar concepts (such as cost savings through scale economies or the acquisition of new products) and reserve "synergy" for intangible qualities that cannot be better described in terms of other variables.

References to synergies abound in the auto merger literature. Former BMW executive Bernd Pischetsrieder (appointed head of VW in 2002) talked of "cross fertilization" benefits from acquiring Rover.[31] Daimler-Chrysler executives constantly referred to synergies in justifying the merger. GM Chief Executive Officer Rick Wagoner has suggested that his firm's strategy of alliances "allows us to realize synergies faster than we could have in a full buy-out."[32] The term "synergy" in many cases is simply a synonym for complementarities involving division of labor of a kind already discussed (for example, firm A provides engineering expertise and firm B marketing skills).[33] At best, it refers to some sort of superadditivity involving intangible variables such as human capital, whereby the value of A and B combined is somehow greater than their separate sums for reasons that cannot be conveniently reduced to familiar factors. Sometimes the term appears to refer to the possibility of miraculous transformations of a sickly company into an automotive star—the toad will turn into a handsome prince when kissed by the princess. At worst, such arguments end up as the last refuge of those who cannot identify any tangible benefits of the action they desire for reasons that they cannot or will not articulate.

There is also a possibility that whatever intangible synergies exist are negative ones. Corporate alliances suffer from a 70 percent failure rate mainly because of poor communication, according to a consulting study by Vantage Partners.[34] They appear to share the unreliability of human marriages and military alliances between states.[35] Much has been said about the clash of corporate cultures resulting from combinations of BMW and Rover and of Chrysler and Daimler. Chris Brady and Andrew Lorenz present the image of an "intransigent, arrogant and grasping" Rover management interacting with BMW managers hobbled by "strategic blindness," "factionalism," and (intra-BMW) "personal rivalries."[36] Daimler's "formality and hierarchy" interacted poorly with Chrysler's "cross functional teams" engaging in "free form discussions."[37] An earlier merger between Fiat and Citroën suffered from similar negative synergies. GM, despite its belief that alliances yield more rapid synergies than mergers, has had its own problems. GM has reportedly had problems getting Fiat and Opel to cooperate because of cultural and nationalistic clashes. Opel and Fiat are market rivals that have difficulty cooperating, and Opel itself has a troubled position within the GM framework (one that, for example, creates conflict between the heads of Opel and GM Europe).[38]

When pressed to give examples of synergies in the Daimler-Chrysler merger, executives cite examples of what are mostly component sharing (such as Mercedes engines in Chryslers) or intracorporate specialization (such as pooling small-car development in Hyundai and Mitsubishi).[39] Yet Daimler executives also confess that they worry about the Mercedes image being "contaminated" by association with Chrysler and have worried about it becoming public knowledge that Chrysler Jeeps and Mercedes SUVs share an assembly line in Austria.[40] The latest showcase for synergies is the new Chrysler Crossfire, a midmarket sports car that Chrysler executive Wolfgang Bernard has called "the first true child of the merger."[41] Yet it is difficult to see how sourcing 40 percent of the components of a Chrysler vehicle from Mercedes qualifies as a novel synergy or even a synergy at all, given that division of labor and component sharing is a strategy automakers have been employing for several decades without full mergers. In any case, Daimler-Chrysler expects to sell fewer than 20,000 Crossfires annually,[42] and the vehicle is clearly not going to bring benefits of great magnitude to the company, synergistic or otherwise.

Merger for Entry into New Markets

Firms invariably become enthused over the prospect of entering new geographic territory, whether as a base for lower cost production or, more usually, for sales and market growth. Just as the nineteenth-century English cotton textile producers looked to the empire for new markets, the automakers of today's developed countries look to the less developed areas of the globe for similar gains. The postwar British government expected a huge export market for its auto manufacturers in the Soviet Union, predicting sales of 20 million vehicles during the five-year period 1949–1954.[43] Such a vision, with the benefit of hindsight, inspires caution in assessing the vistas of new and uncharted markets in the Third World.

The same optimism may be found in contemporary market forecasts predicting "rich opportunities for mature enterprises in emerging markets where car density is low, such as China and Russia."[44] Typical market projections suggest that the Asia-Pacific region and eastern Europe will provide manufacturers with the largest market growth during the first decade of this century.[45] These developing countries are also thought to have production cost advantages that might make them attractive as centers of large-scale production for export, particularly if they are located within free trade areas in which they will have tariff-free access to the markets of other members. Ford, GM, Honda, and BMW are either establishing or concentrating manufacturing for the Asian market in Thailand partly because of that country's location within the Association of Southeast Asian Nations (ASEAN).[46]

Some part of the consolidation of the auto industry has been attributed to the lure of these new markets. One motivation behind the Daimler-Chrysler merger was that Chrysler was weak in the European and Asian markets, where Daimler had a strong dealer network. Chrysler was thought to have the low-cost autos that could be sold through Daimler outlets, particularly in developing countries. Yet Daimler's products in many of these markets were mostly commercial vehicles, the sale and distribution of which is unlikely to easily lend itself to selling Chrysler cars. Some Chrysler managers were highly skeptical of such ambitions. Chrysler's head of international operations, Jim Holden, on a premerger tour of global markets, observed that India had "hardly any cars, . . . just an extraordinary number of extremely poor people," concluding that "the market's just not there" in developing countries.[47] More plausibly, Chrysler would enhance Daimler's position in the U.S. market. The two companies were seen by the proponents of merger as geographically complementary, at least insofar as their respective geographic footprints had little overlap. The claim that Daimler and Chrysler could each provide the other with easy access to new markets was often reiterated by proponents of the merger.

Bids for South Korea's major auto companies (Daewoo and Hyundai) were made largely in the belief that ownership of these companies would not only permit entrance into the protected Korean market but also facilitate entry into China.[48] The willingness of the Bank of China to extend a $500 million credit line to Hyundai in December 2001 supports this reasoning and indeed the importance of diplomatic and political factors that may indirectly encourage some auto mergers.[49] It is noteworthy that GM's takeover of bankrupt Daewoo included very little of Daewoo's assets outside Korea and only required GM to take over Daewoo's two modern factories in Korea and one in Vietnam. The agreement makes it clear that what GM values in Daewoo is its presence in Korea and its possibilities as a base from which to export to China. GM has no interest in the rest of Daewoo's far-flung global empire, including its U.S. marketing and sales operation.[50] Similarly, the alliance of Renault and Nissan may be helping both of them in Russia and China. Renault plans to enter the Chinese market by way of Nissan's joint venture with a local partner, the Dongfeng Motor Corporation. Nissan vehicles will be sold by Renault's sales network in Russia.

Daimler's overture to Chrysler was pitched partly in terms of penetrating third markets, mostly in the developing world.[51] The idea was that their talents would be combined to build an inexpensive vehicle to be sold in low-income countries. There have been earlier manifestations of this imperative. In the 1970s, some corporate alliances were driven by the quest for the illusive "world car" that would be sold in the same form around the world and particularly in lower-income countries. The Ford Escort/Mazda 323 was one such venture, begun in the early 1970s using Mazda engines in the subcompact Ford Escort platform. The world car concept seems to have largely vanished, partly because different markets demanded different vehicle characteristics and perhaps also because modular construction now makes it easy to tailor vehicles for particular markets. Ford made so many changes to the European and American versions of the Escort that they ended up sharing only two parts: the ashtray and an instrument panel brace.[52] GM's first world car, the "J" car of the 1980s (known as the Chevrolet Cavalier and the Opel Ascona), was also subject to so much redesign for individual markets that many benefits of standardization were lost.[53] VW has abandoned the idea of a world car based on the VW Lupo and will produce cars tailored for the individual markets. The Chinese version of the VW Polo, for example, has been produced in Shanghai since early 2002.[54] GM has also announced that the forthcoming Opel Vectra will be its last attempt at a world car to be sold in the same basic form in many countries. Henceforth, it says, the products of GM, Opel, and Saab will share only engines, transmissions, and air conditioners. GM had found that the demands of different markets were sufficiently different that projects started as world cars evolved to be so distinct that they had to incur extra tooling costs in each market, and thus much of the savings from the world car concept disappeared.[55] The failure of the world car concept might well cast doubt on the extent to which mergers will yield the kinds of cost-sharing benefits cited in chapter 2. Of the major producers, only financially troubled Fiat remains wedded to the idea of a car for all markets, and it plans to replace its Palio (sold since 1996) with a new world car in 2005.[56]

Another variation has been joint ventures with indigenous firms, though not always with agreeable outcomes.[57] The "infant industry" model of economic development has always been popular in developing countries, as it was to late industrializing countries (notably Germany and the United States) in the nineteenth century, struggling to catch up to Britain. The basic idea is that an underdeveloped economy may industrialize behind high tariff walls. However, since capital is required to develop these infants, an appeal is made to foreign corporations to enter into partnerships with local firms. Much of the auto industry in poor countries has been developed in this manner, generally yielding high cost and poor-quality autos that could never compete in world markets. The infants remain stunted, and the political leadership is ultimately faced with the dilemma of continuing to foster an uncompetitive, high-cost industry or to open it up to international competition and see the industry disappear, with all the undesirable domestic political consequences that such a decision entails. The government of India is grappling with precisely this problem as it offers ownership of its largest automaker, Maruti, to foreign auto companies. China is in effect having the decision made for it as membership of the World Trade Organization (WTO) forces it to open its markets. China's domestic automakers will be exposed to the very bracing effect of global competition, both from imports and from foreign auto production within China, albeit with the transitional cushion of the WTO's graduated entry conditions for Third World countries and a residual tariff of 25 percent after entry conditions are met.

It is not only developing countries that have found themselves in this conundrum. Australia made the decision after World War II to develop a domestic auto industry. Given a small population, offering little opportunity for scale economies in production, it could do so only with high levels of tariff protection, forcing foreign companies like Ford and GM to manufacture locally in order to penetrate the market. The predictable result was that Australians paid much higher prices for motor vehicles than if they had been permitted to buy at world market prices undistorted by tariffs. Protection of the auto industry in Australia has gradually been reduced since the 1970s to 15 percent in 2002. Domestic producers (primarily GM's subsidiary Holden and Ford Australia) are lobbying against a planned further tariff reduction to 10 percent by 2005.[58]

Third World Auto Markets
To what extent might it be rational for auto companies to pursue global consolidation as a means to penetrate Third World markets? There are two principal questions here: Does the goal justify the effort, and is consolidation necessary to meet the goal? Were the prospective gains in these new markets largely a mirage, one might doubt that the lure of these markets would be a motive for global consolidation. However, as noted earlier, auto

executives are subject to wishful thinking just like the rest of us. Showing that auto sales in developing countries will be modest in the near future does not necessarily mean that the lure of sales could not be a motive for merger. Assuming that these new markets will bear fruit, there is the secondary question of whether firms need to consolidate in order to reap the harvest.

The attraction of developing-country markets appears to be based on speculations about the effect of population size on sales. Dazzled by the populations of the larger developing countries, such as China and India, the naive automaker looks no further. As they become immersed in these markets, they soon find that the reality of the situation is more complicated. Foreign automakers in Russia have been daunted by several factors. Bureaucracy and corruption make both importing and local production a slow and painful process. Once in the market, "Western automakers have trouble finding customers in a market where 90 percent of locally produced vehicles are priced under $5000."[59] What automakers from rich countries may fail to appreciate is the lack of effective purchasing power in the markets they are attempting to penetrate.

On the supply side, local production in emerging markets generally presents multinational automakers with much higher costs of production than they experience in their home countries or in other developed-country markets. Low wages may appear to be an attraction of poor countries, but the benefits are likely to be vitiated by low labor productivity, low levels of human capital (skills and knowledge), and the fact that automaking is a fundamentally capital-intensive industry in which low-wage, unskilled labor may confer little cost advantage. One study estimates the cost disadvantage in 1997 of local building to have been about 40 percent in Argentina, Poland, and Mexico; 170 percent in the Philippines; and 30 percent in India.[60] These cost disadvantages may well be overcome, especially as developing countries build up their stock of capital. BMW exports from South Africa, Honda from China, and GM from Thailand, but all do so in very small quantities, in some cases merely to keep factories running when local demand is low.[61] Total auto exports from the Third World were only 100,000 in 2001.

In addition to conditions of weak demand and high-cost production, developing countries may present idiosyncratic factors that typically resolve into matters of political intervention into the investment environment. In a rare skeptical comment, *Wall Street Journal* reporter Philip Segal asked, "Does it make sense any more for a foreign company to build a car factory in China (if it ever did)?"[62] Noting that most foreign automakers have been drawn to China by tariffs as high as 100 percent and 80 percent local content rules, all of which will eventually be significantly reduced when China is fully integrated into the WTO, Segal suggests that producers of capital-intensive goods like autos have little reason to invest in a labor-rich and capital-poor country when these politically motivated rules are withdrawn. He concludes by citing a remarkably atypical consultant who believes that China will be a "graveyard" for multinational auto companies.[63]

Auto ownership is driven by income and urbanization. A World Bank study has estimated car ownership in developing countries to be predicted by per capita income and urban population.[64] Table 3.1 displays per capita income, urbanization, and auto ownership data for a sample of developed and developing countries. The average urban worker's annual wage in China is about $1,200.[65] Most large developing countries have a long way to go before they reach the income and urbanization levels that will produce close to the modest levels of car ownership exhibited by even the upper tier of developing countries such as Korea, Mexico, Brazil, and Russia. Car ownership in these four newly industrializing countries still averages less than 25 percent of the ownership levels in the United States, Germany, France, and Britain. The increase in numbers of cars in China, India, and Nigeria over the past two decades has been large but only because it was starting from an insignificant base. Auto company executives who are dazzled by the size of the populations of these countries are likely to be disappointed. Table 3.2 provides further evidence, showing that the largest-growing market in the last five years of the twentieth century was in the urbanized and wealthier (relative to the Third World) market of eastern and central Europe.

Nevertheless, there is considerable faith that auto companies are about to strike gold in emerging markets, particularly those of Asia. The consulting firm PricewaterhouseCoopers predicts that annual global automotive production will grow by 10.9 billion vehicles between 1999 and 2006 despite noting that there is overcapacity in the industry of about 24 million vehicles annually. Most of this growth (40 percent) will, they predict, come from Asia-Pacific countries and secondarily from eastern Europe (18 percent). Regardless of whether the auto companies' optimism about emerging markets is warranted, there remains the question as to whether this optimism can account for the global wave of mergers and alliances in the international auto industry in recent years. The following discussion considers each of the major world markets in turn.

Table 3.1. Income, Urbanization, and Auto Ownership

Country	GNP per Capita, U.S.$ 1999	% Urban Population 1998	% Increase 1980–1998	Cars per 1,000: 1998	% Increase 1980–1998
United States	31,900	77	4.1	483	−9.9
Germany	25,620	87	4.8	506	70.4
France	24,170	75	2.7	442	29.5
United Kingdom	23,590	89	0	375	39.9
Korea	8,490	80	40.4	163	2228.6
Mexico	4,440	74	12.1	97	61.7
Brazil	4,350	80	21.1	77[a]	−9.4[a]
Russia	2,250	77	10.0	120	n/a
China	780	31	55.0	3	300.0[a]
India	440	39	77.3	5	250.0
Nigeria	260	42	55.6	9	200.0

[a]All motor vehicles.
Source: World Bank, *World Development Indicators,* www.worldbank.org/data (July 10, 2002).

Asia

The largest auto market in Asia, outside of Japan, is Korea, with 1 million car sales in 2000. Yet automakers' hopes focus on China, where 2.3 million vehicles were sold in 2001, of which 1.6 million were commercial vehicles. China is forecast to have vehicle sales of 2.6 million by 2005, or 38 percent of Asian sales, excluding Japan.[66] Automobile sales alone surpassed 1 million in 2002. China is now the fourth-largest world market for motor vehicles, after the United States, Japan, and Germany. More than 90 percent of auto production China comes from five partnerships between foreign and domestic Chinese firms: Shanghai Automotive Industry Corporation (collaborating with GM and VW), First Automotive Works (VW, GM, and Toyota), Dongfeng Motor Corporation (PSA, Nissan, and Kia), Beijing Automotive

Table 3.2. World Auto Sales (1,000s) in 1995 and 2000

Area	1995	2000	% Increase
Western Europe	12,021	15,192	26.4
Japan	4,444	4,225	−4.9
NAFTA	9,424	10,561	12.1
Pacific Rim	3,267	3,807	16.5
South America	1,898	1,650	−13.1
East-central Europe	1,711	2,370	38.5
Other	1,072	1,198	11.8
Total	33,837	39,003	11.8

Source: Graeme Maxton, "Global Car Forecasts to 2005—The Outlook for World Car Sales," www.just-auto.com (2000), 5.

Industry Corporation (Daimler-Chrysler, Mitsubishi, and Hyundai) and the Tianjin Automotive Industry Corporation (Toyota and Daihatsu).

VW, having entered China in 1985, has long been the foreign market leader, its subsidiary Shanghai Volkswagen having 53 percent of the passenger car market.[67] Entry into China is proceeding rapidly at the beginning of the twenty-first century. Toyota's joint venture with Tianjin is expected to produce 30,000 compact cars a year from 2002 in addition to the 5,000 cars Toyota already imports and sells in China each year.[68] Ford has a 50/50 joint venture with Chongqing Changan Automobile Company to produce 50,000 Ford Fiesta cars annually. Fiat's Nanjing plant, a joint venture with Yuejin Motor Group, is to launch the Palio family car into the Chinese market in 2002, and its Magneti Marelli power-train subsidiary in Shanghai will provide engine management systems for China's major car producers, including VW, GM, Citroën, and Honda.[69] GM has ambitious plans to expand its 50/50 joint venture with Shanghai Automotive Industry Corporation. Nissan has a 30 percent stake in Zhengzhou Nissan Automobile Company and a joint venture with Dongfeng Automobile Group, producing both commercial vehicles and the Nissan Bluebird sedan, with production levels expected to reach 50,000 to 100,000 per year, spread across several automobiles and commercial vehicles.[70] Early in 2002, Hyundai announced a 50/50 joint venture with Beijing Automotive Industry Holding to build a new auto plant near Beijing, expected to produce 200,000 autos per year in 2005.[71] What is most striking about all these arrangements is the lack of obvious economies of scale in all but the most optimistic production plans.

Until China joined the WTO, entry into the Chinese market had been almost exclusively through alliances with local companies to both produce autos and sell imported vehicles, a pattern driven by local content rules and high import tariffs combined with restrictive import quotas. As China becomes increasingly bound by WTO rules, which include the removal of restrictions on foreign investment in 2003, foreign-controlled auto plants may become more common if foreign auto companies decide to continue producing in China rather than exporting to the Chinese market from lower-cost production sites such as Thailand. Honda, for example, has been allowed majority ownership of a new auto plant that may export up to 50,000 cars per year. Nissan has been allowed management control of a new venture with Dongfeng.[72]

While the enthusiasm is evident, there is little indication of a significant causal relationship between global mergers and the goal of entering the Chinese market. All the alliances have been with local firms, producing vehicles already made by the foreign partners in other parts of the world. One exception may be

GM's takeover of Daewoo. The vehicle on which GM has been pinning its hopes, the Buick Sail, is a GM-designed compact car. The acquisition of Daewoo may provide GM with models suitable more for the Chinese market and allow GM to benefit from possible Chinese government favoritism toward Daewoo. In May 2002, GM announced that it will build a new Daewoo model in China using Isuzu engines.[73] One of Daewoo's Chinese assembly plants is being retooled to produce GM's popular Sail model that sold 45,000 units in 2002.[74] Renault plans to use its Korean acquisition (Samsung) to export autos to China and to other emerging markets, including Chile and Jordan. Renault has also announced that it may join Nissan's joint venture with Chinese automaker Dongfeng Automobile Company, which will produce both Nissan and Renault products,[75] though it is doubtful that the absence of a relationship with Nissan would have prevented Renault from entering China. Mitsubishi is to manufacture vehicles in China in a plant owned by Daimler-Chrysler.[76]

The artificial nature of multinational auto investment in China prior to China's WTO entry (forcing the development of a capital-intensive industry in a labor-abundant economy) is likely to lead to a situation in which the Chinese market has even less connection to the pattern of global consolidation in the auto industry. In the absence of tariffs, quotas, and local content rules and given the high cost of capital in this capital-poor country, most multinational auto companies will retreat to a strategy of simply contracting out appropriately labor-intensive components and subsystems to local Chinese companies, depending on how much production they wish to keep in China. These local companies will be in a much better position to manipulate local factor costs in a way that might keep them competitive with each other and potential foreign entrants.[77] Toyota, for example, plans to use locally produced sheet steel, saving 30 percent on the cost of steel imported from Japan.[78] Proton, a protected Malaysian producer (16 percent owned by Mitsubishi) that has so far been limited in its ability to sell outside the Malaysian market by high costs, has acquired a 49 percent stake in a Chinese components maker, Gold Star Heavy Industry.[79]

Yet it is still questionable how much scope there is for cost-effective subcontracting in China. VW claims that components made in China are 10 to 80 percent more expensive than those purchased on world markets.[80] McKinsey & Company has estimated that while auto production in China benefits from lower labor costs (80 percent less than in the United States) and cheaper interior and electrical components (20 and 10 percent, respectively, less than U.S. prices), other categories of more capital-intensive auto production are more expensive than in the United States: power trains (39 percent), chassis (14 percent), and auto bodies (100 percent).[81] More capital-abundant economies, such as Thailand, offer auto companies and their suppliers significantly lower production costs than China. Despite the apparently higher cost of local production, Honda plans to export 50,000 cars per year from China to Europe, beginning in 2005, and VW has also claimed that it may be able to export autos from China.[82]

Even ignoring the comparative disadvantage of producing autos in China, the demand is much too low to enable even a half dozen major world companies to attain economies of scale in Chinese production facilities. Even sales of nearly one million autos in China in 2002 imply very small annual outputs for the foreign companies now producing in China. In 2002, there were more than 100 automakers in China.[83] Toyota's partnership with Tianjin, for example, is expected to produce only 30,000 subcompact vehicles annually, starting in October 2002. Honda produced 51,000 vehicles in China in 2001, hoping to raise production to 120,000 by 2003. GM's Shanghai plant produced only 50,000 cars in 2002. Only one foreign producer (VW) has (in 2002) reached the production level thought to attain minimum efficient scale for Chinese conditions, namely, 150,000 units per year. Profitability is achieved by charging much more than world market prices (for example, $36,000 for a Honda Accord that would sell for $20,000 in the United States).[84] Once WTO-mandated reduction of import barriers occurs, it remains to be seen whether these companies will still have an incentive to maintain Chinese assembly plants. Yet most auto companies that produce in China have high aspirations with regard to volume production. Two of Dongfeng's partners, PSA and Nissan, expect to produce, respectively, 150,000 autos in 2004 and 550,000 in 2006. Toyota hopes that its joint venture with First Auto will produce 400,000 units in 2010.

It is ultimately questionable as to whether foreign auto companies would wish to produce in China at all if import barriers and local content rules disappear. This is unlikely in the near future. China's agreement with the WTO requires import duties to be cut from 70 to 43.88 percent on vehicles with engine capacity of three liters or less and from 80 to 50.7 percent for vehicles with engine capacity in excess of three liters, both effective January 2002. By 2006, quotas are to be abolished and auto tariffs reduced to 25 percent. Tariffs are not likely to be further reduced to European or U.S. levels.[85] Furthermore, some provinces and regions of China have their own taxes on vehicles from other regions of China, barriers to intra-China trade that may be more difficult to eradicate.[86] It is also to be expected that China will increasingly resort to nontariff barriers to slow down the foreign penetration of its domestic auto market, as it did in July 2002 by restricting the trade in import licenses. [87] If it does so, it will be following a well-trodden path. The General

Agreement on Tariffs and Trade (GATT, the predecessor to the WTO) was so successful at negotiating away postwar tariffs that by the end of the 1960s formal tariff barriers (at least among industrial countries) were well below 10 percent. During subsequent decades, much of the protection that had been lost was rebuilt with nontariff barriers, most notably by the use of quotas in the international automobile trade.

Regardless of the long-term outcome, the Chinese auto market will experience considerable turmoil under the combined impact of internal market growth and entry into the WTO. One effect has been the rapid decline in auto prices following China's entry into the WTO. In early 2002, GM's Buick reduced prices in China by 12.5 percent, VW by 6.5 percent, Hainan Mazda by 33 percent, and Suzuki by 20 percent, all presumably in anticipation of falling import barriers.[88] Another effect is the intense competitive pressure being put on local Chinese companies. One of the most popular local partners for foreign auto companies has been Brilliance China Automotive, a firm sufficiently successful during the past decade of rapid entry into China by foreign firms to have its shares listed on the New York Stock Exchange. During the twelve-month period in which China completed its entry process into the WTO, near the end of 2001, Brilliance China's share price fell by nearly 60 percent.[89] Part of this decline is, of course, systematic risk (that is, the decline in world stock markets), but part is undoubtedly due to investors questioning the long-term viability of auto production in China.

Elsewhere in Asia, the role of governments has been similar, whether it be India, Korea, or Thailand, the other major auto markets. Foreign firms generally have to construct joint ventures with local firms in order to enter. India has, since the mid-1990s, been opening up its markets to wholly owned foreign plants and is to sell its stake in India's largest manufacturer, Maruti, of which it owns 50 percent, Suzuki having the other 50 percent.[90] In April 2002, the Indian government announced that it would sell half its stake in Maruti to Suzuki, leaving the latter with 74 percent. Maruti held 54 percent of the Indian market in 2000, followed by Hyundai (14 percent). Ford plans to enter India on its own.

All the major global manufacturers already have large manufacturing operations in Thailand, bases from which they hope to export throughout Asia. BMW already assembles vehicles in Thailand and plans to make the country its production hub for the entire ASEAN market.[91] Honda has chosen Thailand as the site for manufacturing subcompact cars for export to Japan, Australia, and New Zealand. Honda eventually plans to reduce the number of production locations in Asia, concentrating auto assembly in Thailand and ending production in Indonesia and the Philippines. Thailand's greater capital abundance and endowment of human capital will make it a likely export base to China. This trend will be reinforced when ASEAN manages to achieve its stated aspiration of free trade with China. Over the next ten to twenty years, Thailand is likely to be a much more attractive production location than China, at least insofar as the Chinese government is unable to maintain artificial incentives for multinational auto companies to locate production in China.

Plans for an Asian free trade area have been moving very slowly during the past two decades. Global manufacturers hope that regional free trade will enable them to supply the entire Asian market from one source country, presumably that with the lowest cost of capital and other factor advantages. The ten members of ASEAN have frequently stated their desire to attain free trade in autos, though implementation is likely to involve long internal and international political battles as domestic manufacturers (like Malaysia's Proton) resist being subjected to competition from established large international manufacturers. Free trade within the larger Asia Pacific Economic Cooperation (APEC) group is even farther off in the future.

As noted elsewhere, the only obvious cases where entry into an Asian market is clearly linked to the merger of two internationally known companies are GM's purchase of Daewoo and possibly Renault's acquisition of Samsung. Daewoo will give GM (and its partner Fiat) a retail base in Asia's second-largest market. It may provide competitive advantages in the Chinese market. The acquisition may also help GM and Fiat move into other Asian markets because of Daewoo's lower production costs than GM's Japanese partners (Suzuki, Isuzu, and Subaru).[92]

Eastern Europe

Eastern Europe's largest market is Russia. Like China, most existing foreign-owned production is aimed at upper-income customers. In 1999, 85 percent of autos sold in Russia were priced below $5,000.[93] Most models made by foreign companies cost considerably more. The Ford Focus, for example, is priced at $13,000 to $15,000, putting it well out of reach of the typical Russian buyer. Foreign investment has followed the same pattern as in China: joint ventures with local manufacturers, enforced by government rules relating to foreign ownership and local production content, and import restrictions that increase the cost of exporting to the Russian market. Ford, which has had a presence in Russia since 1907, has begun producing the Ford Focus at a wholly owned plant in St. Petersburg. Though unique among major producers in its strategy of no local partner, Ford has pledged local content of 50 percent by the fifth year of production.[94] GM plans to begin auto production in cooperation with Russia's largest car firm AvtoVAZ. VW plans an assembly plant near Moscow.

As in the case of China and other developing markets, economies of scale are a distant goal, so that local production is being sustained primarily by government regulations that restrict imports. Renault investment plans (with no local partner) envisage making 50,000 cars annually in Russia by 2007. GM's AvtoVAZ venture will produce only 30,000 vehicles in 2003, rising to 75,000 by 2005. Ford's St. Petersburg plant has a capacity of 25,000 cars per year.[95]

Yet there are at least two differences between Russia and China with regard to foreign direct investment by global automakers. The first is that China has been given developing-country status in its terms of entry into the WTO and has a transition period for reducing its import barriers to foreign made vehicles, giving foreign automakers a continued, albeit transitional, incentive to seek entry through joint ventures. Russia will be entering the WTO as a developed country and will be required to make large reductions in import barriers, partially removing one incentive to engage in joint ventures rather than simply importing vehicles into Russia. Adjustment costs may well be more severe than in China, being compressed into a shorter time period. Foreign investors will much more quickly have to recalculate the benefits of direct investment relative to exporting to Russia, compounded by the proximity of Russia to the more capital-intensive (and hence capital-cheap) economies of Europe.

The major problems Western automakers have in finding suitable Russian partners provides another reason why importing may be a better strategy. A task force representing Fiat, GM, Ford, and Renault visited 127 potential Russian component suppliers and failed to find any that met quality standards.[96] BMW has attempted to avoid these problems by assembling BMWs from imported kits in Russia's Baltic "special economic zone," Kaliningrad, where such kits enjoy reduced tariffs. BMW executives openly admit that local content sourcing is difficult.[97] Renault's plans to renovate and use a Moskvitch plant in Moscow to produce a $5,000 auto from its Romanian brand, Dacia, have been troubled by local government insistence on using local suppliers that may not be able to meet Renault's quality standards.[98] The problem is one of long standing. In the 1970s, Citroën abandoned plans to produce vehicles in Romania because of the local partner's inability to maintain PSA's quality standards.[99]

The second difference is the participation of international government organizations in promoting the Russian auto industry. The most well known of these projects is the agreement in June 2001 between GM, Russian automaker AvtoVAZ, and the European Bank for Reconstruction and Development (EBRD) to fund a $340 million project to build a Russian-designed SUV (the Chevrolet Niva) at Togliatti, 600 miles southeast of Moscow.[100] Fiat's partnership with Gorkovsky Avtomobilny Zavod (GAZ), formed in 1997 and canceled in 2002, had 20 percent participation by the EBRD (Fiat and GAZ equally dividing the remaining 80 percent) in an auto plant in Nizhny Novgorod.[101]

As in the case of China, there is little evidence that entering the Russian market was a motivating factor in global mergers or alliances. VW intends to produce Skoda vehicles in Russia[102] in addition to its own VW models, but VW's acquisition of Skoda predates VW's entry into Russia and is more part of VW's larger strategy of having a low-cost entry-level vehicle for all markets. The same would apply to Renault producing in Russia models from its Romanian Dacia acquisition. Nevertheless, it is clear that both VW's acquisition of Skoda and Renault's acquisition of Dacia are aimed at providing them with low-cost models suitable for marketing as entry-level vehicles in eastern European markets. Dacia, acquired by Renault in 2000 for $270 million, produces in Romania versions of a Renault model produced in the 1970s. These autos are sold for $3,000 to $4,000 and meet only 15 percent of Renault's normal quality standards.[103]

Whether the entry of eastern European countries into the European Union enhances or reduces the profitability of these local acquisitions remains to be seen. Both WTO membership and entry into the European Union will force these state-managed economies into an intensely competitive environment in which the global automobile oligopoly may see some eastern European economies as little more than potential suppliers for local outsourcing of labor-intensive components. Furthermore, these local sources will be subjected to considerable monopsony power on the part of global manufacturers.[104] If local sourcing cannot match imported parts on price and quality and if the relative scarcity of capital makes direct investment costly, foreign firms may feel they would have been better off simply importing vehicles from western Europe. While many suppliers to the volume automakers are moving production to eastern Europe, the activities they are moving are mostly low-technology, labor-intensive processes making standardized products.[105]

VW's Skoda is one of the few of these acquisitions likely to shine in the future since Skoda's factories in the Czech Republic appear to be capable of matching western European cost and efficiency, most likely because Czechoslovakia had long been (since the 1920s) one of the most industrialized areas of central and eastern Europe.[106] The Czech Republic and Hungary are likely to be favored by auto manufacturers and suppliers because of the abundance of skilled labor. BMW, Toyota, and Peugeot have also been drawn to the Czech Republic's abundance of human and physical capital, relative to other eastern European countries, and by 2002 the auto industry accounted for 13 percent of the country's manufacturing output and 14 percent of its exports. Daewoo's extensive eastern European operations with local partners are generally unprofitable, and GM refused to buy Daewoo's eastern European assets under the terms of its takeover agreement in 2002. GM will prefer to rely on its partners, Opel and Fiat, for more efficient local production.[107] Similarly, Toyota and Peugeot have decided to collaborate with each other rather than with local producers in eastern Europe, and they plan to assemble 300,000 vehicles per year in the Czech Republic by 2005.[108]

Latin America

After World War II, many Latin American countries pursued policies of "import substituting industrialization," a variation on the "infant industry" argument, and attempted to force industrial development behind high-tariff walls. In the Brazilian auto industry, for example, this took the form of offering foreign companies tax incentives and a protected market in exchange for a high local content. Yet consumer purchasing power was insufficient for the auto firms to sustain economies of scale in production volume. The predictable result was high-cost autos that were not competitive on world markets and could not be exported. Rapid trade liberalization from the 1970s left these multinational auto companies unencumbered by requirements for local partners. In Brazil, for example, the market leaders are local subsidiaries of Fiat, VW, GM, and Ford, in that order.[109] In 1986, VW and Ford merged their Brazilian operations under the name Autolatina, but the joint venture was dissolved in 1994.

With import barriers falling, both through Mercosur[110] and the North American Free Trade Agreement (NAFTA), some parts of Latin America are becoming attractive bases for auto manufacturers seeking to produce for export to global markets. This may be partly due to the ability of multinational auto companies to import components without attracting prohibitive tariffs and to the accumulation of capital stock (both physical and human) in some Latin American economies. VW's New Beetle, for example, is supplied to all world markets from its plant in Pueblo, Mexico,[111] and eventually all world production of VW's Jetta and the new Bora model will be sourced from this factory. Renault's Brazilian subsidiary is to export engines to France from 2004, and supply engines for locally produced Renault and Nissan vehicles.[112] Fiat's Brazilian operation is the largest supplier of components to

Fiat's Chinese joint venture producing the Palio subcompact car.[113] The advantage of less state regulation and access to larger markets has led to major investments by the world's largest auto companies. Between 1998 and 2000, Daimler-Chrysler, Renault, GM, Ford, and PSA/Citroën all announced major investments in Brazil.[114] Toyota, hitherto absent from Mexico, is to start selling (and possibly producing) its autos in Mexico as a result of NAFTA.[115] GM announced in February 2002 that it will invest $1 billion in modernizing and expanding production of compact cars in Brazil.[116] The fact that multinational auto production continues to expand in Latin America in the absence of state support, as has been the case in China and Russia, suggests that the area has appropriate factor advantages, and the further reduction of market impediments will increase the area's locational attractions for global manufacturers.

Has the Latin American market been a causal factor in encouraging global auto mergers? The lack of state-mandated requirements for local partners has perhaps allowed more scope for non–Latin American firms to combine forces to enter this market. Though perhaps not a major factor in the merger, Nissan's tie with Renault has enabled Nissan to enter Latin America at a much lower cost. Nissan is to begin with an assembly line at an existing Renault plant in Brazil, preparatory to launching new models for the Mercosur market, using Renault's operations in manufacturing, financial services, and sales outlets.[117] Suzuki (20 percent owned by GM) is to increase production in Latin America, selling its vehicles under the Chevrolet name.[118] Such alliances may help one partner enter the Latin American market but are unlikely to have been major considerations in the formation of the relationship. Total auto sales in Central and South America were less than 2 million in 2000, considerably less than the 11 million sales in North America and the 15 million autos sold in western Europe.

Africa

Low incomes and a lack of urbanization suggest that Africa presents little market potential in the near future, with the possible exception of South Africa. Even in this richest country on the continent, a highly skewed income distribution (white incomes average $4,300 per year and black incomes $500) limits effective market size.[119] Almost all auto production in South Africa is by subsidiaries of major global manufacturers, including VW, BMW, Daimler-Chrysler, Ford, GM, and Renault-Nissan. Whatever interest these companies have in Africa, and South Africa in particular, it is less because of domestic consumption than as an export base. Total car production in Africa in 2000 was 306,713, of which 219,813 were made in South Africa, almost half of which were exported. Domestic sales for Africa were 643,928, of which 222,092 were in South Africa.[120] It has the supply conditions that make it suitable as an export base to regional markets but lacks the demand conditions to be a major market.

Given the small size of these markets, any connection to global merger activity is likely to be minor. Daimler-Chrysler has taken over Mitsubishi's sales and production in South Africa.[121] Volvo has liquidated its production in Botswana and is to restart production, at 2,000 vehicles per year, in a South African Ford factory.[122]

Developed-Country Markets

Insofar as penetrating new markets is discussed in the context of auto mergers, it is usually in reference to emerging lower-income markets where a European, American, or Japanese manufacturer may not yet have a significant presence. Mergers may also help some firms establish themselves in developed-country markets.

Ford plans to make the Ford Escape SUV in Mazda's plants for the local Japanese market.[123] Ownership in Subaru (20 percent), Isuzu (49 percent), and Suzuki (10 percent) has given GM a foothold in the Japanese market, supplemented by agreements to develop new propulsion technologies with Toyota and to buy engines from Honda.[124] Given the many complaints by U.S. and European industries about nontariff barriers in Japan, such as collusive arrangements between Japanese suppliers and retailers, it is understandable that some auto firms would see links to Japanese manufacturers as a means to enter the Japanese market without having to jump real or imagined hurdles allegedly having the tacit approval of the Japanese government. Some of the activity cited earlier may well stem from the acrimony between Japan and the United States during the early 1990s, when the U.S. government demanded that Japan purchase more auto components from the United States and American auto executives (notably Chrysler's Lee Iacocca) accused Japanese auto companies of denying them access to the Japanese market. A common response was that U.S. auto companies do not produce vehicles of the size and quality characteristics demanded by Japanese auto buyers. Access to the Japanese market, with vehicles that are attractive to Japanese consumers, is a very plausible contributing factor to decisions by U.S. and European automakers to ally with Japanese firms.

Renault mistakenly hoped that its purchase of AMC in the 1970s would establish it in the U.S. market. Now Renault hopes to use its link to Nissan to enter Japan and the United States through Nissan's 17 and 5 percent share of those markets, respectively.[125] When VW was at its nadir in the U.S. market during the 1980s, it seriously contemplated a formal link with Chrysler. The Daimler-Chrysler-Mitsubishi-Hyundai alliance may help some firms in the group enter the United States at lower cost. Hyundai, for example, is to establish a manufacturing capacity in the United States of 300,000 vehicles per year and hopes to distribute through Chrysler dealerships.[126] Isuzu is moving all its SUV production to North America, where it shares an assembly plant with GM's other major Japanese partner, Subaru.[127] Daimler also hopes to sell its Smart minicar through Chrysler's more extensive chain of dealerships, which may give it an edge over BMW's Mini.[128] Mazda is to produce autos with unused Ford capacity in Europe.[129] Volvo is to distribute Land Rovers in Scandinavia.[130]

It should be noted that some automakers have stubbornly refused to make links to others. BMW, burned by its Rover experience, is close to making one million cars a year, doing so alone and by both exporting and producing in local markets, including low-income countries like South Africa and China (though with local partners in the latter market). PSA is another manufacturer that eschews mergers and alliances.[131] Toyota has managed to achieve the largest world auto market share in the absence of global mergers.

Some alliances contribute more than others to the combined entity's global market reach. The Fiat-GM alliance, for example, probably does little for GM because Fiat is a volume producer in markets in which GM already has an established presence. Nissan and Renault, though they have similar product portfolios, benefit more because their presence varies across geographic markets.

Conclusion

Mergers and looser forms of integration have provided some global auto manufacturers with a larger portfolio of products and expeditious access to new markets. Nevertheless, there remains the question of how important these factors were in motivating mergers, acquisitions, or alliances. It is also evident that much of what has been acquired, whether products or markets, could have been acquired by the consolidation-seeking firms without any formal linkages to other firms, albeit perhaps more slowly. Put slightly differently, did companies pay too high a price for quick access to new markets or new products?

Access to some large developed-country markets was clearly important in much of the consolidation during recent decades, such as the Daimler-Chrysler merger and the GM-Fiat alliance. Yet the importance of the geographic market expansion factor may be somewhat weakened by the lack of strong sales potential in developing-country markets. There is a lack of significant comparative advantage in auto production in most parts of the Third World, though some may be useful for outsourcing labor-intensive components. Furthermore, as WTO rules encompass more countries and regional free trade arrangements expand, states will be forced to retreat from rule-setting behavior that in the past has exercised a considerable influence on the location of production by international manufacturers.

CHAPTER FOUR

The Lure of Market Power

The rapid consolidation of the international auto industry in recent decades presents several opportunities for controlling and manipulating the structures and processes of the international auto markets, the markets that supply inputs of capital and labor, and related industries such as commercial vehicles, consumer financing, and auto rentals. Being able to control the prices and quantities of traded goods and services is one of the most obvious links between politics and economics. It gets to core issues of power both in the sense that the term "power" is used in political science (getting people to do things they would not otherwise do) and in the sense it is used in economics (allocating resources in a way that is different from that of a competitive and free market allocation). Control over markets is an obvious motive for corporate mergers and alliances. But do these opportunities constitute a motive that explains auto mergers? And if so, are multinational auto firms willing and able to exploit these potential gains? Governments may well set limits on the ability of firms to act on these incentives, a constraint that is considered in chapter 5.

This chapter examines four forms of market power that may provide an incentive for global industrial consolidation in the auto industry. First, and most obviously, a well-known motive for merger is to reduce competition, perhaps even leading to near monopolization of a market or at least some form of oligopolistic collusion. A second possible motive is that vertical integration allows firms to control markets for inputs, the production of the good itself, and sales to the final consumer, allowing the vertically integrated

firm to capture more of the "value added" or "value chain" (the more collo-
quial business consulting term) at different stages of production and distribution. A third form of market control is monopsony power, or merger for the
purpose of presenting suppliers of inputs with a dominant buyer of their factors of production. Finally, mergers may enable auto companies to extend
their power into other markets, some related to autos (for example, commercial vehicles) and some unrelated (for example, financial instruments, such
as credit cards).

Monopolization and Collusion

In American economic history, merger to acquire monopoly power is the
classic motive for industrial consolidation and the impetus behind the antitrust legislation of the late nineteenth and early twentieth centuries. The
Sherman Act of 1890 prohibited monopolization and restraints on trade.
The Clayton Act of 1914 clarified the Sherman Act by specifically banning
some activities not included in the Sherman Act, such as exclusive dealing
arrangements. Also in 1914, Congress established the Federal Trade Commission, giving it quasi-judicial powers to investigate unfair competitive
practices.

Theoretically, the gains from monopolization are simple and familiar to any
undergraduate in economics. A firm in a competitive market will produce
that output at which the market price (average and marginal revenue) equals
average cost, and in a long-term equilibrium that output will also place each
firm at the minimum point of its long-run average cost curve. The monopolistic firm reduces production to the level that maximizes profits by equating
marginal cost and marginal revenue, yielding a price (also average revenue)
that is greater than marginal revenue, average cost, and marginal cost at that
output. The monopolist then collects monopoly profits on a smaller volume
of output than in a competitive market, that profit being the difference between the monopoly price (average revenue) and average costs, summed
across the entire output. Income (or "consumer surplus," the gain to the consumers from paying less in total for a good than they would be willing to pay)
is shifted from consumers to the producer. The motive for monopoly pricing
is to redistribute the gains of trade from consumers to the producer.

There is, in addition, a "dead weight" loss to society. Wealth is being destroyed because in addition to the redistributive effect of monopolization,
there is a net loss of income to the society as a whole. This loss occurs because the amount of the gains from trade (consumer surplus) that is lost to
the consumer is greater than the amount transferred to the monopolist as

monopoly profit. The rationale for government regulation of monopolization rests mainly on these net social losses and the assumption that it is undesirable to redistribute income away from consumers, though there may well be additional objections to monopolistic markets (such as that monopolies may stifle innovation). An oligopolistic market, one with few suppliers, attempts to capture some the benefits of monopolization subject to the problems of coordinating the efforts of two or more firms.

Concern about competition in the national auto industries of the world is not new. During the middle decades of the twentieth century (the interwar period from 1918 to 1939 and extending into the 1950s), when there was little international trade in autos, most national markets were dominated by a small number of firms. This was nowhere more evident than in the United States. During the 1950s, a time when import penetration was low, tacit collusion in the oligopolistic American auto industry raised auto prices by about 6 percent.[1] The rush of imports in the U.S. markets in the 1960s and 1970s effectively precluded such collusion. Quotas imposed on Japanese auto imports in 1980 partially restored the market power of U.S. automakers, allowing them to sustain very large price increases (39 percent over the period 1979–1981) and experience a surge in profits.[2]

The historically larger number of manufacturers in Europe inhibited collusion and may have benefited consumers, though it has not prevented market manipulation.[3] Outside the developed industrial countries, national industrial organization strategies are common, obviating the need for separate or additional competition policies in most developing countries. Nevertheless, cases sometimes arise in which developing countries appear to place some value on maintaining competitive markets. Daimler-Chrysler's ownership of Hyundai may well have undermined its bid for Daewoo; as such, an acquisition would have allowed them to control both major Korean car producers.[4]

Antitrust laws notwithstanding, consolidation in the global auto industry increases the ability of the remaining producers to collude, creating oligopolistic (if not monopolistic) market conditions. The much higher degree of global concentration, as measured by the Herfindahl index (see chapter 1), has already been noted. Whether they would actually collude on vehicle pricing is another question. There are at least two possible patterns of behavior for a global auto industry with a half dozen major producers. One conjecture is that the global market might begin to operate much as the U.S. domestic market did when dominated by a few firms, unthreatened by imports. In the postwar decades before large-scale import penetration, the U.S. market exhibited a "stylized and well-understood pattern of price leadership,"[5] with Ford and Chrysler attempting to match or predict General Motors' (GM's) prices at the introduction of each model year. Though the greater diversity of types of vehicle models and differentiation within model categories is a complicating factor, it is not inconceivable that a similar pattern of global price coordination could emerge. Given the GM group's current global market share of 22 percent (see table 1.2), it would again be the global price leader, with the Ford, Daimler-Chrysler, and Volkswagen (VW) and Toyota groups following GM prices.

There is a second possibility for global market behavior. Oligopolists may collude, but they may also like to put each other out of business.[6] The collusion scenario is consistent with the conclusions drawn from an analogy to the famous "prisoners' dilemma" game. In the short term, each oligopolist (or duopolist, to make the analogy more accurate) may have a dominant strategy of reducing prices and undercutting its rival, leading both players to an outcome that is individually and collectively inferior to one of mutual cooperation (that is, both end up losing money). If they take a longer-term perspective, the warring oligopolists may see the mutually destructive effect of competition and collude on setting price and output, maintained by the threat of retaliating if one of the group cheats and cuts prices. However, there is another game-theoretic parable that may be equally appropriate: the "chain store paradox," drawn from the idea that oligopolists may engage in severe price competition with a new entrant in order to drive it from the market despite the high short-term costs—hence the discrepancy between the two scenarios.

The prisoners' dilemma scenario suggests that the short-term and myopic strategy is to compete and that the sensible longer strategy is to collude. The chain store story suggests the opposite: A player should seek to collude if trying to maximize short-term profits is the desired goal, but for higher long-term profits, it is better to incur large short-term costs and drive the competitor out of the market. One reason why the two stories offer different behavioral prescriptions is that the chain story argument allows players to exit; the dynamic prisoners' dilemma typically assumes that the players may not leave the game. The relevance of these two stories to competition in the auto industry is simply that the collusion scenario, analogous to the dynamic prisoners' dilemma, assumes that firms cannot drive each other out of business. If they might be able to do so, the chain store image becomes more appropriate. If auto companies believe that they may be able to drive each other out of markets and are considering the longer-term outcome, it may be more reasonable to predict intense competition rather than collusion.[7]

The Japanese auto market, historically insulated from imports, is fiercely competitive despite the small number of producers. This is not to suggest that Honda, Toyota, and Nissan have ever actually tried to drive each other out of business but simply that their domestic market in Japan retains a high level of competitive pressure without active or tacit collusion. The three major German automakers (Daimler, BMW, and VW) and the high-volume German subsidiaries of Ford and GM (Opel) exhibit little evidence of American-style tacit collusion. BMW and Mercedes are particularly competitive. Porter notes that global competitive advantage often comes from industries that are very competitive in their home markets even with a small number of firms.[8] The Japanese economy in particular is often depicted as being dominated by collusive industrial oligopolies, yet the degree of competition in these industries can be very high despite the small numbers of firms. Similarly, the German economy is, at least in popular image, thought to be prone to manipulation by industrial and banking cartels.

Creating a collusive global oligopoly is an implausible motive for auto mergers and is an unlikely outcome whether intended or otherwise. The American style of collusive pricing in the 1950s appears to be a historical aberration, most likely the result of other factors, such as clearly defined market segmentation, almost identical types of vehicles produced by each manufacturer, and a lack of competition from imports. The much higher degree of product differentiation across global brands today, combined with wide variation in market shares in different areas of the world, would make such collusion difficult. The segmented national markets of the 1950s that made collusion feasible, at least in the United States, no longer exist. Quite apart from these considerations, the gradual emergence of global antitrust policies, or at least coordination of the policies of the United States and the European Union (discussed in chapter 5), would further inhibit collusion.

Vertical Integration: Capturing the Value Chain

The typical form of vertical integration for an auto company would be "upstream" ownership of the production of major components, such as engines, transmissions, axles, fuel injection systems, and air-conditioning systems. This is sometimes called backward vertical integration to distinguish it from forward vertical integration toward the consumer, the latter including such activities as financing and after-sales service. Despite the possible benefits of buying from specialized vendors (such benefits are mainly lower costs because the vendors could attain economies of scale by producing for more than one manufacturer), U.S. auto companies have historically preferred to remain vertically integrated and produce components themselves or in wholly owned subsidiaries. Such an arrangement may yield lower transaction costs, being those costs of acquiring information about suppliers, bargaining with them, and enforcing contracts. The primary goal was to avoid being exploited by bilateral monopoly power from specialized vendors. Scherer notes how Ford decided to produce its own transmissions in the 1940s because of fear of dependence on Borg-Warner, despite the fact that its price bid was less than Ford's cost of internally producing transmissions.[9]

Japanese auto companies have their famed *keiretsu* relationships with favored groups of suppliers that, though not necessarily owned by the automaker, have close traditional ties to the company and would be unlikely to attempt to exploit any bilateral monopoly power that might be available to them. However close their relationship with the auto assembler, supplier members of the auto *keiretsu* are expected to be independently profitable.[10] They are also not subject to complete monopsony power since they are usually encouraged to sell to other auto assemblers outside the *keiretsu*. It has been part of the conventional wisdom of management analysts that the *keiretsu* system has been a major ingredient in the global success of the Japanese auto companies. The following passage from Altschuler is fairly typical in its praise, claiming that the *keiretsu* system

> simultaneously attains the scale and coordination advantages of Western-style vertical integration and the flexibility of decentralization. Its aim is cooperation and mutual information flow between the parts, rather than top-down hierarchy. Its distinctive capabilities are tight production scheduling, cooperation on research and product design, and sharing of staff and production capacity, all while the independence of supplier firms in general management and in the setting of wages is maintained.[11]

Despite such lavish praise, few auto companies are actually increasing their vertical integration either in the traditional Western sense of the term or in the form of imitating the *keiretsu*. This may be partly because there is little scope for more vertical integration of either type and because the disadvantages of vertical integration appear to be more salient in a global market. Toyota is one exception and is increasing its stakes in supplier companies, notably Denso (electronics), Toyoda Automatic Loom Works (vehicle assembly and engines), Toyoda Gosei (plastic and rubber parts), and Aisin Seiki (power-train parts).[12] This has not been without costs, and Toyota still subsidizes loss-making members of its industrial group.[13] In at least one case, backward vertical integration into components is due to fortuitous factors.[14] Ford's Land Rover, for example, purchased its insolvent chassis supplier UPF-

Thompson in 2002 simply in order to avoid having to halt production of its vehicles.

However, the prevailing trend today is for vehicle manufacturers to shed their semicaptive suppliers. GM began the trend by spinning off its major parts supplier, Delphi, in 1999. Ford followed in 2000 by divesting itself of its primary in-house auto parts supplier, Visteon. Both Delphi and Visteon must now compete for parts contracts with their former owners but are also free to supply other vehicle manufacturers. The relationship of Ford to Visteon and GM to Delphi now appears to more closely resemble that of a loose Japanese *keiretsu*. Under new Renault management, Nissan began to dismantle those parts of its *keiretsu* in which it had direct ownership stakes, selling its seat-making operations to a U.S. company (Johnson Controls), its driveshaft and power-train operations (Tochigi Fuji) to a British company (GKN), its fuel tank business (to Solvay) and its 37 percent stake in Exedy, Japan's second-largest auto parts maker.[15] In 2002, Nissan sold its 25 percent share in its major auto electronics affiliate, Unisia Jecs, to Hitachi.[16] As it increased its stake in Mazda from an initial 25 percent to 33.4 percent during the early 1990s, Ford also began to sell off the wholly owned parts of Mazda's *keiretsu* relationships. As Daimler asserted control over Chrysler, it began to sell many of Chrysler's captive suppliers. In February 2002, for example, Chrysler sold Dayton Thermal Products, which made heating, air-conditioning, and engine cooling systems for Chrysler vehicles to the German company Behr.[17] European companies have been less salient in shedding captive suppliers, though Fiat, under financial strain, plans to sell all or most of Magneti Marelli (its major parts subsidiary) and Comau (a maker of robotic and other specialty auto assembly equipment).[18]

The global pattern emerging appears to be one in which automakers may retain a close relationship with some favored suppliers but with the freedom to solicit outside bids and suppliers are free to sell to any assembler. The passing of these remnants of semifeudal guild relationships and exclusive dealing presents a more complex pattern of bargaining between assemblers and suppliers. It is also worth noting that many of the captive suppliers that have been sold are going to other, larger suppliers, increasing concentration in the supplier industry, a development of some importance and taken up later in this chapter.

There is a second, perhaps more currently contentious form of vertical integration in the auto industry—that involving the stream of revenue generated downstream from the manufacturing of the auto, activities such as distribution, consumer financing, maintenance, insurance, and related businesses, such as car rental. It has become commonplace for auto consulting firms to prescribe that vehicle manufacturers must "migrate downstream toward the consumer."[19] The rationale is that there is more profit to be made in these downstream activities than in simply selling new cars. The revenue stream of a typical midsize auto in the United States during the first ten years of ownership is over three times the initial purchase price of the auto. Automakers currently capture about 43 percent of that stream through the traditional activities of sales, financing, repair, and maintenance. More extensive vertical integration would enable the auto companies to acquire revenues that currently go to oil companies, repair facilities, tire makers, after-market parts and accessories manufacturers, insurance companies, and banks.[20]

Some auto companies are buying up and consolidating their existing dealerships, including Ford, Mazda, and Mercedes (in the United Kingdom). Daimler has moved to eliminate independent Mercedes dealerships in Britain and to sell Mercedes only in large company-owned dealerships in major metropolitan areas, supported by service sites in smaller towns.[21] Toyota has purchased its U.K. distributor (Inchape), a majority holding (74.9 percent) of its South African manufacturing partnership (Toyota South Africa), and plans to take over its Spanish distribution system.[22] Saab is cutting its 1,200 worldwide number of dealers by half, consolidating them into partially owned "Saab Unlimited" partners.[23] VW has purchased full ownership in both the exclusive Swedish importer and distributor Svenska Volkswagen and the retailer Din Bil, the latter selling VW brands and Porsches in several large Swedish cities.[24] Mitsubishi has purchased the German auto wholesaler MMC Auto Deutschland.[25]

Ford, GM, and Fiat have all announced plans to sell autos directly to the public through the Internet.[26] Both Ford and GM have websites that allow consumers to access dealer inventories around the United States (www.forddirect.com and www.gmbuypower.com), though they do not yet sell directly to the public through websites. The existing dealership networks are strenuously resisting both trends.[27]

Vertical integration downstream toward customers has extended to related activities. Fiat bought the remainder of an auto insurance company in which it already had a stake.[28] VW acquired the auto leasing business of the Dutch financial services group ABN Amro.[29] In 2001, Ford purchased 18.5 percent of Hertz, completing its full ownership of the auto rental company. Daimler-Chrysler announced in 2002 that it plans to set up a unit to trade in used cars of all brands, not just those made by its own group.[30] These investments may not always pay off. Ford announced in December 2001 that it had written off $199 million of investments in electronic web-based commerce ventures following the dismissal of its chief executive officer, Jacques

Nasser.[31] In 1999 in the United Kingdom, Ford purchased Kwik-Fit, a chain of auto repair shops, and sold the chain at a loss in 2002.[32] As in the case of the conglomerate mergers of the 1960s, auto companies are finding that some attempts to vertically diversify along the revenue stream may lead them into activities in which they lack the experience and expertise to add value to the activity.

What is the relevance of either form of vertical integration to global merger activity? Do mergers facilitate vertical integration and therefore provide another motive for mergers? It is doubtful that this is the case to any significant extent. Vehicle manufacturers can pursue vertical integration backward toward sources of inputs and forward or downstream from the production of a vehicle, toward the final consumer, independently of whether they are merging or allying with other manufacturers. Nevertheless, merger may make possible some forms of vertical integration that might otherwise be difficult. A few examples may suffice to make this point.

GM is to set up an auto service network in Korea in cooperation with Korea's LG-Caltex Oil Corporation.[33] In the absence of its planned purchase of Daewoo, GM would have had fewer motives to enter into the auto repair business in Korea since part of the motivation of entering the service business is to capture the revenue from servicing GM-produced vehicles. A service network will both enable GM to capture downstream revenues from the sale of Daewoo vehicles (presumably more so than if it did not own Daewoo since owners of Daewoo vehicles can now be steered to an in-house service supplier) and provide it with an alternative to Daewoo's own troubled service and distribution network. Another example is the cross shareholding between GM and Fiat, an arrangement in which both companies will use some common platforms, engines, and power trains.[34] This yields a form of vertical integration: If, for example, GM had purchased engines or other components from Fiat in an arm's-length transaction, then an equity stake in Fiat gives it partial ownership rights and provides a weak form of vertical integration.

The Daimler-Chrysler merger has led to plans to merge all European dealerships into company-owned outlets, a plan that may extend to other markets and include the Mitsubishi and Hyundai brands.[35] The intent appears to be to put all the Daimler-Chrysler group brands into company-owned dealerships. This might have been done by the separate brands without mergers, but the mergers of these four companies provided the scale necessary to make consolidated company-owned dealerships a cost-effective proposition, presumably through economies of scale or cost sharing in "mega"-dealerships. GM's purchase of Daewoo will have a similarly concentrating effect in some retail markets. In the U.S. market, for example, GM refused to include Dae-woo dealerships in the purchase and intends to sell Daewoo products as GM products from GM dealerships.[36] GM's European subsidiary Opel announced in 2002 that it would terminate its 900-unit German dealership system and regroup them into 470 larger dealerships.[37] Renault plans to cut its European Renault/Nissan dealer network from 2,400 to 800 by 2005, partly by consol-idating sales into larger factory-owned dealer groups.[38] Selling both Renault and Nissan vehicles from the same outlets enables the company to reduce the total number of dealerships. Similarly, GM Europe has encouraged Opel, Saab, and Daewoo to combine retail outlets into common dealerships that will sell all three brands.[39]

It should be noted that vertical integration can still be attained by independent firms without any need for formal integration through mergers or acquisi-tions. Firms may, as already noted, simply vertically integrate by themselves if they do not destroy economies of scale by doing so (that is, by producing com-ponents or services in house on a smaller scale rather than purchasing from in-dependent vendors who may derive economies of scale by selling to multiple manufacturers). It is also possible for firms to vertically integrate in cooperation with other firms while remaining independent. GM and Toyota plan to both participate in a web venture, gazoo.com, to sell vehicles and service directly to the Japanese public and obviously see no need for a merger or even a formal al-liance to capture a segment of this part of the value chain.[40]

Political factors may limit the ability of automakers to vertically integrate or to use vertical integration for the purpose of restraining trade and hence reduce any motivation to merge for such purposes. In September 2002, the European Commission partially removed the automakers' exemption from certain anticompetitive trade practices. The European Union's Block Ex-emption had hitherto allowed auto manufacturers to restrain trade in both the retail markets and the supply of auto parts for repairs and maintenance.[41] The exemption had allowed automakers to prevent the growth of large multibrand dealerships by requiring dealers to deal exclusively in one brand, giving manufacturers both monopoly power and effective vertical integration with respect to retail dealers. Under the proposed new rules, car dealers will be able to sell multiple brands, outsource repairs, and sell throughout the Eu-ropean Union, and repair shops will be allowed to perform "authorized" ser-vice and use after-market parts. The proposed reforms remove from manu-facturers the right to exclude after-market parts suppliers from authorized service centers, effectively preventing that manufacturer from being a mo-nopolistic, vertically integrated supplier of parts (as well as vehicles) to deal-ers and service centers.[42]

As the Block Exemption disappears, European manufacturers may face the market power of large dealers and groups of dealers with the power to bargain down wholesale prices of vehicles, conferring on these retail dealers some degree of bargaining power that the manufacturers could deny them under the old rules. Vehicle manufacturers will no longer be able to sustain downstream vertical integration by way of market restrictions that formerly allowed them to coerce retail businesses with threats of withdrawal of supplies of vehicles—hence the movement, noted earlier, for them to acquire ownership of these downstream activities so that they can regain the downstream control that was lost with the removal of their exemption from some anticompetitive practices.

Automakers fear that the balance of market power between retail dealers and manufacturers may swing from a vertically integrated monopoly favoring manufacturers to a more open retail market, potentially favoring dealers and other buyer groups. Manufacturers will have to compete for floor space in these "mega"-dealerships, and presumably this will put downward pressure on wholesale auto prices. The European Automobile Manufacturers Association has, in opposing the revision of the Block Exemption, raised the fear of "accelerated and uncontrolled distributor concentration."[43] Canceling the contracts to supply independent dealerships and regrouping retail supply under a smaller number of company-owned "mega"-dealerships (as Mercedes is doing in Britain and Opel in Germany), are attempts to regain vertical integration and market control.

This is becoming a global problem for most auto companies. The ability of auto companies to vertically integrate downstream toward the consumer is increasingly limited by the rise of large independent dealerships that stock many brands. Some of these dealerships are becoming multinational and may ultimately present auto companies with a formidable amount of market power. The United Auto Group, for example, owns 105 dealerships with 114 vehicle franchises in nineteen states in the United States, 7 dealerships with 9 franchises in Puerto Rico, 42 dealerships with 50 franchises in the United Kingdom, and 3 dealerships with 4 franchises in Brazil, the total operation selling thirty different brands of vehicles.[44]

Monopsony Power: Controlling Input Markets

When sellers face a single buyer, the market is a monopsony in which the buyer can exploit a bargaining advantage analogous to that enjoyed by a single monopoly seller. Monopsony is an example of an "external economy" or a pecuniary economy of scale. It is closely related to Porter's notion of "clustering," in which industries that trade with each other agglomerate together in geographic space. A cluster, as Porter notes, will typically focus on a core industry that "is often the most sophisticated buyer of the products and services it depends on."[45] He cites the example of the paper industry in Sweden, which promoted the development of a cluster of supplier industries producing machinery for wood handling, pulp making, papermaking, and paper drying. Curiously, Porter does not discuss the monopsony power that may be conferred on the core industry buying from the rest of the cluster. Auto mergers clearly have the potential to confer monopsony power on auto companies with respect to their purchasing of both labor and capital.

Controlling Labor Costs with Bargaining Power

Monopsony power with regard to labor may be difficult to attain, primarily because it is rare for a single firm to be the dominant employer in a particular labor market. Even in an area such as that around Detroit, Michigan, where auto companies are major local employers, there are other employment opportunities, and, as a last resort, labor is geographically mobile within a large national market.[46] Furthermore, auto workers are well organized, represented in the United States by the United Auto Workers (UAW) and in most other major auto-producing countries by peak labor organizations that may partially offset whatever monopsony bargaining power auto companies might otherwise possess. Even in countries with relatively authoritarian governments, such as South Korea, auto workers can be well organized and militant. Large-scale mergers, such as that between Daimler and Chrysler, have not obviously affected the bargaining power of organized labor in the United States. As Chrysler announced job cuts of 26,000 in January 2001, following the replacement of top Chrysler managers by Daimler executives, the UAW followed with a statement assuring its members that all existing contracts would be "fully enforced."[47] Whatever loss of bargaining power the UAW has suffered as a result of the Daimler-Chrysler merger is more likely to be a longer-term erosion of that power due to the greater international mobility of Chrysler's production under German management.

Monopsony power with regard to labor in the international auto industry is usually manifested in a slightly disguised manner by way of the geographic mobility of the auto companies, a mobility enhanced by international mergers and alliances. An auto company facing high labor costs in a particular market can threaten to shift production elsewhere if workers refuse wage concessions. The fact that such threats often do seem to work is evidence that monopsony power exists despite the still-significant power of trade unions in the major auto-producing countries.

The long postwar decline of the British auto industry was marked by an increasing number of days lost to strikes, peaking in the early 1970s.[48] The companies that weathered these labor situations were ones (like Ford and GM) that could shift production to other European locations. After one particularly long and bitter strike in 1969, Ford held down British production and boosted output elsewhere in Europe, particularly Germany. Ford unions could still inflict some damage on operations in the United Kingdom by blocking imports of Ford vehicles and supplies from European factories. In 1971, the Ford unions did this by securing the cooperation of unions representing seamen, dockworkers, and delivery workers.[49] GM followed the same strategy with its British Vauxhall brand as it raised production from its German company, Opel.

In the current environment of a high geographic mobility of capital, British union behavior has moderated considerably. GM unions backed away from strike threats when GM announced plans to shed 2000 jobs at its plant in Luton, England, in 2002, settling on a plan to "urge" the company to reduce job losses and find a new model vehicle to produce at Luton.[50] Ford unions were similarly moderate in their muted reaction to the announcement that Ford would close its operations at its large plant in Dagenham, England, the scene of major strikes in the 1960s.[51] On February 20, 2002, Ford ceased producing automobiles in Britain.[52] The ability of Ford and GM to shift production around Europe, enhanced by the tariff-free frontiers within the European Union, has undoubtedly helped both companies' bargaining power with the traditionally powerful and belligerent British unions.

The contrasting case is the Rover group (known as the British Motor Corporation in the 1960s and then British Leyland from 1968), which was unable to shift production out of Britain, sank into a steep decline, and was ultimately sold to BMW in 1994. BMW's reluctance to antagonize the management and workforce of Rover's Longbridge factory contributed to the major financial losses from this acquisition and ultimately to divestment. Only in the last year of ownership did BMW begin to resort to threats of utilizing its capital mobility, suggesting that it would move production of Rover vehicles to Hungary.[53] Unable to make the company profitable again, BMW sold much of the remains of Rover in 1999. Unions opposed the sale and possible closure of Rover's main plant at Longbridge, calling for a consumer boycott of BMW in sympathy with the union.[54] Interestingly, union leaders mistakenly thought that German unions might strike at BMW plants in Germany to help force BMW not to reduce production in England.[55]

The sale of Rover to the British consortium MG Rover has reduced capital mobility, and Rover is once again more exposed to union threats. In

March 2002, Rover's unions threatened to go on strike over the system of flexible working hours imposed by BMW and retained by Rover's new owners.[56] Rover unions subsequently voted overwhelmingly (85 percent) against the strike.[57] Despite MG Rover's current lack of geographic mobility, its lack of bargaining power in this respect was offset by its perilous financial state, paradoxically conferring on it some strength through weakness. MG Rover's motivation to develop production facilities in China, in cooperation with Brilliance China, may well enhance its bargaining power with respect to British labor unions.

British unions are not alone in their vulnerability to footloose multinational auto companies. Fiat's unions opposed the cross-shareholding link with GM and particularly the option for GM to buy Fiat presumably because GM could move Fiat production outside Italy. Continental European companies have been moving production to lower-wage areas of Europe, such as Spain and eastern Europe. VW, Europe's largest automaker, settled wage talks with its German unions in 2001 partly by threatening to move production out of Germany.[58] Plans such as Peugeot's joint venture to make small cars in the Czech Republic with Toyota[59] will have the same effect on labor power in western Europe. Successful strike actions simply accelerate this tend. The German metalworkers union IG Metal won 7.1 percent wage increases as a result of a strike in 2002, giving German companies more incentive to move operations to eastern Europe. VW's plans for auto assembly in Russia and Poland now call for local procurement of components rather than merely assembling parts imported from Germany.[60] Auto parts companies making labor-intensive components are particularly attracted to those countries that offer cheap skilled labor, such as Poland, the Czech Republic, Hungary, and Slovakia. As it has already been noted in chapter 3, low wages alone will not make a country attractive to a capital-intensive industry.

These pressures on labor power are even evident in the United States, where the UAW long held a powerful position with respect to the three major U.S. automakers. Foreign manufacturers like Honda, Nissan, BMW, and Daimler benefit not only from international mobility but also from placing their plants away from large population centers, presenting employees with fewer employment alternatives. In October 2001, the UAW lost, for the second time, a ballot to unionize Nissan's plant in Smyrna, Tennessee.[61] The UAW hoped that victory at Smyrna would help it gain entry into other European- and Japanese-owned plants in the United States, particularly Daimler's plant in Vance, Alabama; Toyota's in Georgetown, Kentucky; and Honda's in Marysville, Ohio. Perhaps to emphasize its international mobility, Nissan announced just days before the vote that it planned to move production of its

Maxima sedan from Japan to Smyrna. Though beneficial to its Smyrna employees, the move might also be interpreted as a signal that Nissan could also move production from Smyrna elsewhere in the world if the UAW were to unionize the plant.

American unions have long recognized the bargaining power conferred on U.S.-based multinationals by the ability to shift production outside the United States. They strongly supported the failed Burke-Hartke Bill of 1971, which proposed restrictions on corporate investment outside the United States. The major source of opposition to the North American Free Trade Agreement (NAFTA) came from a coalition of environmentalists and trade unions.[62] The latter feared loss of jobs to Mexico. Ford subsequently shifted production of the Ford Escort to Mexico, and Volkswagen chose to produce the New Beetle in Mexico rather than the United States despite its previous investment in an assembly plant in Pennsylvania in the 1970s.

The strong and sometimes violent opposition of Daewoo's unions to the proposed takeover by GM may have been motivated, in addition to nationalism, at least partly by the specter of monopsony power (Daewoo's largest factory in Pupying employs one-quarter of the local workforce),[63] compounded by GM's international mobility. GM as a new owner might well feel less political obligation to keep production in Korea than would Daewoo's Korean management. GM could also move the production of Daewoo vehicles to its own facilities (or those of partners specializing in small-vehicle production, such as Opel or Fiat) outside Korea, as Ford has done in moving Mazda production to Ford plants elsewhere in the world. Early in 2003, GM announced plans to sell Daewoo autos under the Opel name.

Capital Inputs: Beggaring Your Suppliers

Large size and market control may also allow a vehicle manufacturer to exercise monopsony power with respect to suppliers of capital, both financial (for example, with respect to banks or other lenders) and real capital (for example, suppliers of components, such as instrument panel assemblies, and raw materials, such as steel). Currently beleaguered automakers have been attempting to use whatever market power they have to force suppliers to reduce prices. The pressure on suppliers has been severe enough to induce some suppliers to turn down business from a few auto manufacturers or to reduce the quality of their products.[64] Some decline to bid for supply contracts. In 2002, Michelin decided not to supply tires to GM because of pricing demands, as did Tower Automotive in declining to continue supplying frames for the Ford Explorer.[65] Suppliers also claim to be cutting back on research and development as automakers refuse to commit to new technologies until they are developed, tested, and validated (which Ford refers to as the new "pay on production" principle) and suppliers refuse to commit resources to research and development without assurances of subsequently selling the technology.

The increasing size of automakers may be helping them lower the cost of financial capital. Ford has used its market power both to demand lines of credit from investment banks and to sell bonds over the Internet directly to the public.[66] Nissan's additional market power through its alliance with Renault may well have encouraged it to look for financial capital beyond its traditional "house" banks associated with its domestic Japanese *keiretsu*, seeking lines of credit from a more diversified set of international banks, including Citibank.[67] Without the Renault ties, Nissan might well have lacked the power to negotiate sufficiently favorable terms to enable it to break away from its traditional sources of financial capital.

Chrysler, Ford, and GM have been particularly salient in attempting to exploit monopsony power with respect to suppliers of components. Chrysler unilaterally reduced payments to suppliers by 5 percent in 2000.[68] In March 2001, several months after the announced price cuts, Chrysler claimed that 40 percent of suppliers had agreed to the price cuts, and those that did not were being replaced.[69] During 2000–2001, Ford demanded 4.5 percent price cuts from suppliers and asked them to forgo payment until after the parts would be installed in a vehicle. The Visteon Corporation, Ford's former parts arm that still sells 80 percent of its output to Ford, became sufficiently distressed to make public a price dispute with Ford.[70] Visteon's bargaining power was weakened by the 2000 spin-off agreement that gave Ford the right to receive from Visteon, for the years 2001 to 2003, price cuts equal to those received from other suppliers. Visteon argued that the value of price cuts demanded by Ford would exceed its cash reserves by $125 million.[71] For the third quarter of 2001, Visteon had reported a net loss of $95 million, compared with a year-earlier profit of $48 million.[72] Visteon hopes to break even in 2002.[73] Throughout 2002, Ford was engaged in a continuous public debate with suppliers over the prices and quality of components, Ford blaming suppliers for poor-quality components and suppliers blaming Ford's enforced price cuts for any quality problems.[74] For 2003, GM asked suppliers for price cuts of between 4 and 10 percent, though by the beginning of that year it was expecting more modest cost reductions of 2.3 percent.[75]

Automakers in other countries have followed these practices, though perhaps not quite so publicly. BMW hoped to reap gains from joint purchasing with Rover, decreeing in 1996 that all Rover parts procurement would be sourced through BMW's purchasing department in Munich.[76] Under Renault's management, Nissan reportedly cut its components cost by 10 percent by dropping costly suppliers, many of whom had been part of Nissan's *keiretsu*. By the middle of 2002, Nissan was encountering increasing resistance from suppliers as it attempted to raise price cuts to 15 percent.[77] Toyota aims to cut costs by 30 percent by 2005 by diversifying its sources of supplies, forcing its traditional local suppliers to compete with large international parts makers like Delphi and Bosch.[78] Monopsony power is being exercised in this case by Toyota pointing out to its local suppliers that it can buy parts on a global market, but the local suppliers are selling only to the Japanese parts market and some even mostly to only Toyota. In a similar move, VW's Brazilian subsidiary refused to accept a price increase from local steel suppliers and threatened to import steel from outside Brazil.[79] Japanese auto companies have been notably successful in obtaining cost reductions from Japanese steel companies, partly by importing steel from South Korea and China.[80]

Large auto companies would, of course, be attempting to cut supplier prices in any event regardless of whether they had been engaging in merger activity. The mergers simply increase the capacity of merged entities to exercise such power. In the case of the Renault-Nissan alliance, the relationship has become quite explicitly expressed in terms of market power with respect to suppliers. In March 2001, Renault and Nissan announced that they were setting up a joint purchasing organization, covering about 30 percent of their components (with the expectation that the proportion of jointly purchased supplies would rise to 70 percent), including power trains, parts, raw materials, and services. The venture was publicly justified as a device to obtain greater discounts from suppliers through larger-volume purchasing.[81] Chrysler and Mitsubishi claim to have attained from suppliers cost reductions of 6 percent on components for two new car platforms (the C and D platforms) to be shared between the brands, starting with the Mitsubishi Lancer and Dodge Neon on the C platform in 2005, with 65 percent commonality of parts.[82] Since planned production of these two models is expected to be 600,000, shared equally between the brands, and clearly well above that necessary for production economies of scale, the motive of pecuniary economies of scale (that is, monopsony power) is evident. Daimler-Chrysler, Hyundai, and Mitsubishi hope to jointly procure more than $13 billion of parts annually from 2003.[83]

These price-cutting pressures should have affected the profitability of suppliers. One study estimated that the profitability of the median U.S. supplier fell from 6.4 percent in 2000 to 2.9 percent in 2001.[84] These results should be interpreted with caution. Two data points do not, of course, make a trend, and the data aggregate the profits of failed firms with those that stayed in business. Nevertheless, the evidence is consistent with mergers generating some monopsony power.

Countervailing Market Power: Limits on Monopsony

The extent to which auto mergers may increase the ability of automakers to exercise monopsony power may be limited by at least four factors: concentration in the supplier industries, Internet markets for components, the increasing proportion of the value of vehicles being outsourced to suppliers, and the asymmetric access to political influence possessed by some supplier industries.

Consolidation in the supplier industry, occurring partly because of the increasing pressure from cost-cutting auto assemblers, provides countervailing market power. The number of suppliers fell from 30,000 in 1988 to fewer than 8,000 in 1999 and continues to decline.[85] Concentration is occurring through merger, acquisition, and takeover and by firms simply exiting the industry. Harvard Industries, a maker of transmissions and frame components, announced in 2002 that it was leaving the automotive sector.[86] Thompson-Ramo-Wooldridge Corporation (TRW) derived two-thirds of its $16.38 billion revenue in 2001 from its automotive unit, one of the world's largest suppliers of braking systems, air bags, seat belts, and steering columns. When TRW was bought by Northrop in 2002, the auto supply business was sold so that TRW could concentrate on its defense and aerospace activity.[87] One consulting firm predicts that the number of "tier one" suppliers will drop from around 800 in 2000 to about thirty in the near future.[88] Two formerly captive subsidiaries of GM and Ford (Delphi and Visteon) are now among the three largest independent parts manufacturers in the world; Delphi had the largest sales in 2000 ($29.1 billion), followed by Bosch ($20.6 billion), and Visteon ($19.5 billion).[89]

Many of the supplier mergers are domestic, such as U.S. giant Delphi acquiring for $300 million the electronics division of Eaton, a smaller U.S. supplier.[90] Parts suppliers are also emulating the automakers and engaging in global mergers. American parts maker Johnson Controls has purchased Japan's largest maker of auto seats, Ikeda Bussan.[91] Visteon has purchased most of Fiat's major parts supplier, Magneti Marelli, a maker of fuel injectors, engine control computers, suspension components, cooling systems, and instrument clusters.[92] The French parts maker Valeo purchased the Japanese auto lighting company Ichikoh.[93] Many of these acquisitions are parts suppliers that are being sold off by the auto companies themselves. The European company Continental, for example, purchased 60 percent of Daimler's automotive electronics subsidiary, Temic.[94] In 2002, JP Morgan Partners (the global private equity arm of JP Morgan Chase) purchased a number of auto suppliers, including Teksid (from Fiat), Rhythm (from Nissan), and Mando (from Hyundai).[95]

International alliances have formed. Globalization (through foreign direct investment or by exports) might actually weaken the bargaining power of suppliers by offering automakers more alternative sources of supply. Global supplier alliances may offer suppliers access to new markets without necessarily offering automakers greater diversity of independent sources of components. Nippon steel, Japan's largest steelmaker and dominant supplier to the Japanese auto industry, is allying with Usinor, Europe's largest steel producer, to produce sheet steel for automakers.[96] When the U.S. parts maker Tenneco announced an alliance with two Japanese parts makers (Tokico and Futabe), the president of Futabe specifically linked the development to consolidation in the auto manufacturing market and the consequent need by suppliers to form alliances in order to avoid being played off against each other by global auto assemblers.[97] Similarly, a German and a Japanese electronics company (Siemens and Yazaki) plan to combine some of their global operations in dealing with three of their customers: Ford, Renault, and BMW.[98]

The increasing incidence of international consolidation in the components industry is of some importance. It will further enhance the bargaining power they are attaining through mergers since the truly multinational supplier will be less vulnerable to threats by automakers to source parts from other countries. Concentration in a domestic market alone may do little to give a supplier monopoly power with respect to that country's auto companies if the automakers can source components internationally. The Japanese steel industry is highly concentrated, but the consequent market power afforded them in the past has rapidly eroded as Japanese car companies began to buy steel from China and South Korea.

Internet markets between auto companies and suppliers will reduce the market power conferred by concentration on both sides of the market. The primary effect of electronic markets is to lower transaction costs. Just as eBay enables buyers and sellers to come together over great geographic distances and engage in a low-cost bidding process, so electronic markets for auto parts create a larger market, one that is more transparent and with much lower transaction costs. Increasing the size of markets will reduce the ability of parties on both sides of the exchange to exercise monopoly or monopsony power. The efficiency and speed of such exchanges will instantly reveal supercompetitive pricing and expose it to arbitrage. For companies on both sides of an electronic market, it will reduce procurement costs, allow better supply chain management, and make possible tighter inventory control. Monopoly and monopsony depend on the existence of barriers to competition, and electronic markets greatly reduce a major example of such barrier. Electronic exchanges effectively put all transactions into a larger market—larger in physical volume of transactions, geographic space, and numbers of participants. Lower transaction costs bring in participants who might otherwise stay out or be restricted to more localized markets where they are vulnerable to large buyers or sellers with localized market power.[99] Again, consider the analogy to a private individual buying an automobile. Previously restricted to scanning local or regional newspaper advertisements, the auto buyer can now use the Internet to search for a car within the entire U.S. market, and even abroad.

The most well-known electronic exchange in auto components is Covisint, created in 2000 by GM, Ford, and Daimler-Chrysler (later joined by Peugeot, Nissan, and Renault), all promising to direct their combined annual parts spending of $250 billion to this new forum. The world's largest parts maker, Delphi, announced that it would participate. By the middle of 2002, about 7,000 suppliers had registered to participate in Covisint auctions. In May 2001, Daimler-Chrysler reported that it had conducted the largest Covisint transaction, spending $3.1 billion on parts orders from five suppliers.[100] VW established its own electronic parts procurement exchange. Suppliers have created other electronic market exchanges. A group of German suppliers (including the world's second largest, Bosch) established Supply Chain Online, with about 209 participants.[101]

Prior to the existence of such electronic auctions, bidding for parts contracts could take weeks to yield completed transactions. Suppliers would mail or fax bids to the assembler, who might request multiple rounds of new bidding in order to obtain the lowest prices. Covisint auctions last about forty-five minutes, and suppliers can instantly view competitors' bids. As a result of a Covisint auction in January 2002, Chrysler claims to have saved 40 percent on the opening prices of some parts.[102] The promise of reducing transaction costs to nearly zero will have major consequences for the structure and process of commerce.

Covisint has not evoked universal enthusiasm. As in any auction, there is the "winner's curse" problem. The form it takes here is that if the lowest bid wins and if the winner is less informed than some other bidders about the true cost of producing the component, the supplier can actually lose money from being the winner. Another factor that may reinforce the pressure to offer low bids is that some suppliers feel that Covisint is being run in a way that actually reinforces monopsony power on the part of manufacturers. The main objection of suppliers is that the automakers select, prior to the opening of bidding, a group of suppliers who are designated "preferred bidders." These suppliers are then invited to compete against each other. As one supplier complained, "If that [automaking] customer represents 30 percent of your business and you walk away, they could tell you that you will never be a preferred bidder again."[103] Suppliers also worry about automakers revealing sensitive information to competitors and playing off the competitors against each other because of asymmetric knowledge of the bidding process. Whether this asymmetry is a structural flaw in the operation of Covisint or simply a sign of institutional immaturity remains to be seen. There is almost certainly too much concentration on the demand side for Covisint to ever be as close to a perfectly competitive market as eBay.

The primary rationale for the existence of any business organization (in contrast to multiple transactions by individuals) is transaction costs.[104] In the absence of transaction costs, many of the forms of social and business organization that we take for granted would be unnecessary. Insurance companies, for example, exist only to match up individuals with differing degrees of risk attitude (that is, the risk-neutral person sells an insurance policy to the risk-averse person). If such individuals could transact bilaterally at low cost with each other, insurance companies would not exist. Hence, sophisticated electronic markets reduce the optimal size of firms by reducing the transaction costs that make firms necessary for commerce to take place efficiently in the first place. Insofar as the global merger process is driven by a need to reduce transaction costs, electronic markets reduce not only the bargaining power of large firms (on both sides of the exchange) but also the need for large firms to even exist. Transaction costs are, of course, not the only reason global mergers are occurring.

A third factor limiting the monopsony power of producers is the increasing amount of the value of their product that is being outsourced to suppliers (see table 2.2), especially to those who produce preassembled modules that the auto assembler simply attaches to the vehicle, rather like "plug-and-play" computer peripherals. The bargaining power of a vehicle maker is, ceteris paribus, inversely proportional to the amount of value that is farmed out to suppliers as long as individual suppliers are not dependent on particular auto assemblers. An automaker that outsources 10 percent of the value of the vehicle to suppliers faces a lower opportunity cost or vulnerability than the automaker that outsources 90 percent to independent suppliers. The role of the brand name–owning automaker is shifting to that of coordination, sequencing, and final assembly, rather like the maker of personal computers that simply gathers and assembles a small number of basic components, like the motherboard, disk drives, memory modules, and so on. Automakers are moving away from being true vehicle manufacturer to being brand-name owners that may confine themselves largely to assembly and marketing.

Along with outsourcing and modularization comes standardization of these components, a cost-saving measure that has shifted some market power toward suppliers. Suppliers are producing homogeneous components and subsystems sold to many auto assemblers that may have previously used their own proprietary systems. As automakers become dependent on these suppliers of standardized components, an increasing degree of monopoly power is conferred on the largest suppliers of the most important components. Bosch, for example, has for more than a decade sold its Motronic electronic ECM (engine control management) systems to a variety of automakers that would have difficulty finding a close substitute.[105]

As the proportion of a vehicle consisting of "plug-in" modules rises, this favors further consolidation in the supplier industry. Part of this imperative comes from the need for module suppliers to have expertise in the many different areas necessary to provide a manufacturer with a complete module for, say, the cockpit of a vehicle. Many automobile dashboards, for example, are now purchased as a complete unit from the supplier, so that the manufacturer's assembly-line workers no longer attach dozens of small instruments, switches, and wiring harnesses during assembly. Modularization also reinforces the need for economies of scale in suppliers' production management. Finally, insofar as modularization increases the proportion of a car's value that is outsourced from manufacturer to supplier, it also increases the amount of risk that is passed to the supplier. Manufacturers may be more eager to embrace new technologies when they can pass the development costs on to the suppliers. Size—and diversification across various types of components—is a way of coping with this added risk. The large diversified auto supply and components manufacturer is both less exposed to the risks of fluctuations in any one part of the components market and better able to bargain with larger brand-name manufacturers.

Component makers are following the auto companies into emerging markets, and this may increase the market power of those suppliers insofar as they face little credible competition from local suppliers. Automakers encourage suppliers to follow them into these markets both because they can then be assured of the quality of components and because it may help them comply with host country foreign investment rules. In Russia, for example, Western automakers not only have trouble finding Russian suppliers that can meet their quality standards but also can import parts duty free if they procure 50 percent of their components locally. GM's main supplier, Delphi, has moved into Russia to supply components for GM's joint venture with Avto-VAZ.[106] Delphi is also supplying engine parts from its Chinese and other Asian plants to Brilliance China Automotive, a local Chinese auto producer that has partnerships with several foreign auto companies.[107] Internationalizing their production facilities will help major global suppliers to maintain their share of automakers' procurement of inputs and enable the automakers to continue to increase the proportion of their value added that is outsourced to those suppliers. Both of these developments might reduce automakers' monopsony powers with respect to those suppliers and increase the market power of those suppliers who choose to follow the automakers into new markets, unless the move brings multinational component suppliers into competition with other multinational suppliers rather than merely displacing inefficient local suppliers.

There may well be ways in which auto manufacturers can draw back to themselves, intentionally or otherwise, some of the monopsony power lost due to outsourcing. One of these is through the increasing size of contracts. As the numbers of independent manufacturers and distinct platforms shrink and commonality of parts across different brand names increases, vehicle makers are offering contracts of much larger size to suppliers. The large size of individual contracts generates heavy competition among suppliers and effectively restores some monopsony power to the automakers, even as outsourcing increases.[108] Nissan, for example, cut its number of suppliers from 1,145 to 700 from the beginning of 2001 to June 2002 and twenty-eight of its remaining suppliers rely on Nissan for more than 20 percent of their sales.[109] Insofar as mergers result in joint purchasing, the trend toward larger contracts is further enhanced. In 2002, Nissan and Renault increased the size of their joint components, purchasing from $15 billion to $21 billion.[110]

Finally, some supplier industries possess political power that auto industry consolidation cannot overcome for the purpose of exercising monopsony power. The steel industry in the United States may be one such example. Long in a state of secular decline, the steel industry retains formidable political power because of both its geographic concentration in states with a large number of electoral votes and its critical importance in some electoral districts. The industry enmeshed itself in a destructive bargain with politicians. The industry wanted protection from import competition, but once obtained (such as the steel import quotas under the Reagan administration in 1984), the protection removed much of the incentive to modernize. Furthermore, some politicians made support conditional on the industry not modernizing since that would involve abandoning old steelmaking technology in the northern and northeastern states and moving to smaller mini-mills in the southern states. The announcement in March 2002 that the Bush administration would protect the steel industry with tariffs of up to 30 percent was simply another step in this decades-old political saga.

Whatever monopsony power U.S. automakers may have in their relationship with the U.S. steel industry is of little help in the face of the steel industry's electoral power. The auto industry is damaged by steel protectionism in at least two respects. One is the obvious increase in the costs of production. About 15 percent of the steel produced in the United States goes to the motor vehicle industry.[111] As a result of the tariffs, contracts between U.S. steelmakers and automakers were renewed in 2002 with price increases of 5 to 10 percent, with some as high as 15 percent, and some makers of auto components claim their steel costs have gone up by as much as 80 percent.[112] An indirect but perhaps more serious longer-term cost is the competitive advantage to foreign automakers who not only can buy steel unencumbered by the tariff but may experience the further benefit of having low-cost steel diverted from U.S. factor markets into their own, lowering the price of steel to these foreign producers even more.

In addition to political power, the steel industry also benefits from increasing concentration, similar to auto components suppliers. Some of this activity is international. When Renault and Nissan formed their joint purchasing organization, the move was specifically linked to mergers between steel companies that supplied the two firms. Renault in Europe buys much of its steel from Arcelor, a steel producer established from the merger of four European steel companies, including Germany's Thyssen-Krups. Two of Nissan's steel suppliers, NKK and Kawasaki, also merged. GM has reportedly been encouraging foreign steel companies to establish production within the United States, a move that may be related both to the tariff increase of 2002 and to concentration within the steel industry.

Diversification beyond Autos

The reduction in the number of global automakers has been accompanied by some efforts to diversify away from autos. Toyota and Ford are offering credit cards.[113] Toyota is also seeking to move into theme parks, movies, and music.[114] Fiat seeks to diversify farther away from its core auto business into areas such as insurance and telecommunications.[115]

Diversifying outside of the auto business may reduce some kinds of risk. Nonsystematic risk is the risk that is unique to a particular activity (for example, a shift in demand between auto brands is nonsystematic risk to an auto company). Systematic risk is the risk imposed on all economic agents by, for example, macroeconomic fluctuations. Diversification beyond core auto-related activities can reduce nonsystematic but not systematic, risk. However, it also introduces the danger of moving beyond a management's area of core competency, a problem raised by the conglomerate mergers of the 1960s. VW briefly diversified, unprofitably, into office equipment with its ownership of Triumph-Adler from 1974 to 1986. Daimler made costly acquisitions in the aircraft and aerospace sectors (for example, the Dutch aircraft maker Fokker and Deutsche Aerospace).[116] Daimler has in recent years been shedding such noncore assets. In 2002, for example, its sold its unit dealing with commercial financing of ships, aircraft, and commercial real estate.[117] In 2001, Ford reported a $199 million charge to write down investments in electronic commerce and other ventures largely unrelated to its core automotive business.[118] Ford's "Consumer Connect" electronic business was ended in July 2002, and functions directly relevant to the auto business were folded into its traditional marketing operations.[119] Whether such diversification is desirable is beyond the scope of this analysis, particularly since it does not appear to have any direct bearing on the reasons for global consolidation in the auto industry itself, except perhaps for the reason that expansion within the industry may be less risky than diversification outside the firm's area of expertise and experience.

Consolidation in the auto industry has had some impact on the commercial vehicle sector. The latter has become particularly important to automakers because of the increasing substitutability of autos and trucks, manifested primarily in the fashion of the sport-utility vehicles (SUV) and minivans of the past decade, a trend that has proliferated into new types of "crossover" vehicles blending the characteristics of trucks and autos. The higher profit margins on these vehicles have been particularly important to automakers in recent years. Even Porsche has succumbed, releasing in 2002 its Cayenne SUV.[120] Expanding into the truck and commercial vehicle market has helped automakers acquire some new technologies, such as all-wheel drive. Marketing both cars and trucks for the same dealerships may have some scale and marketing benefits. Insofar as cars and trucks are displaying convergent technologies there may be scale economies in components and monopsony power in purchasing. Finally, having a product range that includes trucks may help an automaker penetrate emerging markets where the characteristics of trucks may be more desirable than in the urban environments of developed countries.

One of the attractions of Chrysler to Daimler was that 40 percent of the former's sales were in light trucks, including minivans and SUVs. Chrysler's success in this sector was perhaps even more attractive given Daimler's continuing losses at it own U.S. truck maker, Freightliner, purchased in the early 1990s. In 2001, Daimler-Chrysler bought Volvo's 3 percent stake in Mitsubishi's truck operations (Mitsubishi Fuso) and announced plans to increase its commercial vehicle operations with both Mitsubishi and Hyundai, of which it already owns 43 and 50 percent, respectively. Daimler executives cited scale and distribution networks as the rationale.[121] In 2002, Daimler indicated that it may take a much larger stake of 30 percent in Mitsubishi Fuso.[122] The group plans a Hyundai truck factory in western China as part of strategy to open new factories in China to tap demand for both small cars and trucks in addition to exporting to China from Hyundai's Korean factories.[123] Daimler's long-term goal is to increase its share of the Asian truck market, an area where Mitsubishi Fuso is already well established.

The European truck market continues to regroup. After selling its car division to Ford, Volvo's takeover of Scania (another Swedish truck maker) was vetoed in March 2000 by the European Union on the grounds that it would result in an unacceptable reduction in competition. VW then moved to acquire a 34 percent voting share of Scania, approved by the European Union in 2000.[124] Scania and the Japanese truck maker Hino (50 percent owned by Toyota, Japan's largest manufacturer of commercial vehicles) subsequently entered into an alliance (without any cross-equity holdings) to share development costs and share their product lines, Hino specializing in smaller engines and Scania in larger power plants.[125] During the following year, the truck operations of Volvo, Renault, and the U.S. company Mack were combined under the Volvo name, with Renault holding a 15 percent stake in the combined operation, making Volvo the world's second-largest truck manufacturer after Daimler's Mercedes truck division.[126]

Conclusion

It is unlikely that oligopolistic collusion, monopsony power, and vertical integration have been primary motivating factors in the consolidation of the industry even if only because it would be difficult to estimate in advance how successful a merged firm would be in reaping the benefits of added market power, particularly given the scrutiny of governments when this motive is suspected. Any such gains are more likely to have been fortuitous bonuses from merger.

Artificial constraints on competition, including oligopolistic collusion and monopolization, are limited by government competition policies. Furthermore, an oligopolistic market can still be intensely competitive despite the presence of possible benefits from collusion. Vertical integration downstream toward the auto consumer has had a mixed record. Technology, electronic markets, and the lower transaction costs that promote "unbundling" of corporate activity are likely to restrain downstream vertical integration.

Integration back toward sources of supply may well be easier with fewer auto manufacturers in the market, but they might be just as likely to see benefits in divesting themselves of captive suppliers and engaging in arm's-length transactions with a larger group of suppliers in a competitive market for inputs, such as that which occurs within Covisint exchanges.

Monopsony power, particularly when combined with increasing geographic mobility, is clearly present in the auto sector. When applied to component purchasing, the net effects are ambiguous because of countervailing consolidation in the supplier sector and increasing supplier power, particularly as automakers outsource more of their production activity. Much more clear is the loss of bargaining power by labor as fewer multinational automakers move production around the world to take advantage of lower costs, especially with regard to skilled labor. Despite the stridency of many of the critics of globalization, they may well be correct in pointing to the adverse effects on the bargaining power of labor. Yet again, beneficial as they may be, none of these effects is likely to have figured largely in companies' motivations to merge, acquire other auto companies, or form alliances. Companies do not merge to outmaneuver trade unions. These are largely fortuitous side effects.

CHAPTER FIVE

Sovereign States
and Corporate Governance

The capital of a corporation comes from either debt or equity. The obligation to debt holders is a fixed payment of principal and interest, the residual benefit accruing to shareholders.[1] It is reasonable to start any analysis of corporate behavior with the presumption that firms are trying to maximize profits both to service debt and to maximize returns to the shareholders who ultimately determine the governance of the firm. Previous chapters have discussed arguments that the global consolidation of the auto industry may be the result of firms seeking to maximize profits by reducing costs, increasing revenue with new product offerings and sales in new markets, or enhancing their ability to manipulate market structures for the purpose of influencing input or product prices. All these are familiar and conventional reasons that fall within reach of the standard microeconomic theory of the firm. This chapter attempts to step beyond the assumption of rational profit-seeking behavior that follows from the classical theory of the firm and examine the possibility that global mergers in the auto industry are the outcome of people or organizations seeking to maximize some goal other than corporate profits.

Two categories of such conjectures are examined. The first consists of factors that are exogenous, or external, to the firm, typically incentives or constraints that are presented to firms by sovereign states seeking to exercise the ultimate coercive power that states have over firms, to induce them to allocate resources in ways that they would not otherwise. The instruments that governments use may be positive (such as subsidies) or negative (such as antitrust policies). The second category comprises factors that are endogenous, or internal, to the firm but not directly conducive to profit seeking. Firms may consolidate to maximize their size, revenues, product line, or geographic market presence regardless of the implications for the magnitude of profits accruing to shareholders. Some interests within a firm may gain from mergers even as others (and possibly even the firm as a whole) suffer pecuniary losses as a result of mergers. The most general term for this area of study, the internal structure of incentives within firms, is "corporate governance."[2]

Governments, Politics, and Industrial Consolidation

There are at least four categories of ways in which governments may have helped to promote or inhibit global consolidation in the auto industry. First, there are policies that indirectly affect the auto industry, even though that is not the primary goal of the policy (for example, monetary, fiscal, and exchange rate policies). Second, most governments, particularly those in developed areas of the world, have policies designed to promote competition and discourage monopolistic practices, and some of these policies specifically affect the auto industry. Third, governments may act so as to directly allocate resources toward or away from the auto industry with instruments such as taxes, subsidies, government equity in the industry, or regulations on investment, particularly foreign ownership. Finally, foreign trade policies may have specific provisions relating to industrial sectors, such as autos, typically in the form of tariffs and nontariff barriers, such as quotas.

Indirect Effects of General Economic Policies

The macroeconomic policies of governments, principally monetary and fiscal measures, have a multitude of effects that may unintentionally affect the propensity of auto firms to consolidate. Britain experienced a long postwar economic decline, and by the 1970s its per capita income had slipped below that of Italy, the poorest of the original six members of the European Economic Community, or Common Market. This decline contributed to the weakness of British auto firms, even if only by reducing domestic demand relative to other developed countries. Constant balance-of-payments crises (financial outflows exceeding inflows) led both to higher taxes to cut demand for imports and to devaluations of the pound to make British exports more price competitive, the former further lowering the effective demand for autos and the latter lowering the cost to foreign firms of acquiring British firms. The selling off of the remnants of the British auto industry from the 1970s into the 1990s occurred during a period when the value of the British pound languished around or below $1.50, significantly lower than its pre-1967 devaluation level of $2.80.

Paradoxically, the unusually high value of the pound with respect to the euro in recent years has also contributed to a further decline of the (by now almost entirely foreign owned) British auto industry as foreign producers threaten to transfer production elsewhere in Europe because of the cost of procuring inputs from within Britain. When BMW sold Rover in 1999, it openly blamed the high value of the pound for making Rover unprofitable,[3] though BMW obviously had many other reasons for being unhappy with Rover. Nissan's threat to move production from its Sunderland plant to France helped it get a pledge of £40 million financial assistance from the British government.[4] Nissan was not the only foreign company threatening to shift production out of Britain. Ford, General Motors (GM), Toyota, and Honda had been doing the same.[5] What distinguished Nissan from the others is that its alliance with Renault enabled it to credibly suggest that it could easily shift production to Renault plants in France.[6] Ford and GM were already shutting down production in Britain, and Honda and Toyota did not have assembly plants elsewhere in Europe. This may not be a motive for merger, but geographic mobility is certainly a benefit of global integration. Toyota has indicated that it is opening a factory in France so as to have the same flexibility.[7]

During the 1990s, the Japanese economy has languished, also lowering domestic demand for autos. In recent years, the weakness of the Japanese yen has helped the Japanese auto companies compete on world markets[8] but has also made their assets cheaper for foreign firms to acquire. The coincidence of a decade of a weak yen with an increasing foreign stake in the Japanese auto industry is surely causally connected.

Competition Policy

Industrial concentration is influenced by governments' competition policies relating to mergers and what are perceived as the anticompetitive practices that might emerge from consolidation. Discussion here focuses on the United States and the European Union as the auto-producing countries with the most active and explicit sets of competition policies. While other countries in which mergers take place may regulate competition, implementation and criteria tend to be ad hoc and less transparent. In South Korea, for example, the state-run Korean Development Bank first indicated that it would not allow Hyundai to bid for bankrupt Daewoo but reconsidered and suggested that a Hyundai monopoly in Korean auto production would be acceptable as long as Hyundai brought in a foreign partner, presumably the Daimler-Chrysler-Fiat group that already had a stake in Hyundai.[9]

During the immediate postwar years, at least until the late 1960s, western European countries encouraged mergers in the belief that it was required for international competitiveness. Since the 1970s, mergers in the European Union have been guided primarily by the competition rules implemented by the EU Commission. The members of the European Union reached agreement in June 2001 on a set of common rules to govern takeovers within the European Union, and members are expected to pass the required legislation by 2005.[10] The measure is intended primarily to restrict the ability of members to block takeovers in order to protect national companies and to ensure transparency. The European Union hopes to prohibit, for example, rules that grant disproportionate rights to some shareholders (often governments) so as to block takeover bids. There are indications that Germany may block the new rules because they would force the removal of the so-called Lex VW law, a statute that protects Volkswagen (VW) from a hostile takeover both by requiring that trade union and government representatives have a majority of seats on VW's governing board and by the provision that no shareholder may have voting rights in excess of 20 percent, slightly more than the proportion held by the state of Lower Saxony.[11] Early in 2003, the EU Commission suggested, following a ruling by the European Court of Justice, that it was contemplating legal action against the German government as part of a larger campaign against state-owned "golden shares" that some member states used to protect domestic firms against foreign takeover by giving particular groups of shareholders blocking power over the disposition of the assets of the firm.[12] Lower Saxony has indicated that it will increase its stake in VW to 25 percent if the law is overturned.

Mergers of motor vehicle makers have been relatively unrestrained by competition policies, though the commercial vehicle market is scrutinized more closely in Europe because of the much smaller number of manufacturers. The EU Commission prohibited in 2000 the merger of commercial vehicle makers Volvo and Scania,[13] though it did not object to VW's purchase of 34 percent of Scania votes. The objective of the Commission was to prevent one company from having a monopoly in the Swedish market and a dominant position in the Nordic market.[14] The European Union also required Renault to undo its joint commercial vehicle venture (Irisbus) with Fiat before collaborating with Volvo.[15] The European Union is apparently much less concerned about cross-border ventures in the auto sector, perhaps believing that there is still a substantial amount of competition even after the various collaborations of which it has approved, most recently GM's purchase of the remaining 50 percent of Saab in 2000,[16] GM and Fiat's cross shareholdings and collaboration in power trains and component purchasing,[17] and Ford's takeover of Mazda's distribution network.[18] In September 2000, the EU Commission gave Toyota permission to buy out its partner (Inchcape) that distributed Toyota cars and vans in the United Kingdom.[19]

In addition to scrutinizing outright mergers, the European Union monitors competitive practices generally. In 1995, manufacturers were enjoined from maintaining price differentials between countries. In 2000, the European Union fined both Opel and VW for obstructing the exports of vehicles from dealers in one country to consumers in other EU member states.[20] Individual member states have also taken unilateral action. Britain ordered vehicle manufacturers to offer the same volume discounts to dealerships that they offer to fleet buyers, with the intention of causing consumer auto prices to decline.[21]

The major competitive issue in Europe has been the Block Exemption that allowed vehicle manufacturers to engage in vertical restraints on trade. Specifically, manufacturers have been allowed to restrict their supplies of vehicles to only selected, franchised dealers and to restrict consumer warranty work to these authorized dealers. The European Union is reforming the Block Exemption (which expired in September 2002) so as to allow more opportunity for multibrand dealerships and for existing dealers to expand beyond the geographic markets initially designated to them by manufacturers, though it will still allow manufacturers to bar supermarkets and Internet merchants from becoming volume auto sellers.[22] Under the new rules, manufacturers will have to choose between two modes of distribution: "exclusivity," in which the automaker may give a retail dealer an exclusive territory but the dealer must be willing to sell to other professional retailers, and "selectivity," where dealers may open as many outlets as they wish, anywhere in the European Union, but the manufacturer may restrict them from selling to anyone but private customers. Hence, automakers are still allowed some market restraints. The exclusive system is closed territorially but open with regard to types of customers; the selective system is open geographically but closed as to type of customers.[23]

The reforms are most likely to be delayed and softened to favor the auto manufacturers because of heavy lobbying by auto manufacturers for a long transitional period and to the objections of some member states, particularly Germany. Chancellor Gerhard Schroeder argued to the European Commission that implementation of the reforms would lead to job losses and "huge competitive disadvantages to the German car industry,"[24] implying that the German government believes that the distribution systems of German auto companies are unusually uncompetitive. Auto prices in Germany are roughly 20 percent above those of the rest of the European Union. In May 2002, the

European Parliament voted to advise the EU Commission to delay until 2005 allowing dealers to sell outside the regions currently allocated to them by manufacturers, though it did endorse the Commission's plan to allow dealers to sell more than one brand of vehicle.[25] The European Union's Competition Commissioner Mario Ponti agreed to delay the reform until 2004.[26]

Competition policy in the United States has evolved from its traditional emphasis on formal measures of industrial concentration as a means of predicting the likelihood of price collusion to a new emphasis on promoting innovation. Recognizing that innovation is not necessarily inconsistent with industrial concentration since oligopolies may be highly competitive, policymakers now ask whether the degree of competition in an industry is sufficient to promote innovation rather than focusing on objective measures of concentration and seeking the lowest prices for consumers. Such a policy shift may well reduce the possibility of antitrust objections to mergers in the auto industry from either the Department of Justice or the Federal Trade Commission since it is manifestly very competitive despite the small number of major producers.[27] Chrysler attempted to have GM's cooperative production arrangement with Toyota in 1984 (NUMMI) blocked on antitrust grounds.[28] When the effort failed, Chrysler moved to ally itself with Mitsubishi, importing the latter's autos for sale under the Chrysler brand name.

American and European antitrust authorities are increasingly working together on individual cases in the hope of avoiding jurisdictional conflicts, and the United States has formal agreements on antitrust enforcement with the European Union, Brazil, Canada, Japan, and Mexico. The goal would be a set of common rules to enable firms to comply with antitrust regulations in all the geographic areas party to the agreement, an objective advocated in a report by the Department of Justice's International Competition Policy Advisory Committee.[29] Standardization of reporting and policy convergence on criteria for approval may yield both transparency and "one-stop" shopping for international firms. Insofar as a truly multinational antitrust policy comes to exist, auto companies may well be major beneficiaries. Any industry whose major firms have a market presence in many countries is less likely to have mergers stymied by inconsistent competition policies in its major markets.

Subsidies and Government Equity in Auto Companies

Governments have on occasion taken a financial interest in auto companies—indirectly with varying forms of state aid and directly through partial equity ownership. The U.S. government is loath to enter this game, though it did give Chrysler a $1.2 billion loan in 1980. More typical are small indirect forms of aid, such as a $500,000 federal grant to Missouri in 2002 to use in ways to encourage Ford to refrain from shutting an auto assembly plant in St. Louis.[30] State governments have been active in luring auto companies to locate within their borders. In 1992, South Carolina gave BMW $130 million in support of its local plant. Kentucky gave Toyota $125 million in 1985, and early in 2003 Arkansas and Texas were competing for another Toyota plant.[31] Alabama gave Daimler incentives worth $253 million in 1993 to establish a manufacturing site, and in 2002 the state legislature gave Hyundai $118 million for its first U.S. assembly plant.[32] Also in 2002, the Michigan Economic Development Corporation gave Auto Alliance International (a Ford-Mazda joint venture) a $94.9 million tax credit over twenty years.[33] These forms of aid are unlikely to have had any direct impact on consolidation in the industry, though for Daimler a manufacturing presence in the United States might have been considered complementary to the capacity of its Chrysler partner. With Hyundai now associated with the Daimler group, all three firms have more production flexibility within the United States.

European governments have done the same, though the European Union must approve such aid. The British government offered Nissan aid of $76 million in 2000 not to close down its Sunderland plant.[34] Nissan had threatened to relocate production to a Renault factory in France,[35] an exercise of bargaining power that would have been impossible in the absence of the corporate alliance with Renault. The European Union approved the aid despite protests from Peugeot.[36] The corporate alliance of Nissan and Renault conferred on the two firms a degree of bargaining power that financially benefited both to the competitive disadvantage Renault's major domestic rival. Auto mergers must considerably increase the bargaining power of auto companies in extracting such subsidies from both national and subnational governments. As "buyers" of investments, these governments are faced with more concentrated oligopoly power.

Yet the European Union is not always so indulgent. In 1996, it blocked aid to VW from the state of Saxony, and courts ultimately rejected VW's appeals.[37] In 2002, the European Union indicated that it would block the Italian government from giving direct aid to Fiat as it became clear that the company was struggling to stay in existence and the holding company's debt holders were pressuring it to sell off the car business.[38] While the European Union will allow national aid to auto companies to locate in depressed regions of Europe, it also requires a demonstration that in the absence of the aid, the firm would relocate existing or proposed production. German aid to Daimler and Mitsubishi for an engine plant in eastern Germany was reduced in 1991 at the request of the European Union.[39] In May 2002, the European Union ruled that Spanish aid to Ford exceeded the allowable limits and that its proposed aid to VW was unnecessary because VW had not demonstrated the existence of a lower-cost production site.[40] At the same time, the European Union was questioning aid to BMW from the German federal government and the state of Saxony (allegedly to induce BMW not to move production to the Czech Republic) and a Portuguese plan to provide aid to GM for a factory near Lisbon.[41] In June 2002, the European Union allowed Spanish government aid to Renault because the auto company demonstrated that it could produce engines more cheaply in Turkey than in Spain and that the proposed aid would be less than the incremental cost of continuing production in Spain.[42]

Government equity stakes in auto companies clearly present the ability to facilitate or block consolidation. No foreign company would be able to acquire Renault without the active approval of the French government, which owns 44.2 percent of Renault's shares. The French government announced in October 2001 that it intends to reduce its holdings of Renault to 37.6 percent and is prepared to further reduce its share to 25 percent in the future in conjunction with Renault increasing its share of Nissan to 44.2 percent from 36.8 percent, while Nissan will take a 15 percent stake in Renault. The French Finance Ministry stated that the purpose of its action was to help in "strengthening the alliance between Renault and Nissan, and consolidating Renault's prospects within the group."[43] The alliance with Nissan has reduced the vulnerability of Renault to foreign takeover, allowing the government to itself partially withdraw from direct holdings in the company. In April 2002, the French government began the process by selling a 10.7 percent stake in Renault to institutional investors.[44] Even without such a stake, the French government will block foreign takeovers, as it did in the case of Fiat's move to absorb Citroën in 1972.

Partial state ownership may also be used to resist consolidation. The federal government of West Germany held a 16 percent stake in VW until sold in 1988. The state of Lower Saxony owns nearly 20 percent of VW, and federal statutes prohibit any shareholder from owning more than 20 percent of the company. This gives Lower Saxony a great deal of power to block takeovers of VW in addition to using its voting power to manipulate VW's corporate policies to meet its political objectives (such as in the area of employment and industrial relations). New EU laws on takeovers may well prohibit rules such as those that protect VW, though the government of Lower Saxony has suggested that if the rule is overturned, it will simply acquire enough shares of VW to have the power to block takeovers.[45] Lower Saxony is clearly determined to prevent any foreign takeover of VW.

In a few cases, governments are directly involved in merger activity of auto firms. The British government spent decades pouring subsidies into the

British auto industry as it gradually consolidated many companies into the single company that by the 1990s was called the Rover Group. The government strongly supported Honda's equity stake in Rover during the 1980s (up to the BMW takeover in 1994), hoping it would relieve the burden on taxpayers. Prime Minister Thatcher had tried to interest Ford in buying Rover in 1985.[46] Again in 2000, it had been prepared to offer BMW $236 million in aid to maintain Rover as a volume producer, though the European Union indicated that it would not allow the aid to be forthcoming.[47] Between 1964 and 1967, Chrysler purchased a majority interest in the British automaker Rootes, owner of the Humber and Singer brands. During the following decade, it lost increasingly large amounts of money in the company, and in 1975 Chrysler forced the British government to subsidize its operations under threat of liquidating the company.[48] In 1978, Chrysler sold its U.K. operations to Peugeot to the chagrin and surprise of the British government, which had just offered further aid to keep Chrysler's U.K. operations viable.[49] During the 1980s, Britain gave Nissan aid of over $200 million to invest in its Sunderland plant.

The Italian government arranged Fiat's purchase of Alfa Romeo at a time when Ford was seeking to acquire Alfa Romeo.[50] Unlike the British government, Italy seems to prefer to keep its major automaker in national hands. As Fiat's financial condition continued to deteriorate at the beginning of 2003, Italian Prime Minister Berlusconi repeatedly stated his interest in having the Italian government take an equity interest in Fiat (as an alternative to aid that would be blocked by the European Union) in order to prevent the company from being absorbed by GM, a sentiment enthusiastically shared by the latter. The European Union reminded the Italian government that it could invest in Fiat only if it were to be on the same terms as a private investor, with no hidden subsidies. As an alternative, Berlusconi was reported to be supporting a bid by Italian entrepreneur Roberto Colaninno to arrange an $8 billion rescue package that would both release GM from its obligations and replace the Agnelli family as the largest shareholders in Fiat.[51] The governments of France, Germany, and Italy all appear to have a strong preference for preventing mergers that would allow a major domestic auto producer to fall under foreign ownership.

The government of South Korea has been intimately involved in the sale of Daewoo to a foreign automaker. After pressing domestic creditors and suppliers to extend credit to the ailing company, the government's Korean Development Bank, Daewoo's main creditor, took over the task of selling its assets as an alternative to bankruptcy or nationalization. After Ford withdrew its offer and negotiations with GM dragged on for months, the Korean government attempted, without success, to speed up the process by offering tax breaks to GM.[52] Daewoo was a *chaebol*, or industrial conglomerate, the breaking up of which can be exceedingly difficult because of the many links between the constituent parts. This is especially so when one or more parts of the *chaebol* are to be sold to foreign companies, often inspiring xenophobic reactions.

Similarly, the Indian government has been attempting to sell its 49 percent stake in its large national automaker Maruti since 1999.[53] Maruti's dated but inexpensive subcompact autos, made under license from Suzuki since 1982, have dominated the Indian market since the early 1980s, though by 2001 its market share had dropped to 43 percent under competitive pressure from Hyundai, Daewoo, and Ford, who are undoubtedly offering the Indian consumer more modern products. Suzuki owns 49 percent of Maruti and has the right of first refusal to buy the Indian government's share, though it appears to be in no hurry to do so. However, acquiring the remnants of obsolete local producers may be an increasingly unattractive strategy for multinational auto companies in an age during which trade barriers and local content rules are being whittled away by the World Trade Organization (WTO). Nevertheless, Suzuki is likely to buy up to 55 percent of Maruti.[54]

Finally, governments may control the flow of resources into the auto sector with regulations on investment, particularly with regard to foreign ownership. The Japanese government did not permit foreign ownership in its auto industry until the 1970s.[55] Developing countries typically regulate foreign investment. Only in 2002 did the government of India permit wholly foreign-owned auto production.[56] The Malaysian government has made it equally clear that its national car company Proton (which also owns the British car company Lotus) is not for sale despite widespread interest that some global automakers have in Proton, primarily as a way of getting a foothold in the prosperous but tariff-protected Malaysian market.[57]

In 1994, China set out its policy for regulating foreign investment in the auto industry, prescribing a ceiling on foreign ownership and mandating increasing local content and the transfer of technology to local partners. Joint ventures with Chinese firms have been the only way for foreign firms to be volume sellers in China. Entry into the WTO is almost certain to drastically reduce the incentive for international joint ventures in the Chinese market because import tariffs on autos are to fall to 25 percent by 2006. Entry into the WTO is likely to force on the domestic Chinese auto industry a process of painful intranational consolidation, compounded by competitive pressure from foreign producers no longer required to serve the Chinese market through joint venture local production. However, even after becoming fully compliant with WTO rules, the Chinese government will still have many instruments at its disposal to force international auto producers to continue production in China, even if it would be cheaper to serve the Chinese market from other locations. These would include the lower 25 percent tariff (still a considerable obstacle by international standards), various nontariff barriers (such as setting auto construction standards unique to the Chinese market[58]), and restrictions imposed by subnational local and provincial governments.

The Chinese auto market may well follow the recent pattern of change in India, where the Indian government is not only being obliged to offer uncompetitive national auto companies for sale to foreign firms but also having its domestic investment rules challenged as inconsistent with membership in the WTO. The United States and the European Union filed successful complaints with the WTO over India's policy of requiring foreign vehicle manufacturers to invest at least $50 million if they own more than 50 percent of the equity in the venture and attain 50 percent local content within three years and 70 percent local content within five years.[59] In general, as developing countries open up their economies, the practice of joint ventures to produce vehicles is likely to diminish both because the foreign firm may prefer to import rather than produce locally, and because if it does produce locally, it may prefer the freedom and potentially greater efficiency of a wholly owned subsidiary.

Trade Policy

It has been common for countries to have provisions in their trade policies that specifically target the auto sector. Quotas on exports of Japanese cars to the United States began in 1981 and continued into the 1990s. The disappearance of the quotas was related less to any diminution in the political power of U.S. automakers than it was to Japan's investment in the United States (making the quotas less helpful in determining market shares) and to moves by U.S. manufacturers to engage in coproduction arrangements with Japanese automakers in the 1980s. Ford began importing Mazdas, Chrysler importing Mitsubishis, and GM importing Toyota, Isuzu, and Suzuki vehicles. From 1995 to 2001, Japan and the United States had an auto pact in which the United States called for more openness in the Japanese domestic auto market under threat of unilateral import restrictions on Japanese cars. American pressure for the pact was motivated by a bilateral trade imbalance in the auto sector. A country needs to strive for an overall balance on its international trade and capital accounts if it does not wish to be a net international lender or borrower, but the notion that it should bilaterally balance trade in specific sectors or with a specific country makes little economic sense. Nevertheless, bilateral balancing has been a politically appealing concept in the populist domestic politics of trade policy in the United States. In 2001, the Japanese government refused to renew the pact.[60]

Since the 1970s, the European Union had restricted Japanese auto imports with quotas that were not finally removed until 1990. By the late 1970s, Britain had an 11 percent market share quota on Japanese imports, France a 3 percent quota, and Italy a numerical annual sales quota of 2,200 autos. Italy also sought to block imports of British Leyland autos made under license from Honda. In 1983, an informal agreement between Japan and the European Union restricted Japanese autos to 9 percent of the EU market.[61]

It may well be that increasing cross ownership has reduced corporate pressure for such trade arrangements. American companies with equity stakes in Japanese auto firms have less interest in forcing their Japanese partners to buy higher-cost American parts. European companies like Renault, with a stake in the profitability of Nissan, have little incentive to continue to attempt to restrict the access of Japanese autos to the European market. Indeed, the underlying logic of European countries trying to keep out Japanese autos began to crumble rapidly after Nissan became the first Japanese auto company to set up production facilities in Britain in the late 1970s. The French government had suggested that it would keep British-built Nissans out of the French market but eventually backed down.

Auto import tariffs in developed countries (0 percent in Japan and the United States and 10 percent in the European Union) have been too low in recent decades to be a compelling motive for merger in order to gain quick entry to a tariff-protected market. However, as recently as the 1960s, developed-country tariffs were high enough to provide such a motive. In 1960, auto import tariffs were 8.5 percent in the United States, 35 to 40 percent in Japan, 30 percent in France, 13 to 16 percent in Germany, 31.5 to 40.5 percent in Italy, and 30 percent in the United Kingdom.[62] Chrysler's purchase of Simca, Rootes, and the Spanish producer Barrerios was directly related to the need to jump over import tariffs.[63] Similarly, U.S. import quotas encouraged Honda's decision to produce in the United States in 1980. Of the developed countries, Australia is one of the few to still have high auto import tariffs (15 percent in 2002 due to fall to 10 percent in 2005 and 5 percent in 2010), the legacy of an earlier "infant industry" policy for forcing the development of an industry in which Australia had no comparative advantage. The four major Australian auto producers (Toyota, Mitsubishi, Ford, and GM-Holden) will continue to receive large government subsidies (over $400 million in 2002) to employ only 55,000 people. The result in the case of Australia has been not merger with existing firms (as in the case of Korea) but rather the development of an industry that would not otherwise have existed—and at a considerable cost to consumers.

Developing countries have much higher tariffs that offer more incentive to invest in local production or merge with a local company to jump over tariff barriers. Foreign firms may be able to jump a tariff or nontariff barrier with wholly owned direct investments without a local partner, but tariffs are often combined with investment barriers, and mergers or joint ventures are quicker than starting from scratch. South Korea is a case that stands out as an example of how a country's trade policy may directly encourage corporate mergers in the auto industry. American and European automakers have long complained that nontariff barriers, assisted by an 8 percent tariff, close the South Korean market to them. In 2001, Korean auto companies had domestic sales well in excess of a million vehicles, while imports were less than 3,000 units. Korean auto buyers were allegedly deterred from purchasing foreign vehicles by government-inspired publicity campaigns urging them to buy domestically produced vehicles, by domestic taxes that discriminate against autos with large engines, and on occasion by implicit threats that buyers of foreign vehicles would be subjected to tax audits.[64] Purchasing an interest in domestic Korean producers appeared to be the only way for a foreign automaker to participate in Asia's second-largest market.

These distortions and nonmarket incentives may be moderated by free trade and customs union agreements. Outside the developed countries, auto provisions in trade agreements are common.[65] The Association of Southeast Asian Nations (ASEAN) has long had plans for an Asian Free Trade Area (AFTA), intended to include a reduction of auto tariffs to 5 percent among members. There is some potential for these agreements to diffuse more widely. Singapore, for example, has concluded an Economic Partnership Agreement with India to facilitate trade and investment.[66] In principle, this would enable producers to concentrate production in one member. Companies such as BMW and GM are betting that Thailand will be the auto hub of AFTA, presumably because of its high-factor intensity in human and physical capital, and have invested accordingly. Malaysia is resisting free trade as a threat to its indigenous producer Proton and is continuing its import tariffs of between 42 and 300 percent in addition to making it clear that it would block any attempt to take over Proton.[67]

The Latin American common market Mercosur has subagreements specific to free trade in autos. Brazil and Argentina, for example, have a bilateral auto pact within Mercosur that calls for zero tariffs on autos, subject to balanced trade in that sector.[68] Brazil and Mexico have a trade agreement that confers lower tariffs on auto trade between the two.[69] Such agreements may encourage corporate consolidation because the enlarged single firm may be better able to treat these larger subareas of the world as single markets. In 2000, Nissan and Renault announced that they would pursue a coordinated strategy in the Mercosur countries of Brazil, Argentina, Paraguay, and Uruguay.[70] It would be unconvincing to argue that Mercosur provided a significant part of the incentive for Nissan and Renault to establish an alliance. Nevertheless, it does suggest that this aspect of globalization, the establishment of larger areas of free trade, is seen by auto companies as an opportunity to gain from consolidated operations.

Why should a movement toward free trade areas and customs unions[71] produce an incentive for auto companies to merge? Cannot two separate companies serve a large market just as well as one combined company? Perhaps an alliance gives the companies an opportunity to exploit real or imagined economies of scale. Free trade between two countries allows an auto company with a presence in both countries to combine previously separate production, sales, and distribution groups into single units to serve the combined market, possibly allowing the combined entity to benefit from cost savings through economies of scale (in production, sales, and distribution), reduced organizational duplication, cost sharing, and pecuniary economies of scale in purchasing. Two firms that each had a presence in the two countries might see a further incentive to merge so as to be able to serve the larger market with one set of organizations for each activity and reap even more economies-of-scale gains or cost-sharing gains than separate companies serving the combined market. Segmented markets would reduce the potential for realizing economies of scale or savings through cost sharing.

It should be noted that, insofar as the logic of these arguments relies on assumptions about economies of scale, one must assume that both each individual country market and the combined markets of the two countries are too small to yield economies-of-scale gains or significant cost-sharing opportunities for the individual firms. It must be assumed that the combined markets of the two countries will yield economies of scale if the two firms merge operations. While this may well be true for firms serving small tariff-protected developing-country markets (such as those of Latin America or ASEAN), it is unlikely to apply to firms serving large developed-country markets where single-firm operations serving single countries are likely to already be large enough to reap economies of scale in most areas of the firm's operations (as in most of the large countries in the European Union).

Corporate Size Maximization

Corporations are political as well as financial entities. When considering the possibility that international consolidation in the auto industry is driven by political motives or non–profit maximizing motives in general, we must also consider the possibility that these motives are endogenous, generated internally within the corporation, rather than incentives externally imposed by the rules or other incentives offered by sovereign states or by international organizations like the European Union or the WTO. Hence, the question at hand is whether auto companies might simply wish to expand in size for reasons that have no direct connection to the well-being of the corporation, its employees, or shareholders, particularly when that well-being is measured by the conventional criterion of profit.

A common cliché is that political empires inevitably overexpand and collapse, possibly leading to global cycles of "hegemony" in which great powers emerge from periods of war and instability, rise to world or regional domination, and then collapse for a variety of reasons that many political historians attribute to excessive expansion.[72] Thucydides attributed the Peloponnesian War of the fifth century B.C., in which Sparta defeated Athens after thirty years of fighting, to imperial overexpansion by Athens, motivated by a drive for power and domination.[73] How one could ever predict when an empire is too large, apart from the historical hindsight of observing its demise, is left unexplained. Since the medieval period, the world has seen successive domination by the empires of Portugal, Spain, England, and (more arguably) the United States.

Why would rational national leaders pursue imperial expansion to the point of collapse? Obviously, none would deliberately do so. Some are apparently able to recognize what they see as indications of overexpansion. British Colonial Secretary Joseph Chamberlain warned in 1902 that Britain was a "Weary Titan [that] staggers under the too vast orb" of its empire.[74] The Romans cleverly attempted to adjust the size of their empire to that of an optimal tax collection area, pulling back the boundaries when the revenues fell short of the costs of holding on to a piece of territory.[75] Some empires have arguably been good business ventures. One scholar who has examined the modern empires of Germany, Japan, and the Soviet Union has suggested that they were profitable,[76] which would imply that they eventually collapsed for exogenous reasons beyond the control of imperial managers.

There are many factors that could drive empires to expand beyond optimal size. Lack of information may be one reason. If everyone had perfect information, there might be no wars because the side that would be defeated would know this in advance and presumably seek a settlement to save the human and physical cost of actually going to war and getting defeated. We know only with hindsight that an empire was not sustainable or that a particular investment or merger was not profitable. Economic historians have shown that much of the British and other empires were a net drain on the home country and benefited only particular sectional interests at the expense of the nation as a whole.[77] Yet this may not necessarily have been obvious at the time. Perverse psychological motives may also be a factor. An early twentieth-century political economist, Joseph Schumpeter, argued that imperialism was simply an "objectless disposition" to "unlimited expansion," an irrational, atavistic relic of a warrior culture. By this reasoning, empire building is little more than a demonstration that a country or its leadership has "the right stuff."

Could it be that corporate mergers are driven by the same impulses, perhaps because expansion provides financial or psychic benefits to groups or individuals within the corporation at the expense of shareholders and probably most employees? If so, we would expect to see corporations try to expand in size, perhaps through mergers, maximizing sales revenue or market share (or some other index of size) regardless of the implications for profits and the interests of shareholders. The notion that businesses try to maximize firm size or sales rather than profits is an old one.[78] Is there evidence consistent with such a goal?

Studies of mergers reveal that acquirers pay too much, many mergers fail, and few are profitable.[79] A McKinsey study found that in 61 percent of the mergers examined, the acquisition did not earn a rate of return sufficient to cover the cost of the capital required for the investment.[80] Mueller's cross-national study of mergers in the United States and western Europe during the 1960s and 1970s found little evidence that profits improved as a result of mergers, and he concluded that the pursuit of growth (that is, size maximization) was left as "a sort of residual explanation for why mergers might take place."[81] More recent work by Sirower found, in a sample of mergers and acquisitions of the 1980s, that in 66 percent of the cases the merger reduced the value of the acquiring firm and that the damage was greater as the size of the firm being acquired increased. No wonder, then, that a larger study of mergers between 1950 and 1976 found that 47 percent of acquired units were later sold off, which suggests that the profit motive will at some point reassert itself, perhaps through shareholder distress.[82] Managers will sacrifice profit in order to grow, and, worse still, in one study merger-prone firms even failed the goal of sales expansion.[83] A recent study sponsored by McKinsey found that of 160 acquisitions by 157 companies during the period 1995–1996, only 12 percent of the acquirers increased their rate of growth during the three years following the acquisition.[84] The general record of mergers is, in the words of Scherer, "widespread failure, considerable mediocrity, and occasional success."[85]

What motives would drive managers to pursue a goal of size maximization through merger, acquisition, and alliances, even perhaps to the extent of sacrificing corporate profit and the interests of shareholders? Managers are obviously unlikely to be forthcoming about motives that make shareholders worse off. Furthermore, "they may be unconscious of deep seated drives which affect their actions . . . [and] . . . it is rash to place much reliance on the overt utterances of industrialists."[86] The weight of evidence that mergers are generally unprofitable suggests that lack of information, while it might explain the overexpansion of political empires, is much less plausible as a source of corporate imperialism. The numbers of empires from which would-be world leaders may learn are few. Markets may not be perfect, and business managers may not have "rational expectations" (that is, very good forecasting abilities about the future value of economic variables), but data on the success or otherwise of corporate mergers are large in volume and sufficiently widely disseminated that ignorance of the normal unprofitability of such activity is not a compelling explanation of mergers, though it may apply to some individual cases. Three more reasonable categories of explanations are natural selection, sectional interests within the firm, and innate psychological drives.

Some observers of the auto industry suggest that in the long term only the largest firms will be left standing. Some sort of natural selection imperative is being invoked: Only the fittest survive. Yet such arguments beg the question of how we should measure fitness. Size is not a measure of fitness in the animal world, nor is it in the corporate world. In a controversial piece written in the early 1950s, Milton Friedman suggested that natural selection in markets ensures that in the longer term only profit-maximizing firms will survive regardless of whether they are doing so by accident or by design.[87] Do we have any reason to assume that size correlates with profitability? Recent corporate history suggests not. If there is any correlation at all between size and profitability, it would appear to be negative. Some of the prominent smaller companies, such as Honda, Porsche, and BMW, are the most profitable.

A more defensible variation on this theme is that large companies have bigger cash reserves that will enable them to weather the financial storms of intense competition and macroeconomic recessions.[88] This is perhaps true in an absolute sense, but unless it is also true relative to their size (namely, that large firms have large cash reserves, even after controlling for size), absolute measures of cash reserves are unlikely to be a reliable measure of market "fitness." Large companies will obviously have more cash reserves and other resources than small firms. Large firms also face financial problems of a larger absolute magnitude. Unless the larger firm's resources are also larger in a relative sense (for example, as a proportion of sales), then the larger size of their resources is not particularly meaningful. Put in terms of the prevailing nautical metaphor, larger ships may have more lifeboats, more watertight compartments, and more bilge pumps, but they also have more people to save, more areas to get holed, more weight to support, more places to leak, and so on. Perhaps fewer large ships sink than small ships, but there are fewer large ships afloat in the first place. If very large companies constitute, say, the upper 5 percent of the tail in a size distribution for the entire industry, there are obviously going to be fewer of them than in the lower 95 percent of the distribution. Assuming that sinkings are random occurrences, one would expect to see fewer large ships sinking. It is also worth noting that even if very large business firms do go under at a lower rate (relative to their total number) than small firms, this is not necessarily because they are in any economic sense "fitter." Governments and the financial community may simply be more reluctant to see them sink, a motive illustrated by U.S. government loans to Chrysler in the 1980s, taxpayer subsidies to British Leyland from the 1960s into the 1990s, and the Italian government's current dilemma over the imminent foundering of Fiat Auto.

In a related argument, *BusinessWeek* has suggested that possession of large cash reserves by some of the large world auto companies has been driving the consolidation of the industry because they feel compelled to spend these reserves on acquisitions.[89] Is *BusinessWeek* suggesting that car companies are like profligate consumers who cannot bear to have positive bank account balances and must compulsively spend any cash reserves on the first familiar object that catches their attention? Again, the rationality of the imperative is obscure. Why would managers assume that buying another auto company is the most efficient or, in this context, "fit" use of cash reserves? It would make more sense to think that companies that possess cash reserves or use those cash reserves in unproductive ways would be targets of takeovers. One anonymous poster (a disgruntled Chrysler manager?) on a discussion board at the www.just-auto.com website suggested as much in an opinion posted in December 2000:

> It seems funny that "all of a sudden" there is $10 billion missing from Chrysler's reserves . . . the Daimler side of DCX has used the Chrysler side's cash to go on

a spending spree. They purchased the remaining stock of Detroit Diesel, and dramatically increased their share in Mitsubishi, as well as Hyundai. They've also purchased Western Star and GEM. . . . From what I understand, Germany also charges Chrysler "cost centers" . . . for every single thing they can think of, from information to "services rendered." This includes the diesel engine to replace the Cummins in the new Dodge ram (at DCX German management's direction). Mercedes has charged Dodge for the development and implementation costs of the new diesel, even though Mercedes plans to use that same diesel in their own commercial vehicles. . . . This leads me to believe that Daimler planned to suck Chrysler's reserves dry from the beginning, and if Chrysler foundered . . . , they could blame it all on "American Mismanagement" and dump the Chrysler division off on the highest bidder (while keeping all that Chrysler's finances had helped them to buy).[90]

Economic markets are certainly subject to some of the same kinds of natural selection or survival of the fittest, imperatives that are found in biology, albeit with the caveat that learning behaviors not present in biological natural selection may alter natural selection in markets. Animals do not learn that they have to grow longer legs to outrun predators, but managers can learn that one corporate strategy is more conducive to survival than another. Yet it remains to be demonstrated that maximizing the size of a firm is evolutionarily rational or, even if it is, that it is more fitness enhancing than maximizing profitability. If profit is the ultimate criterion of success, then the size maximizing executive is, in the long run, eroding the firm's market fitness. As Milton Friedman reminded us, in the long run business managers who do not maximize profits, whether by accident or by calculation, will go out of business as surely, one might add, as the animal with too-short legs will not survive to reproduce. The social life of economic markets may make maladaptive corporate strategies endure longer than in the world of biology and even allow time for such entities to learn enough to save themselves, but the long-term equilibrium will be the same.

A second set of incentives relates to the structure and process of corporate governance. Organizations are collections of different and often competing interests. Allison's famous study of "bureaucratic politics" showed how much of the formulation and implementation of government policy is the result of competing bureaucracies battling for power, influence, and resources.[91] Embedded within this general perspective is the argument that individual bureaucratic agencies may attempt to maximize their budgets rather than following the efficiency-enhancing objective of trying to maximize the difference between their budgets and their costs (that is, the bureaucratic equivalent of profit).[92] Bureaucratic leaders may seek to maximize the size of their agencies and their budgets at the expense of competing bureaucracies because size is correlated with power, prestige, and salary.

Executives of private firms may face similar incentives to pursue size maximization goals. Executive benefits and corporate rankings (a proxy measure of power and prestige) are related to size. Executive compensation schemes reward managers in direct proportion to the company's size; salary, bonuses, and pensions are all linked to size.[93] One observer of the lack of profitability in British mergers notes not only the higher managerial salaries in larger firms but also the greater opportunity for managers in large firms to live a "quiet life." The latter observation is reminiscent of Downs's much earlier suggestion that as bureaucratic organizations get larger, the typical managerial style changes from "climber" to "conserver"—the latter being the risk-avoiding manager who simply wants to preserve established routines and distributions of power and resources, even at the cost of reduced organizational performance.[94]

The general term in economics for this type of behavior is "rent seeking," the use of power to transfer wealth and income from one group to another, in this case from shareholders to executives. Rent-seeking is distinguished from profit-seeking behavior because the latter creates wealth; rent seeking merely transfers or redistributes wealth. Firms may vary in the extent to which they permit leaders to pursue rent-seeking goals, such as size maximization, that are at variance with the shareholders' interest in profit maximization. Managers may be less able or willing to attain size-related goals to the extent that equity is concentrated in the hands of a few shareholders, or if the executives themselves derive a large part of their own compensation from shares (or an index linked to long-term share value), or if corporate rules give shareholders a significant role in monitoring management. Shareholders have collective action obstacles to dealing with size-maximizing and resource-wasting chief executive officers who almost invariably have a considerable amount of managerial discretion.[95]

National differences in managerial autonomy are frequently observed. Executives of European and Japanese corporations seem much better protected from shareholder wrath. In German companies, power is in principle divided between two boards: a management board for running daily operations and a supervisory board (including representatives of workers and shareholders) for long-range strategic decisions. In practice, a powerful chairman of the managerial board can exercise great power simply by withholding information. Daimler's management board was informed one month before, and its supervisory board one day before, the merger with Chrysler. Shareholders in Daimler-Chrysler have voiced considerable consternation about the short-term results of the merger,[96] yet its major shareholder, Deutsche Bank (which owns 12 percent of the company's shares), continues to support the management of Daimler. At the 2002 annual meeting of Daimler shareholders, the Association for the Protection of Minority Shareholders unsuccessfully presented a motion to deny renewal of the firm's board of supervisors on the grounds that Daimler-Chrysler was worth less in 2002 than Daimler alone had been worth prior to the merger in 1998.[97]

A third possibility is that corporate executives, and perhaps even many employees and shareholders, are simply afflicted with Schumpeter's "objectless disposition to unlimited expansion," a nonrational desire to pursue bigness quite apart from any private financial (rent-seeking) or natural selection benefits that bigness might confer on the corporation or its management. The classic textbooks on industrial organization cite, but without much examination, the possibility that businessmen may not be fully cognizant of the impulses that drive their behavior.[98] Revealing stories of many corporate mergers suggest the importance of managerial ego in merger actions, as illustrated in such book titles as *Barbarians at the Gate*.[99] The popularity of such terms as "irrational exuberance" to describe investor behavior further suggests that psychological motives may figure prominently in financial markets. The following analysis from a corporate consulting firm is illuminating:

> Corporate managers in general and CEOs in particular are accustomed to winning. Unfortunately, in M&A transactions "winning" is usually defined in terms of which company is the successful bidder, not the effects on the company's stockholder wealth. In a difficult negotiation or protracted bidding contest, it is easy for managers to lose sight of their ultimate goal—the creation of stock-holder wealth. The longer the drama plays out, the more likely the participants develop vested interests in its eventual outcome. What's more, many managers suffer from hubris. In the heat of a bidding contest, ego replaces judgment. Overconfidence that synergies will be realized causes managers to overpay. In certain respects this is the most unfathomable reason of all given the large body of evidence testifying to the difficulty acquirers experience in creating stockholder wealth. In the same vein, CEOs see themselves as leaders, and they are expected to lead. In no other corporate endeavor does the CEO take command and lead his troops into battle as he does in a transaction. Once the adrenaline begins to flow, it is imperative for the CEO to emerge the victor.[100]

Is there evidence that auto executives have been motivated by the emotional lure of building an empire regardless of the financial implications for the firm or for themselves personally? Daimler's merger with Chrysler was the culmination of a long stream of Daimler acquisitions in other areas, including Fokker, Deutsche Aerospace, and the American truck maker Freightliner. All imposed large losses on Daimler. Following the Chrysler merger, Daimler's chairman Jürgen Schrempp failed to persuade his board to also purchase Nissan and then sought to buy Fiat for $12 billion just prior to the latter's alliance with GM.[101] In an unguarded moment, Schrempp revealed that the merger with Chrysler had always been intended as a takeover and that his goal was to create a company that would both cover all regions of the world and produce cars across the entire spectrum of models, from small to large: "The structure we have now where Chrysler is a division . . . was always the structure I wanted. We had to go a little bit in a round about way but that has to do with negotiations and with psychology and things like that. . . . I have the structure I want because we will run this company as an integrated automotive company."[102] Since Schrempp is undoubtedly very well financially remunerated for his services, even in the absence of mergers, it is unlikely that the rent-seeking motive could be plausibly applied to him or to any other chief executive officer of a major international auto company.

Similar anecdotal evidence abounds of auto executives driven by the goal of controlling ever larger corporate empires. Lee Iacocca confessed that he wanted to merge Chrysler with Fiat, VW, and Japanese automakers to create a "Global Motors" company.[103] In a later memoir, Iacocca more modestly said, "My latest vision of Global Motors is smaller than it was a few years ago."[104] Ferdinand Piëch, chief executive of VW from 1993 to 2002, exhibited a management style that to some displayed "a tendency to place empire building over either profitability or Anglo-Saxon style shareholder value."[105] Former Ford President Jacques Nasser expressed similar ambitions—to expand Ford's global reach, including diversifying into auto-related activities such as Internet sales and auto repair store chains, a move that yielded too little profit and partly accounted for his downfall.[106] Carlos Goshn, currently president of Nissan, will become chief executive of both Renault and Nissan in 2005 on the retirement of Renault's chief executive, Louis Schweitzer. Rare indeed is the auto executive who does not aspire to make his company the largest manufacturer in the world. BMW's chairman Milberg, in a moment of introspective hindsight, told *Automotive News* that he saw no connection between size and financial success.[107] Perhaps this lack of hubris has contributed to BMW's superior financial performance.

The competitive allure of size is mostly likely made more intense by the fact that there is a high rate of circulation of top executives within the auto industry. The dynamics of interpersonal competition among a small group of individuals may naturally lead to an emphasis on easily visible indices of superiority, particularly those with the primal appeal of size. Lee Iacocca went from Ford to Chrysler in the 1970s. Longtime Chrysler strategist Robert Lutz was hired by GM in 2002. Ford was remarkably pleased to be able to hire Wolfgang Reitzle away from BMW in 1999 to run Ford's Premier Automotive Group. Before Reitzle left the auto industry in 2002, he claimed to have been wooed by GM with an offer to run Opel and Saab.[108] Another BMW executive, Karl-Peter Forster, had been hired by GM in 2000 to run Opel. Appointed in 2002 to be the new chairman of VW, Bernd Pischetsrieder is also a former BMW executive.

Financial markets and commentators exacerbate this syndrome by themselves focusing on market share as the criterion for judging the success of an auto company. Global auto firms are typically ranked according to market share, not profitability, a habit that cannot be explained solely by the difficulty of specifying an accurate and cross-nationally valid measure of profit. Any discussion of the major global auto companies in the financial press will almost invariably rank them according to size and market share. A recent survey by www.auto.com, for example, refers to "the global seven," being GM, Ford, Daimler, Toyota, VW, Honda, and Renault-Nissan, all ranked by size.[109]

When executives talk of their aspirations for their companies, they usually refer to market share, not profitability. Toyota's 2002 statement of its long-term strategy, titled "2010 Global Vision," expressed the company's major goal as increasing its global market share by 50 percent, to 15 percent, by 2010. Nissan's President Goshn proudly announced to the press in February 2002 that he expected Nissan to increase its share of the Japanese market by 1 percent but quickly added, "We are not aiming to expand market share, but are focusing on profitability."[110] When Daimler finally removed the American chief executive officer of Chrysler, his replacement, Mercedes executive Dieter Zetsche, stated that his goal was to maintain Chrysler's market share.[111] GM chief executive Rick Wagoner, reviewing his company's performance in 2000, expressed great concern that GM's global market share had fallen near the end of 2000.[112] Though it is frequently said that American managers are more closely monitored by shareholders than are European managers, there is no obvious evidence that European auto company managers are any more desirous of size maximization than managers elsewhere in the world, though they may face fewer constraints (such as complaints by unhappy shareholders) in implementing those goals.

Is there any systematic evidence that the auto companies most actively engaged in mergers, alliances, and acquisitions are any more or less profitable than those that are not? Table 5.1 shows, for the major auto companies, the difference between their rates of return (or operating profits) and their cost of capital. Most auto firms have struggled to earn a return over their costs and have been destroying rather than creating wealth by earning less than the cost of capital. The large mergers of most interest are too recent to warrant any conclusions as to long-term profitability. There is also a significant amount of variation over the period examined, 1991–1999. Yet a few comments may be warranted. Daimler and Chrysler were separate companies until the end of 1998, and the apparently poor performance of the merged entity needs to be compared to the financially sound aggregate performance of the constituent parts from 1993 to 1998. Both Renault and Nissan did poorly throughout the 1990s, and that is the benchmark to which the favorable recent results of the alliance (at least in the area of cost cutting as noted in chapter 2) should be compared. The data suggest little reason to be optimistic about the Fiat-GM relationship, as both companies destroyed shareholder wealth throughout the 1990s. Ford and VW fare better than most, perhaps because of their reluctance to make large and very costly acquisitions, limiting themselves in recent years to smaller specialist companies. It is also the case that Ford and VW have had a longer time period to integrate into their operations their larger acquisitions, Mazda and Audi, respectively.

Though it may be too early to conclude that the recent large auto mergers are not conducive to long-term profitability, the evidence to date is not particularly encouraging. A Goldman Sachs report released early in 2003

Table 5.1. Profitability of Auto Companies, 1991–1999

	1991	1992	1993	1994	1995	1996	1997	1998	1999
BMW	n/a	–3.3	–4.0	–1.7	–2.8	–2.4	–2.1	–1.9	0.1
Daimler–Chrysler	–12.5	–3.1	3.8	5.4	1.0	3.9	1.3	3.4	0.4
Fiat	–1.3	–6.6	–10.9	–1.4	–1.2	–1.4	–2.7	–2.7	–3.9
Ford	–9.5	–11.1	–7.4	–0.2	–4.9	–0.9	0.3	–3.3	2.1
GM	–9.8	–7.4	–6.2	–3.1	–1.9	–4.5	–3.1	–5.5	–4.0
Honda	–2.1	–1.3	–2.3	–1.6	–7.3	–4.7	–0.6	2.2	2.5
Hyundai	n/a	n/a	n/a	n/a	n/a	1.1	–2.8	–7.6	–4.6
Mitsubishi	n/a	n/a	n/a	n/a	n/a	–2.7	–3.1	–3.8	–3.8
Nissan	–3.3	–6.1	–7.5	–12.5	–8.4	–4.4	–4.4	–4.6	–4.3
Peugeot	n/a	n/a	n/a	n/a	–1.2	–3.1	–2.4	1.2	0.4
Renault	n/a	n/a	n/a	n/a	–4.6	–11.9	–8.7	–0.8	–2.3
Toyota	–0.7	–2.5	–3.5	–3.7	–6.8	–4.2	–2.2	–0.4	–0.6
VW	–0.4	–3.7	–7.9	–4.3	–4.0	–3.7	–3.7	0.5	0.1

Note: The data report Stern Stewart's calculation of "economic value-added margin," or profitability (rate of return) after deducting the cost of capital.
Source: Stern Stewart Research, *Best of Times, Worst of Times* (New York: Stern Stewart Research, 2000).

noted that there is no correlation between size and returns to invested capital in the auto industry.[113] The evidence is at least suggestive of motives other than profit. Unless there are reasons to view the auto industry as qualitatively different from other sectors, there may be grounds for being doubly pessimistic: The wave of mergers, acquisitions, and alliances may yield neither added profitability (much needed in an industry that has been mostly destroying shareholder wealth during the past decade) nor even the size maximization that may serve the narrower goals of the industry's management and leadership.

Conclusion

Sovereign states clearly have the power to encourage or discourage global consolidation in any industry. They have done so in the case of the auto industry, most directly by subsidies, equity holding, and trade and investment policies that encourage foreign firms to operate in cooperation with domestic investors. Yet the merger cases that may be explained by such incentives are few, and only in the cases of Britain and Korea could one plausibly argue that subsidies (in the British case) or foreign investment policies (Korea) were a major factor in industry consolidation.

Perhaps more persuasive as general explanations of auto mergers are factors internal to the governance of the corporation: a belief that size confers natural selection advantages and personal pecuniary benefits to managers or simply satisfies an intangible psychic need for power, expansion, and domination. Yet the evidence for such explanations is inevitably anecdotal, difficult to test, and hence unsubstantiated by systematic data analysis. Size maximization is the variable left over after everything else has been found wanting, rather like the error term at the end of statistical equation. Such reasons are also ultimately inconsistent with the logic of competitive markets. Is it really possible for firms to pursue strategies unrelated to profit for long periods of time and still stay in business? Perhaps. And perhaps the non–profit motivated mergers will reveal themselves as unsuccessful in the years to come.

CHAPTER SIX

Conclusions:
Economics, Politics, and Strategy

By the beginning of 2003, the pace of mergers, acquisitions, and alliances had slowed down, even if only because the number of possible combinations had considerably diminished, and the results so far may not encourage further consolidation, or at least not at the rate of the past decade. Acquirers are digesting their meals, smaller companies are planning their survival in the interstices between the behemoths, and the industry in general is awaiting the revival of world demand that they hope will save them from their collective overcapacity. Though the consolidation of the industry may not be over and evaluation of the results will obviously continue for years to come, the analysis of the preceding chapters suggests some general explanations, prescriptions, and predictions.

Explaining the rapid global consolidation of this important industry leads to many causes. It is unhelpful to attempt to look for a monocausal explanation or to seek the sort of buzzword type of explanation that abounds with the popularity of terms such as "synergy" and "irrational exuberance." All the reasons for global concentration in the auto industry that have been examined in the preceding chapters have some merit, though some of the factors most commonly cited in the financial press seem to be much less important than conventional business wisdom would suggest. The causes may be categorized into four distinguishable groups: consolidation to achieve reductions in the cost of production, diversification of geographic markets and product offerings, the opportunity to manipulate market structures, and external or internal factors that may lead a corporation to pursue goals other than profit maximization.

Industry journalists and auto company executives (especially by the ones doing the acquiring) usually focus on three types of explanations: variations on the theme of "synergy" (the belief that the whole will somehow yield intangible gains unattainable by the parts if they remain separate), a belief in the need for a larger global "footprint" in terms of offering a wider array of vehicles and technologies or being present in a larger range of countries, and finally, the invocation of natural selection and the assumption that only the large will survive. All these arguments have been examined here and found to be less overwhelming to a dispassionate observer than they are to the executives who enthusiastically offer them up to business journalists, shareholders, and potential partners. The synergy and footprint arguments are most often little more than vague and hopeful speculations. Insofar as they have substance, they typically resolve into more prosaic arguments about the benefits of sharing costs, products, and markets: "We can share the costs of developing a new engine," "We can put my engine in your platform," "I can sell your vehicles in my area of the world," and so on. While often presented as examples of economies of scale, they are usually not. Though not necessarily false, these arguments about synergies, defaulting into hopes for sharing costs, products, and market opportunities, are vulnerable to the following question: Are these not activities that firms could just as easily have pursued by themselves, without all the costly "baggage" of a merger between different organizational interests and cultures? Merger may be an expensive way to acquire new products. Firms may be able to share the cost of developing a new product requiring extensive research and development (R&D) without the need for merger, as examples have suggested. Markets can be entered without mergers, and most companies are already in the major world markets.

In an age in which lower transaction costs (and especially through utilizing the Internet) permit what consultants like to call "unbundling," or the separation of different parts of an economic process, what passes for synergy appears to be an attempt to run against the current managerial wisdom on efficiency. Perhaps the most obvious manifestation of synergy is that consumers will see more product uniformity and less transparency because of brand rebadging (such as Fords masquerading as Jaguars or generic General Motors [GM] platforms bearing Saab nameplates), though in a few cases they will see new products that might not otherwise have appeared (such as the Chrysler-Mercedes Crossfire).

The search for synergies and the perceived need for a larger global footprint often become part of a less tangible assertion that the synergies of merger and the larger geographic and product presence will give the new firm the size it needs to survive. Yet no evidence is presented to demonstrate that size correlates with survival, nor are clear reasons given as to why it should be so. While it is true that many small auto companies have disappeared in the course of the past century, so have some rather large ones (for example, American Motors and British Leyland). The fact that more smaller auto companies have gone out of business than large auto companies means little because there will naturally be more of the former than the latter. The large cash reserves of some auto companies are unlikely to be reliable measures of the probability of survival unless, among other caveats, those reserves are large relative to other measures of size. Financial data yield little reason to believe that large auto firms are more profitable than small ones.

It has been noted that some small auto companies do very well, and those that do seem to fall into two categories. One group (exemplified by companies such as Ferrari, Porsche, and Morgan) sell in niche markets with a low price elasticity of demand that permits high profit margins on very small volumes. The other group (which would include companies like BMW and Subaru) specializes in a market segment large enough to offer economies of scale across a small range of different models. The small companies that fail appear to be those that are too small to attain economies of scale over a range of model variations (selling fewer than 150,000 autos per year) but lack the cachet to sell at high markups over cost. The latter category would include Saab, Volvo, Jaguar, and the former BMW-owned firm of MG Rover, hence the tactic of pushing these marques into the mass market or, in the case of MG Rover, frantically searching for partners in Third World countries to produce derivative cheap variations.[1]

The classic academic or "textbook" rationales for merger focus mainly on economies of scale and the potential for market manipulation. Paradoxically, economies of scale are probably the least relevant motive for auto mergers, given that even small auto companies easily attain them at the plant level (despite the previously cited exceptions) and that much of the activity conducive to economies of scale has been farmed out to supplier industries. It is very unlikely that any major auto merger, at least between firms of significant size, has been motivated by the need for economies of scale. If economies of scale are present, they would be found in the cases of very small automakers being taken over by larger ones and using the components and platforms of the larger company (such as Ford supplying Volvo and Jaguar with engines, platforms, and many components), a tactic that may well have unintended negative consequences, including diluting the brand name of previously prestigious but small automakers. Furthermore, there are small companies that buy components from larger firms without the need to be taken over.

What are often presented as arguments about economies of scale in production actually turn out to be, on closer examination, observations on the sharing of R&D costs that precede production for the market. This is where we may see some of the most plausible reasons for consolidation. The sharing of the costs of developing new engines and platforms has followed most of the major mergers of the past decade. While auto executives may call it synergy, it is really nothing more than the sharing of costs that are more than one firm may wish to bear and has little do with any intangible value added conferred by combining efforts. Nor is it subsumed by economies of scale. Firms like Chrysler, Mercedes, and Hyundai could all get economies of scale with new platforms and engines; what they save by combining efforts are the lesser amounts each spends on the development of these products.

However, as already noted, there are many forms of cost sharing that occur between automakers without the need for any formal integration. Toyota and Peugeot, for example, may share the cost of building a new car in eastern Europe without the need for anything beyond a temporary alliance for a specific project. Daimler and Chrysler are attempting a much more wide-ranging array of cost-sharing activities.

Merger or some other form of integration would presumably be most desirable when there are a variety of sharing activities to be managed and there is a perceived need for central control of the process in order to reduce transaction costs. As Coase reminded us many years ago, transaction costs are the fundamental rationale for the existence of business firms, an insight that some of the more enthusiastic proponents of "unbundling" have forgotten. More recently, Caves applied the same explanation to the existence of multinational business organization as an alternative to arm's-length transactions between independent firms in various countries.[2] Perhaps what appears to some auto executives as synergy is merely the ability of a unified organizational structure to manage the transaction costs of joint activities that might otherwise not take place.

The third set of explanations of multinational auto mergers includes the various opportunities for exerting market power. Collusive oligopolies that raise the prices of automobiles to consumers are a possibility but appear to be extremely unlikely because of both the probability of scrutiny by antitrust authorities (particularly those of the United States and the European Union) and the intense competition between the global auto groups. Yet even in the absence of tacit or active collusion, the fact remains that consumers face fewer choices in the auto market as a result of mergers and alliances, even though the number of brand names they see may not have appreciably diminished. Competition between the surviving oligopolists may remain intense, but it is competition between smaller numbers of basic vehicle alternatives.

Suppliers of components to the auto firms are certainly facing pressure to lower their prices, but they have important elements of market power to countervail the bargaining power of the smaller number of automakers, including mergers in their own industry and the increasing reliance of the auto brand owners on outsourced modular components from the suppliers. If there is any clearly definable group that has lost bargaining power during the period of structural concentration in this market, it is labor in general and trade unions in particular. Consolidation has been increasing the international mobility of the auto companies without any corresponding mobility on the part of labor, which is confined largely within national borders for reasons that are mainly political. Unless there is a significant increase in global labor mobility, auto companies have acquired a large advantage in this area of their cost structures, though whether labor costs alone could be an important motive for merger is quite doubtful. An enlarged European Union, encompassing eastern Europe and perhaps eventually Russia, might partly offset the mobility advantage of the auto companies, at least to the extent that a common European labor market equalized wages within the community.

The final area of inquiry has focused on the relevance of motives and incentives unrelated to the conventional assumption of profit maximization. One might expect, given the size and political visibility of the industry, that governments would have played a major role in the consolidation of the auto industry. Yet that has not been the case in most countries. Governments have largely left the industry to seek consolidation in whatever ways that the industry prefers. Perhaps this is partly because auto executives have what economists call "rational expectations": They know what governments would find unacceptable and avoid doing it. The governments of France and Germany, for example, would most likely intervene if any attempt were made to take over their national champions, however haggard they may become. In a few cases, governments have actively promoted consolidation through subsidies, trade barriers, and investment rules, as in Britain and South Korea, where consolidation with foreign firms was seen as an option preferable to further burdening taxpayers with ailing auto firms. The government of Italy now faces the same question in its attempts to orchestrate a solution to the crisis of Fiat Auto. Governments of developing countries are still prone to force multinational auto companies into local partnerships, but membership in the World Trade Organization is gradually putting an end to such practices, most recently in India and perhaps soon in China. In no cases have mergers in the auto sector been prevented by governments on competition grounds, though the European Union has intervened in the commercial vehicle market to block at least one merger. Again, this may be largely due to the intense competition in the industry despite the fact that five firms hold more than 50 percent of the world market. Consolidation is neither producing the manifest price collusion of the type prevalent in the United States in the 1950s nor obviously inhibiting product innovation despite the smaller range of choices offered to consumers.

Conspicuous by its absence, either from conventional accounts of mergers or from the mouths of auto executives themselves (unless by unintentional slips of the tongue, with soon regretted utterances), is the possibility that managers are driven to seek bigness as a goal in itself. They may do so for private material benefits, such as higher salaries, or for the less tangible glory of empire building. Long recognized in the academic managerial literature, it is a motive that is exceedingly hard to demonstrate, except by default, showing that mergers tend to be unprofitable for shareholders of the acquiring company. While some of the more flamboyant auto executives may exhibit these characteristics more openly than others (Chrysler's Lee Iacocca and Daimler's Jürgen Schrempp come to mind), the syndrome may be more widespread. It is challenging to find any evidence that large auto companies have been more efficient or profitable in their long-term corporate results. Hence, size maximization remains as a residual category of explanation that explains what is left after all the more conventional explanations have been applied. This is perhaps less satisfying than a clear empirical test but certainly not methodologically invalid. Motives other than profit maximization are, as noted earlier, analogous to the error term at the end of a statistical estimation.[3]

In a discursive analysis such as this, it would be unhelpful to attempt to offer spuriously precise weights to the four categories of causes of mergers. Nevertheless, a few generalizations are in order on the subject of perception and reality. Cost reduction (particularly with respect to economies of scale) has been a stated motive in all auto mergers, takeovers, and alliances and evidently is sincerely believed by managers in almost all cases. Yet the cost reductions actually achieved, compared with what the firms could have done in the absence of merger, have been very small. Acquiring new products and markets has been a stated motive in many merger cases, though only half-heartedly believed by the managers arranging the mergers, and an observable outcome in very few cases.[4] Collusive market power in retail markets has never been articulated by executives, and for obvious reasons, nor does it appear to have occurred. Monopsony-type power in procurement costs has frequently been cited by merging firms, but the benefits have usually been much less than forecast, perhaps because of the various offsetting factors discussed in chapter 4, including countervailing concentration in the components sector. Non–profit maximizing motives, at least the most venal variations thereof, are rarely admitted by the executives of merging firms, though almost all will cheerfully admit to believing some variation of the argument that "only the large survive." Size maximization may be the hidden and unacknowledged agenda in almost all mergers. The reality is, of course, that size is no guarantor of fitness and survival, as the cases of British Leyland and Fiat Auto clearly illustrate.

A prescriptive or normative assessment would focus on efficiency and the desirability of the distributive implications of auto mergers. The efficiency aspects reside primarily in the possibility of deadweight loses (see chapter 2) and the possibility that mergers may enhance the extent to which capital in the industry moves from areas of the world where rates of return are low to areas where rates of return are high. Given the unwillingness or inability of auto firms to exercise market structure power, the deadweight losses from mergers are likely to be trivial. Insofar as multinational auto mergers reduce the transaction costs of moving capital internationally (an unproven but reasonable assumption), the merger trend should be at least mildly efficiency enhancing. Though still heavily distorted by government incentives that offer private rates of return unequal to the social return on capital, through subsidies or their equivalent, globalization in the auto industry should be promoting the equalization of returns on capital in the industry and thereby enhancing the efficiency of capital utilization.

The distributive implications of auto mergers are more complex. Though consumers benefit from the intensely competitive nature of the international auto oligopoly despite mergers, they do face a diminution in the range of product choices, which may ultimately be manifested as higher prices. Shareholders of auto firms doing the acquiring have seen little benefit (a view vociferously expressed at Daimler's annual meetings), but shareholders of acquired firms may well be better off than if their firms had been left to languish. As with nineteenth-century European empires, the net flow of resources may paradoxically be from the conqueror to the conquered.[5]

Discussion has focused almost exclusively on causal explanation and to a lesser extent on prescriptions drawn from explanation. Understanding causality should also permit prediction. Will the trend continue, yielding even higher levels of global concentration in the auto industry? There is evidence that increasing concentration in an industry will inevitably occur over time as a result of random luck quite apart from any presumed (correctly or otherwise) natural selection advantages of size. If a firm is lucky and grows

more than its rivals in one period and all firms have an equal chance of growing by a given percentage amount in the next period, the same firm will have
a 50 percent chance of again being lucky and growing by more than the industry average and so on. This stochastically generated process of concentration continues until the industry reaches maturity, at which point concentration slows and approaches a long-term equilibrium.[6]

The approach followed here is to assume that consolidation in the auto industry has not been random but has discernible and perhaps even predictable
causes. If so, the question then becomes one of asking whether these causes
are still present to the same extent as in the past. Some are clearly not.
Altschuler suggested in the early 1980s that the global merger trend in the
auto industry was coming to an end because the economies of scale that had
driven consolidation were exhausted and government interference in the
market (causing, for example, firms to merge to jump over trade barriers) was
coming to an end in an era of global markets.[7] The former prediction, about
scale economies providing little reason to merge, appears to have been quite
accurate and even more apropos today than in the 1980s, though Altschuler
was premature in predicting the end of state interference. Furthermore, some
powerful incentives for collaboration (such as cost sharing) remain. Others,
such as the material and psychic benefits of size maximization, will be present into the foreseeable future regardless of economic, political, or technical
change, constrained only by a diminishing number of combinations for collaboration.

Casual observation of the auto sector in 2003 does not suggest any obvious merger patterns likely to emerge in the near future. The largest group,
GM, has little in the way of further opportunities now that it has purchased
Daewoo in 2002 in addition to its unprofitable portfolio of Saab and Opel
and would like to be relieved of the obligation to purchase the remainder of
Fiat in 2004. Fiat's continued financial decline makes its ultimate absorption
by GM a major resource-absorbing liability. Ford has gradually increased its
hold over Mazda, has expressed great (but as yet unrealized) hopes for its Premier Automotive Group (PAG: Jaguar, Land Rover, Volvo, and Aston Martin), and has occasionally made overtures to BMW,[8] but there is little else to
attract Ford to risk a large allocation of its resources. The automotive press
reported in June 2002 that Ford was considering selling Volvo, most probably because of Ford's financial problems stemming largely from the domestic
U.S. market. Yet Volvo is the largest-selling brand within the PAG, and as
its use of Ford platforms and components continues to increase, it will be of
little value to other manufacturers. Both GM and Ford are, to cite Joseph
Chamberlain's warning to early twentieth-century Britain, "Weary Titans"

staggering under the weight of their unprofitable imperial acquisitions. By the beginning of 2003, Ford had debts of $150 billion and pension fund liabilities that exceeded its shareholder equity and is clearly in no position to contemplate major acquisitions.[9]

Volkswagen (VW) is in the throes of an internal generational change in its management, burdened by a constraining relationship with its largest shareholder (the German state of Lower Saxony), expending considerable amounts of money on its newly acquired but unprofitable "boutique" brands (Bentley, Lamborghini, and Bugatti) and undertaking a resource-consuming internal organizational realignment amongst VW's various brands.[10] Ranked first in global auto sales, Toyota remains stubbornly averse to growth by takeover and uses its reserves to buy back its own shares and to become more vertically integrated with its suppliers. The Renault-Nissan group seems more concerned about protecting itself from takeovers, particularly as the French government sells off its share in Renault, than with becoming a global predator. Late in 2001, Renault and Nissan announced their intention to establish an unlisted 50/50 venture in the Netherlands to manage their collaboration. The agreement allows each partner to issue new stock in the joint venture to protect itself in the event of a takeover of the other company.[11] PSA and Honda have repeatedly and publicly rejected the strategy of growth by acquisition.

Another possibility is that the auto industry is following the textile sector in moving production to the developing countries. As the Third World industrialized, comparative advantage in the labor-intensive textile industry shifted from the developed countries of North America, Europe, and Japan to the previously undeveloped areas of the world. Since the 1970s, other low-technology industries (such as assembling televisions sets) followed. It is now commonplace to predict that the auto industry is following the same tend and that in the not too distant future the auto industries of countries such as China, Russia, India, and Thailand will be the major world producers. Perhaps the auto brand names that are now household words will be forgotten, just as companies like Sony replaced Zenith as global brand names in color televisions. Yet the analogy is faulty, even if only because textiles are labor-intensive commodities and most parts of the auto industry are capital intensive. Textile production moved to developing countries precisely because the developed industrial countries no longer had a comparative advantage in producing these goods.

One should never underestimate the ability of a country, especially those with centrally managed economic plans, to industrialize rapidly and establish a world presence in a targeted industry. Consider the speed with which South

Korea pushed beyond specialization in textiles and became a credible volume producer and exporter of televisions, personal computers, and automobiles during the last two decades of the twentieth century, albeit propelled by heavy government intervention. Nevertheless, there remain formidable obstacles to such a vision coming to reality. Automaking is still a fundamentally capital-intensive activity, and countries such as China, India, and Russia are still capital poor. While automakers can substitute labor-intensive for capital-intensive techniques, it is questionable whether they can do so to an extent necessary to offset the comparative disadvantage of these Third World countries in auto production. Furthermore, most poor countries lack the purchasing power to establish a domestic consumption base and are still largely agrarian societies. The political determination of some governments (such as China) to artificially stimulate an auto industry with trade barriers and investment rules masks this comparative disadvantage and lack of a mass market, and while it may enable them to produce autos for a protected domestic market, it will not make them global producers and exporters. For the latter to occur, genuine comparative advantage, such as that exhibited by Japan from the 1960s, must be present. The case of Japan may be an exemplar for China, but one should remember that Japan has been industrializing since the Meiji Restoration in 1868 and has been developing an auto industry since the 1930s.

What we are left with is, first of all, a simple observation. At the beginning of the twenty-first century, the auto industry, which accounts for a significant share of the national incomes of most developed countries and increasingly the incomes of some newly industrializing countries, has during the past few decades consolidated into five major auto groups: GM, Ford, VW, Toyota, and Renault-Nissan. While the development of this degree of concentration may be consistent with stochastic or random occurrence over time, it is also possible to discern some persisting causes. Some of these causes are exactly what one would predict as "rational" corporate strategies, such as various means of saving costs. Some, such as size maximization, are not those that the industry itself would like to admit, having a vested interest in seeing the development as being a result of good managerial decisions seeking to further the interests of shareholders. Yet neither is the process driven by the overarching political interest of states, though they have obviously had some marginal influence on the process.

Notes

Chapter One

1. An oligopoly market is one in which a small number of interdependent firms have a dominant market share—to be distinguished from monopoly (one firm), duopoly (two firms), competitive markets (where no single firm can affect prices), and monopolistic competition (more firms than in an oligopoly but less than perfectly competitive).

2. Joseph Schumpeter's famous study *Imperialism and Social Classes* (New York: Kell, 1951).

3. International Organization of Motor Vehicle Manufacturers, *OICA Statistics 2001*, www.oica.net (accessed September 1, 2002).

4. R. Vernon, *Sovereignty at Bay: The Multinational Spread of US Enterprises* (New York: Basic, 1971), and J. Servan-Schreiber's apocalyptic and much-imitated *The American Challenge* (New York: Atheneum, 1968).

5. Many of the themes of this now dated literature are explored in Richard J. Barnet and Ronald E. Müller, *Global Reach: The Power of the Multinational Corporations* (New York: Simon & Schuster, 1974).

6. M. Hardt and A. Negri, *Empire* (Cambridge, Mass.: Harvard University Press, 2000).

7. Mercantilism in economic history refers to state goals, common between the sixteenth and eighteenth centuries, of contriving a balance of payments surplus (in order to acquire gold) and selling monopolies to private interests for revenue. In recent decades, the term has been used to refer to more general state objectives of maximizing some combination of power and wealth.

8. The U.S. Department of Commerce reports the narrowly defined auto category as contributing 1.2 percent to gross domestic product in both 1987 and 2000. The

auto sector more broadly defined may account directly for 3 to 4 percent of the U.S. national income, or up to 7 percent if indirect effects (such as linkages to related industries) are included (*Wall Street Journal*, July 10, 2001). A study prepared for the Association of International Automobile Manufacturers calculated that in 1996 the auto industry provided 1 percent of private sector employment and 1.3 percent of private sector income; see Transportation Research Institute, *The Contribution of the International Auto Sector to the US Economy* (Ann Arbor: University of Michigan, 1998). Another study, prepared for the Alliance of Automobile Manufacturers, concluded that the auto manufacturing sector contributed 3.5 percent of total employment in the United States and 4.1 percent of total compensation in 1998; see Institute of Labor and Industrial Relations, *Contributions of the Automotive Industry to the US Economy in 1998* (Ann Arbor: University of Michigan, 2001). Maxton and Wormald state that the auto industry provides 13 percent of the national income of most industrial countries but cite no source; see G. Maxton, and J. Wormald, *Driving over a Cliff: Business Lessons from the World's Car Industry* (Wokingham, U.K.: Addison-Wesley, 1994), 3. The McKinsey Global Institute estimated the automotive sector's contribution to value added in 1999 to be 3.4 percent in Germany, 2.3 percent in Japan, 1.9 percent in France, and 1.6 percent in the United States; see McKinsey Global Institute, *Reaching Higher Productivity Growth in France and Germany, Sector Case: Automobiles* (Düsseldorf: McKinsey & Company, 1999), 4.

9. www.auto.com (accessed February 27, 2002), *Wall Street Journal*, April 4, 2002.

10. Quoted in *The Economist*, June 24, 2000.

11. Transaction costs are the costs of gathering information, bargaining, and enforcing agreements. The amount by which the value of the merged entity exceeds the sum of the values of the parts is sometimes used as a definition of "synergy." Insofar as synergy is relevant to mergers, I will use a more restrictive definition, restricting it to intangible aspects of value added. See chapter 3.

12. A brief history of these merger waves may be found in F. M. Scherer, *Industrial Market Structure and Economic Performance*, 3rd ed. (Boston: Houghton Mifflin, 1990), 154–59. A salient case example from the last period is described in B. Burrough, *Barbarians at the Gate: The Fall of RJR Nabisco* (New York: Harper & Row, 1990) about the hostile takeover of R. J. Nabisco.

13. *The Economist*, February 5, 2001.

14. D. Ernst and T. Halevy, "When to Think Alliance," *McKinsey Quarterly* 4 (2000): 47–55; *The Economist*, December 4, 1999.

15. For example, G. Bloomfield, *The World Automotive Industry* (Newton Abbot, U.K.: David and Charles, 1978); P. Dunnett, *The Decline of the British Motor Industry: The Effects of Government Policy, 1943–1979* (London: Croom Helm, 1980); J. Laux, *The European Automobile Industry* (New York: Twayne, 1992); G. Maxcy, *The Multinational Automobile Industry* (New York: St. Martin's, 1981); and J. Wood, *Wheels of Misfortune: The Rise and Fall of the British Motor Industry* (London: Sidgewick & Jackson, 1988).

16. Maxcy, *The Multinational Automobile Industry*, 87.

17. F. M. Scherer, *Industry Strategy, Structure and Public Policy* (New York: Harper-Collins, 1996), 281.

18. See Laux, *The European Automobile Industry*, 224.

19. Laux, *The European Automobile Industry*, 227.

20. www.autonewseurope.com (accessed March 20, 2001).

21. Despite Olson's attribution of postwar German economic growth to the breaking up of the cartels, this industrial structure remained much intact; Mancur Olson, *The Rise and Decline of Nations* (New Haven, Conn.: Yale University Press, 1982).

22. The Porsche 924, the "poor man's Porsche" of the 1970s, was one such example. Porsche and Volkswagen have again collaborated recently on an upscale sport-utility vehicle (SUV) to be sold under both brand names in 2002, the Porsche Cayenne and the Volkswagen Touareg.

23. The European Court of Justice has ruled that national laws constraining share ownership violate the European Union's single-market laws; *Wall Street Journal*, January 7, 2003.

24. Early in 2000, BMW shares surged on rumors of a Ford takeover; *Financial Times*, February 21, 2000.

25. The *Wall Street Journal* (February 24, 2000) reported that Volkswagen gave up on buying BMW when faced with the opposition of the Quandt family.

26. As Porsche moves from its devoted but small core of sports car enthusiasts into the fashionable but changeable SUV market with its Cayenne model, it may find itself much more exposed to the whims of popular taste.

27. *Wall Street Journal*, May 16, 2002.

28. J. Womack, D. Jones, and D. Roos, *The Machine That Changed the World* (New York: Simon & Schuster, 1990), 50–51.

29. Y. Tsurumi, *The Japanese Are Coming: A Multinational Spread of Japanese Firms* (Cambridge, Mass.: Ballinger, 1976).

30. Maxcy, *The Multinational Automobile Industry*, 110.

31. GM followed Ford into Japan in 1926; Bloomfield, *The World Automotive Industry*, 228, 285.

32. The history of multinational auto companies during the interwar period may be found in Bloomfield, *The World Automotive Industry*; Laux, *The European Automobile Industry*; and Maxcy, *The Multinational Automobile Industry*.

33. Simca had been established in 1934 with help from Fiat; see Laux, *The European Automobile Industry*, 126, 196.

34. Laux, *The European Automobile Industry*, 197. In 2000, the Michelin family held 5.25 percent of the voting rights in Peugeot.

35. Maxcy, *The Multinational Automobile Industry*, 111–12.

36. David Waller, *Wheels on Fire: The Amazing Inside Story of the Daimler-Chrysler Merger* (London: Hodder & Stoughton, 2000), 154.

37. Maxcy, *The Multinational Automobile Industry*, 112.

38. This gave Ford a veto power on the board of directors, and Ford subsequently installed a Ford manager to run Mazda.

39. www.just-auto.com (accessed June 26, 2002).

40. See *Wall Street Journal*, April 30, 2002, and www.autonews.com (accessed May 29, 2002).

41. In what appears to be a quixotic effort to revive the brand, MG Rover announced in 2002 plans for joint production in China with Brilliance China and that it was discussing taking over the Polish operations of Daewoo, unwanted by GM. See www.just-auto.com (accessed June 7, 2002).

42. An account of the Rover–BMW saga may be found in Chris Brady and Andrew Lorenz, *End of the Road: BMW and Rover, a Brand Too Far* (London: Financial Times and Prentice Hall, 2001).

43. See David Kiley, *Getting the Bugs Out: The Rise, Fall, and Comeback of Volkswagen in America* (New York: Wiley, 2002).

44. The Mitsubishi name will no longer be used in the U.S. market from July 2001, and all its vehicles will be sold under the Chrysler name.

45. www.just-auto.com (accessed January 31, 2001). Toyota denied any such intentions.

46. *Wall Street Journal*, March 5, 2002. Fiat had previously sold 20 percent of Fiat to Libya in 1976 but later reversed the deal because of Libya's association with terrorism; see Laux, *The European Automobile Industry*, 228.

47. *Wall Street Journal*, May 14, 2002. In late June 2002, 34 percent of Ferrari was sold to Mediobanca and Commerzbank; *Wall Street Journal*, July 1, 2002.

48. See *Wall Street Journal*, May 28, 2002, and June 5, 2002; www.auto.com (accessed May 29, 2002); and www.just-auto.com (accessed October 18, 2002).

49. www.autonews.com (accessed December 10, 2002).

50. *Wall Street Journal*, January 3, 2003.

51. *Financial Times*, May 14, 2002.

52. *Financial Times*, December 17, 2001.

53. *Financial Times*, July 11, 2002.

54. Quoted in www.autonews.com (accessed September 30, 2002).

55. GM reduced its stake in Isuzu to 12 percent late in 2002 in exchange for a controlling interest in a diesel engine development project in the United States and Poland. This was a prescient move, as Isuzu has been rapidly losing market share in the United States. See *Wall Street Journal*, August 15, 2002.

56. *Financial Times*, September 23, 2002.

57. BMW had attempted to buy Rolls Royce in 1998 but was preempted by Volkswagen. BMW subsequently reached agreement with Volkswagen to acquire the Rolls Royce name by refusing to continue supplying BMW engines for Rolls Royce models.

58. Renault's holding of Nissan increased from 36.8 to 44.4 percent in 2002; *Wall Street Journal*, February 25, 2002.

59. Data from www.hoovers.com (accessed September 1, 2002).

60. GM's agreement in 1999 to buy V6 engines from Honda and a more recent agreement in 2001 to develop a "clean engine" with Toyota raise the possibility of an even more monopolistic combination composed of the GM clan, Toyota, and Honda.

61. *BusinessWeek*, January 25, 1999.

62. In July 2001, the European Union vetoed the $42 billion merger of General Electric and Honeywell on the grounds that the merged firm would have a dominant position in critical sectors of the aviation and avionics markets.

63. Anthony Downs, *Inside Bureaucracy* (Boston: Little, Brown, 1967).

Chapter Two

1. David Waller, *Wheels on Fire: The Amazing Inside Story of the Daimler-Chrysler Merger* (London: Hodder & Stoughton, 2000), 208.

2. Specialization may have limits in contributing to lower costs. The claims made for both "autonomous work groups" (of the kind that Volvo pioneered, having groups of workers be collectively responsible for assembling an auto) and the much-admired Japanese system of "lean production" are premised on practices that would appear to violate principles of specialization since they involve workers diversifying their effort across a range of functions.

3. G. Maxton and J. Wormald, *Driving Over a Cliff: Business Lessons from the World's Car Industry* (Wokingham, U.K.: Addison-Wesley, 1994), 223.

4. PricewaterhouseCoopers, *The Second Automotive Century* (Bloomfield Hills, Mich.: PricewaterhouseCoopers, 2000), 3.

5. *Wall Street Journal*, October 15, 2002.

6. P. Dunnett, *The Decline of the British Motor Industry: The Effects of Government Policy, 1943–1979* (London: Croom Helm, 1980), 23.

7. F. M. Scherer, *Industrial Market Structure and Economic Performance* (Chicago: Rand McNally, 1970), 116, describes multiplant economies of scale as "modest or nonexistent."

8. F. M. Scherer, *Industry Strategy, Structure and Public Policy* (New York: Harper-Collins, 1996), 287.

9. *Wall Street Journal*, February 11, 2002.

10. *The Economist*, April 6, 2002.

11. Scherer, *Industrial Market Structure and Economic Performance* (1970), 116.

12. *Financial Times*, February 28, 2001, and www.autonewseurope.com (accessed June 27, 2002).

13. A. Altschuler, M. Anderson, D. Jones, D. Roos, and J. Womack, *The Future of the Automobile: The Report of MIT's International Automobile Program* (Cambridge, Mass.: MIT Press, 1984), 182; Scherer, *Industry Strategy, Structure and Public Policy*, 286–98; G. Maxcy, *The Multinational Automobile Industry* (New York: St. Martin's, 1981), 201; G. Bloomfield, *The World Automotive Industry* (Newton Abbot, U.K.: David and Charles, 1978), 85.

14. www.autonewseurope.com and www.autonewseurope.com/bol/bolproductivity .htm (accessed March 20, 2001).

15. Bloomfield, *World Automotive Industry*, 48.

16. *Financial Times*, April 29, 2002.

17. www.autonews.com (accessed June 27, 2002).

18. Paul Gao, *Passenger Car OEMs in China: At a Crossroads between Capturing Massive Value and Facing Immense Value Destruction* (McKinsey & Company, internal publication, 2002).

19. See Altschuler et al., *The Future of the Automobile*, 182, and Kim B. Clark and Takahiro Fujimoto, *Product Development and Performance: Strategy, Organization, and the Management of the World Auto Industry* (Cambridge, Mass.: Harvard Business School Press, 1991), 61.

20. Volkswagen had sixteen platforms in 1995 but only four in 2001.

21. Altschuler et al., *The Future of the Automobile*, 136.

22. www.auto.com (accessed March 6, 2002).

23. www.autonews.com (accessed October 14, 2002).

24. D. W. Carleton and J. M. Perloff, *Modern Industrial Organization*, 3rd ed. (Reading, Mass.: Addison-Wesley, 1999), 47, cite estimates of scope economies for U.S. auto manufacturers.

25. For example, in 2002, Toyota began outsourcing some overseas vehicle production to its assembling affiliates Toyota Auto Body and Kanto Auto Works, the first time Toyota had contracted with domestic assemblers to make cars abroad; www.autonews.com (accessed July 5, 2002).

26. www.just-auto.com (accessed March 21, 2001).

27. F. Bouvard, M. Cesar, H. Corlay, and W. Sfeir, *Assessing the Impact of Platform Strategy on Technical Economies of Scale: A Quantitative Simulation Tool* (Paris: McKinsey & Company, 1999).

28. Covisint was created to provide automakers with a large Internet parts market, lowering transaction costs and encouraging specialization among parts makers who could then provide standardized parts to many manufacturers.

29. PricewaterhouseCoopers, *Global Automotive Deal Survey, 1998* (Bloomfield Hills, Mich.: PricewaterhouseCoopers, 1999), 5.

30. This description of Ford's Cologne factory is drawn from www.just-auto.com (accessed June 18, 2002).

31. Scherer, *Industry Strategy, Structure and Public Policy*, 287; Christopher Law, ed., *Restructuring the Global Automobile Industry* (New York: Routledge, 1991); Maxcy, *The Multinational Automobile Industry*, 201.

32. www.auto.com (accessed June 27, 2002).

33. *Financial Times*, September 19, 2001.

34. www.just-auto.com (accessed February 6, 2001).

35. www.autonews.com (accessed March 20, 2000, and October 1, 2001); *Financial Times*, October 16, 2000.

36. *BusinessWeek*, September 17, 2001.

37. www.autonews.com (accessed October 4, 2001).

38. *Wall Street Journal*, April 4, 2000.

39. www.just-auto.com (accessed September 13, 2001); www.auto.com (accessed May 14, 2002); *Wall Street Journal*, July 23, 2002.

40. www.ai-online.com (accessed September 17, 2001).

41. More so in the United States than in Europe, where manufacturers have re-sisted multibrand dealerships and tried to maintain tight control over single-brand distributorships, including ownership of distributors by the manufacturer; see chapter 4.

42. See www.golynch.com. Multibrand dealers in the United States seem to make more extensive use of the Internet than do single-brand dealerships because they ex-ist in a more competitive environment.

43. Sociologist Max Weber (1864–1920) is perhaps most well known for a char-acteristic view of large organizational structures, emphasizing the efficiency of py-ramidal structures, hierarchy, and division of labor.

44. This is Caves's explanation for the existence of multinational corporations as an alternative to arm's-length transactions between separate entities; Richard E. Caves, *Multinational Enterprise and Economic Analysis* (Cambridge, U.K.: Cambridge University Press, 1972).

45. The distinction between functional and multidivisional structures was elaborated by Paul R. Lawrence and Jay W. Lorsch, *Organization and Environment: Managing Differentiation and Integration* (Boston: Harvard Business School Press, 1967).

46. Though Daimler-Chrysler has announced that its dealerships will sell and ser-vice Mitsubishi trucks; *Wall Street Journal*, October 8, 2001.

47. *Wall Street Journal*, May 16, 2000.

48. *Wall Street Journal*, September 25, 2001.

49. www.autonews.com (accessed May 22, 2002).

50. www.just-auto.com (accessed October 11 and December 14, 2001).

51. F. M. Scherer, *Industrial Market Structure and Economic Performance*, 3rd ed. (Boston: Houghton Mifflin, 1990), 165.

52. Scherer, *Industry Strategy, Structure and Public Policy*, 292.

53. www.autonews.com (accessed June 5, 2000).

54. Lotus began as a small-engine tuner and maker of racing cars in the 1950s, surviving into the twenty-first century as a small-scale maker of sports cars that in-corporate its race-developed innovations. It is now 81 percent owned by the Malaysian company Proton. In order to survive near bankruptcy in the early 1990s, Porsche had to begin outsourcing many components and eventually standardized its product line with variations of the same engine by 1999.

55. Robert S. Kaplan, *Porsche AG*, Case 9-193-071 (Boston: Harvard Business School Cases, 1992).

56. *Wall Street Journal*, January 8, 2002, and April 22, 2002.

57. www.auto.com (accessed March 7, 2002).

58. www.autonews.com (accessed December 23, 2001).

59. www.just-auto.com (accessed February 26, 2002).

60. www.autonewseurope.com (accessed April 29, 2002).

61. Though sales are tiny. Fewer than 10,000 Insights were sold in 2000; *Business-Week*, August 14, 2000.

62. www.autonewseurope.com (accessed June 18, 2001).

63. *Wall Street Journal*, May 8, 2001, and September 3, 2002.

64. *Financial Times*, April 18, 2001; *Wall Street Journal*, April 18, 2001.

65. www.just-auto.com (accessed October 5, 2001). Toyota already uses GM's "OnStar" communications technology in the Lexus brand.

66. *Wall Street Journal*, October 14, 2002.

67. *Wall Street Journal*, March 22, 2001.

68. www.just-auto (accessed September 4, 2001); *Wall Street Journal*, May 13, 2001.

69. *Wall Street Journal*, October 3, 2001.

70. PricewaterhouseCoopers, *Automotive Sector Insights* (Bloomfield Hills, Mich.: PricewaterhouseCoopers, 2000), 16.

71. www.autonewseurope.com (accessed March 20, 2001).

72. www.just-auto.com (accessed November 7, 2002).

73. In some network industries, there may be an "empty core" problem in which capacity cannot be reduced because of the nonexistence of a winning bargaining coalition among demanders and suppliers, similar to the famous Condorcet paradox (the absence of an alternative that can win a pairwise majority vote against any other alternative) in the theory of voting. This argument, originally set out by Telser, assumes active bargaining between consumers and producers (such as in air transportation) and does not appear to be applicable to the auto industry; Lester Telser, *Economic Theory and the Core* (Chicago: University of Chicago Press, 1978).

74. Scherer, *Industrial Market Structure and Economic Performance* (1970), 170.

75. PricewaterhouseCoopers, *Global Automotive Deal Survey, 1998*, 3.

76. *Wall Street Journal*, April 20, 2001; www.autonews.com (accessed March 20, 2000).

77. *Financial Times*, March 20, 2001.

78. *Financial Times*, June 29, 2000.

79. *Financial Times*, May 29, 2001.

80. www.auto.com (accessed June 20, 2002).

81. *Wall Street Journal*, December 24, 2002.

82. *Wall Street Journal*, February 26, 2001.

83. *Financial Times*, February 10, 2001.

84. In an oligopoly market, shutting down one among several rivals would provide a public good (that is, a free, nonexcludable benefit) to the other firms in the industry at the expense of the acquiring firm.

85. See A. Aizcorbe, C. Winston, and A. Friedlander, "Cost Competitiveness of the U.S. Automobile Industry," in *Blind Intersection? Policy and the Automobile Industry*, ed. C. Winston and Associates (Washington, D.C.: Brookings Institution, 1987), 6–35. Consistent with Aizcorbe's data, Cohen cites $1,718 as being the Japanese "landed cost advantage" in the United States for a subcompact car in 1973; Robert B. Cohen, "The Prospects for Trade and Protectionism in the Auto Industry," in *Trade Policy in the 1980s*, ed. William R. Cline (Washington, D.C.: Institute for International Economics, 1983), 552.

86. Maryann Keller, *Rude Awakening: The Rise, Fall and Struggle for Recovery of General Motors* (New York: Morrow, 1989), 83. The joint project was the New United Motors Manufacturing Incorporated (NUMMI) venture, begun in Fremont, California, in 1984, producing Toyota Corollas that would be sold as the Chevrolet Nova.

87. Maxcy, *The Multinational Automobile Industry*, observed little correlation between comparative advantage and production location, but he was writing at a time when international trade barriers and government investment regulations in the auto industry were still substantial, causing locational decisions to be strongly influenced by these exogenous political factors.

88. It is important not to confuse comparative advantage with other motivations. Nissan is to close down its Japanese production of the Maxima model and move it to Tennessee (*Wall Street Journal*, October 28, 2001). This decision was not a response to differences in productivity or factor costs but rather an attempt to reduce transportation costs by locating production in the largest market for that particular model.

89. J. Womack, D. Jones, and D. Roos, *The Machine That Changed the World* (New York: Simon & Schuster, 1990), 99.

90. See Womack, *The Machine That Changed the World*, 53–103. In the early 1980s, Toyota factories held a two-hour supply of parts and GM factories a two-week supply of parts.

91. Aizcorbe, "Cost Competitiveness," 16.

92. Womack, *The Machine That Changed the World*, 85.

93. www.just-auto.com (accessed October 25, 2000).

94. *Wall Street Journal*, June 16, 2000.

95. The study by the World Markets Research Centre is summarized in *Financial Times*, July 8, 2002. These rankings appear to be sensitive to the measure of productivity. Table 2.5 (citing hours per vehicle) ranks Honda much lower.

96. www.autonews.com (accessed August 15, 2000).

97. www.autonews.com (accessed April 30, 2001).

98. Maryann Keller, *Collision: GM, Toyota, Volkswagen and the Race to Own the 21st Century* (New York: Doubleday, 1993), 161–73.

99. Gao, *Passenger Car OEMs in China*, 37, estimates auto body production in China to be twice as costly as in a typical world-class manufacturer; only labor and electrical and interior parts are cheaper in China.

100. *Wall Street Journal*, March 17, 2000.

101. R. Brooks and L. Catão, "The New Economy and Global Stock Returns," IMF Working Paper no. 216 (Washington, D.C.: International Monetary Fund, December 2000).

102. *The Economist*, January 9, 1999.

103. *Wall Street Journal*, May 18, 2001; www.autonews.com (accessed May 17, 2001); www.just-auto.com (accessed February 8, 2002).

104. George Kacher, "German Occupation," *Automobile*, November 2001, 74.

105. www.auto.com (accessed May 29, 2001).

106. Quoted in *BusinessWeek*, March 25, 2002.

107. www.autonewseurope.com (accessed October 1, 2001).

108. See, in particular, Scherer, *Industrial Market Structure and Economic Performance* (1970), 103–22.

Chapter Three

1. Michael Burns, quoted in www.just-auto.com (accessed June 27, 2001).

2. See G. Maxton and J. Wormald, *Driving Over a Cliff: Business Lessons from the World's Car Industry* (Wokingham, U.K.: Addison-Wesley, 1994), 60–65, who refer to a shift from market segmentation based on vertical product classes to one based on horizontal relationships between groups of customers.

3. *Wall Street Journal*, June 25, 2001; *Financial Times*, November 23, 2001; *BusinessWeek*, July 23, 2001.

4. A marketing history of VW's presence on the American market may be found in David Kiley, *Getting the Bugs Out: The Rise, Fall, and Comeback of Volkswagen in America* (New York: Wiley, 2002).

5. *Wall Street Journal*, May 3, 2002.

6. See Goldman Sachs, *Volkswagen Automobiles* (London: Goldman Sachs, 2002), 20, 37.

7. *Wall Street Journal*, November 20, 2002.

8. www.just-auto.com (accessed February 27, 2001). This brand strategy has been caustically questioned by some motoring writers; see www.auto.com (accessed December 21, 2001).

9. Audi, BMW, Jaguar, Mercedes, and Volvo all have entry-level models priced well below $30,000 in the U.S. market; see www.autonews.com (accessed June 25, 2002).

10. At the middle of 2002, Ford was rumored to be considering selling Volvo and Aston Martin; www.just-auto.com (accessed June 18, 2002).

11. Enterprising consumer advocates have offered to help them do so with books explaining which name brands are similar. See Jack Gillis, *The Ultimate Car Book, 2002* (New York: HarperCollins, 2002).

12. A. St. George, *Mercedes-Benz in Alabama*, Case 9-199-026 (Boston: Harvard Business School Cases, 1999); *Financial Times*, August 28, 2000; *Wall Street Journal*, March 1, 2001.

13. *Wall Street Journal*, March 1, 2001.

14. A blow-by-blow account of BMW's period of stewardship of Rover may be found in Chris Brady and Andrew Lorenz, *End of the Road: BMW and Rover, a Brand Too Far* (London: Financial Times and Prentice Hall, 2001).

15. Brady and Lorenz, *End of the Road*, 147.

16. www.autonewseurope.com (accessed June 4, 2001).

17. *London Times*, March 24, 2000.

18. *Wall Street Journal*, December 1, 2000.

19. *Wall Street Journal*, July 13, 2001; www.just-auto.com (accessed April 10, 2002).

20. *Wall Street Journal*, April 2, 2002.

21. Survey by Kim B. Clark and Takahiro Fujimoto, *Product Development and Performance: Strategy, Organization, and the Management of the World Auto Industry* (Cambridge, Mass.: Harvard Business School Press, 1991), 67–95.

22. P. Milgrom and J. Roberts, *Economics, Organization and Management* (Englewood Cliffs, N.J.: Prentice Hall, 1992), 576–78.

23. *Wall Street Journal*, April 9, 2001.

24. M. Maynard, "Amid the Turmoil, a Core Success," http://web.lexis-nexis.com (accessed February 1, 2001).

25. www.autonewseurope.com (accessed August 15, 2000).

26. www.autonewseurope.com (accessed January 30, 2001).

27. www.autonews.com (accessed March 5, 2001).

28. C. Purrington, *Chrysler and BMW: Tritec Engine Joint Venture*, Case 9-600-004 (Boston: Harvard Business School Cases, 2001).

29. *Financial Times*, February 1, 2001.

30. Mark Sirower, *The Synergy Trap* (New York: Free Press, 1997).

31. Brady and Lorenz, *End of the Road*, 54.

32. Quoted in *Financial Times*, June 20, 2000.

33. F. M. Scherer, *Industrial Market Structure and Economic Performance* (Chicago: Rand McNally, 1970), 118.

34. Cited in the *Wall Street Journal*, May 9, 2001.

35. During the post-Napoleonic period to the present day, 64 percent of states going to war found that *some* of their allies were willing to fight with them; Bruce Bueno de Mesquita, *The War Trap* (New Haven, Conn.: Yale University Press, 1981), 113.

36. Brady and Lorenz, *End of the Road*, 52, 169.

37. Bill Vlasic and Bradley Stertz, *Taken for a Ride: How Daimler Drove Off with Chrysler* (New York: Morrow, 2000), 249.

38. www.autonewseurope.com (accessed January 30, 2001).

39. *Financial Times*, September 29, 2000; www.auto.com (accessed April 19, 2001).

40. *Wall Street Journal*, June 20, 2000; www.just-auto.com (accessed January 3, 2002).

41. *BusinessWeek*, January 14, 2002.

42. *Wall Street Journal*, March 5, 2002.

43. P. Dunnett, *The Decline of the British Motor Industry: The Effects of Government Policy, 1943–1979* (London: Croom Helm, 1980), 34.

44. PricewaterhouseCoopers, *The Second Automotive Century* (Bloomfield Hills, Mich.: PricewaterhouseCoopers, 2000), 4.

45. *The Economist*, January 8, 2000.

46. ASEAN was the only intergovernmental economic organization in the Pacific basin until the formation of Asia-Pacific Economic Cooperation (APEC) in 1989. Both ASEAN and APEC have expressed aspirations about free trade in autos (and other traded goods) that they have not yet managed to attain.

47. Quoted in Vlasic and Stertz, *Taken for a Ride*, 116–17.

48. *Wall Street Journal*, February 10, 2000.

49. www.just-auto.com (accessed December 13, 2001).

50. *Wall Street Journal*, April 30, 2002.

51. Vlasic and Stertz, *Taken for a Ride*, 97.

52. J. Womack, D. Jones, and D. Roos, *The Machine That Changed the World* (New York: Simon & Schuster, 1990), 212.

53. G. Bloomfield, "The World Automotive Industry in Transition," in *Restructuring the Global Automobile Industry: National and Regional Impacts*, ed. Christopher M. Law (London: Routledge, 1991), 44.

54. www.autonewseurope.com (accessed July 3, 2001).

55. www.auto.com (accessed March 6, 2002).

56. www.autonewseurope.com (accessed June 3, 2002).

57. Ashwin Adarkar, Asif Adil, David Ernst, and Paresh Vaish, "Emerging Market Alliances," *McKinsey Quarterly* 4 (1997): 120–37.

58. www.just-auto.com (accessed June 26, 2002).

59. www.autonews.com (accessed September 12, 2000)

60. Michael S. Flynn, Sean P. McAlinden, Kim Hill, Kara F. Alkire, and Morgan H. Edwards, *Cars, Capacity and Competition in the 21st Century* (Ann Arbor: University of Michigan Transportation Research Institute, 2000). The study offers various measures of cost comparison. The one selected (figure 6, p. 18) compares the cost of sourcing a three-component vehicle entirely from local production with the cost of production when each component can be sourced from a full-scale plant in the United States, should U.S. costs be lower. Flynn et al. refer to the latter as the "optimum mix." On the same comparison, costs in Germany were about 10 percent greater than in the United States.

61. *Wall Street Journal*, July 31, 2002.

62. *Wall Street Journal*, February 15, 2002.

63. The consultant is Graeme Maxton of the U.K.-based firm Autopolis (www.autopolis.com) and coauthor of Maxton and Wormald, *Driving Over a Cliff.*

64. A. Faiz et al., *Air Pollution from Motor Vehicles* (Washington, D.C.: World Bank, 1997; www.worldbank.org/wbi/cleanair), estimated car ownership in developing countries to be predicted by the following equation:

log (vehicles) = –3.6 + 0.8 log (GNP per capita) + 0.9 log (percentage urban population)

65. *Wall Street Journal*, July 2, 2002.

66. Press release from the Autopolis consultancy; www.autopolis.com (accessed April 27, 2001).

67. *Financial Times*, August 24, 2001.

68. *Washington Post,* May 30, 2000.

69. www.just-auto.com (accessed June 12 and December 10, 2001).

70. *Financial Times,* April 8, 2002; *Wall Street Journal,* May 8, 2002.

71. *Financial Times,* February 5, 2002. Note that this output may be below minimum efficient scale.

72. *Wall Street Journal,* September 20, 2002.

73. www.autonews.com (accessed May 24, 2002).

74. *Wall Street Journal,* December 20, 2002.

75. *Wall Street Journal,* October 26, 2001.

76. *Financial Times,* June 7, 2002.

77. This is the view of McKinsey consultant Paul Gao, "A Tune-Up for China's Auto Industry," *McKinsey Quarterly* 1 (2002): 1–3.

78. www.just-auto.com (accessed April 15, 2002).

79. *Financial Times,* March 6, 2002.

80. *Wall Street Journal,* June 6, 2002.

81. Paul Gao, *Passenger Car OEMs in China: At a Crossroads between Capturing Massive Value and Facing Immense Value Destruction* (McKinsey & Company, internal publication, 2002).

82. europe.autonews.com (accessed December 4, 2002); *Wall Street Journal,* April 15, 2002.

83. www.autonews.com (accessed May 2, 2002).

84. *Wall Street Journal,* April 18, 2002.

85. Auto tariffs in the United States are 0 percent.

86. www.autonews.com (accessed January 31, 2002).

87. www.auto.com (accessed July 23, 2002).

88. www.autonews.com (accessed January 29 and May 2, 2002).

89. From $33.85 on June 4, 2001, to $14.90 on June 26, 2002.

90. Note that GM owns 20 percent of Suzuki.

91. www.just-auto.com (accessed February 14, 2002).

92. www.autonews.com (accessed May 31, 2001).

93. www.just-auto.com (accessed January 2001).

94. www.just-auto.com (accessed January 2001).

95. *Wall Street Journal,* November 25 and December 16, 2002.

96. *Wall Street Journal,* April 18, 2000.

97. www.just-auto.com (accessed February 10, 2001).

98. www.autonewsinternational.com (accessed October 1, 2001); *Financial Times,* April 9, 2001.

99. A. Altschuler, M. Anderson, D. Jones, D. Roos, and J. Womack, *The Future of the Automobile: The Report of MIT's International Automobile Program* (Cambridge, Mass.: MIT Press, 1984), 179.

100. *Wall Street Journal,* June 26, 2001.

101. *Wall Street Journal,* September 5, 2000. Cancellation (www.autonews.com [accessed January 16, 2002]) was most likely due to weakness in the Russian economy and to Fiat's financial problems.

102. www.just-auto.com (accessed October 1, 2001).

103. *Wall Street Journal*, January 21, 2000.

104. Monopsony power is the bargaining advantage that accrues to a small number of buyers who can dominate a market and dictate terms to suppliers; it is discussed in chapter 4.

105. europe.autonews.com (accessed November 5, 2002).

106. www.just-auto.com (accessed January 25, 2001).

107. www.just-auto.com (accessed September 28, 2000).

108. *Wall Street Journal*, December 19, 2001.

109. *Wall Street Journal*, July 6, 2000; www.just-auto.com (accessed February 10, 2001).

110. Mercosur is a customs union comprising Argentina, Bolivia, Brazil, Chile, Paraguay, and Uruguay; see www.mercosur.org. A customs union has a common external tariff on each commodity. Members of a free trade area keep their own tariff structures with regard to nonmembers.

111. See N. Pal, *The New Beetle*, Case 9-501-023 (Boston: Harvard Business School Cases, 2000).

112. www.just-auto.com (accessed March 26, 2002).

113. www.just-auto.com (accessed March 28, 2002).

114. *BusinessWeek*, October 23, 2000.

115. www.auto.com (accessed June 22, 2001)

116. www.just-auto.com (accessed February 21, 2002).

117. *Financial Times*, May 30, 2000.

118. *Wall Street Journal*, September 18, 2000.

119. *London Times*, January 15, 2001.

120. Automotive News Data Center, www.automotivenews.com; *London Times*, January 15, 2001.

121. *Wall Street Journal*, October 25, 2000.

122. www.just-auto.com (accessed February 25 2000).

123. *Wall Street Journal*, June 12, 2000.

124. *Wall Street Journal*, January 26, 2000.

125. *Wall Street Journal*, April 25, 2000.

126. *Financial Times*, October 3, 2000.

127. www.auto.com (accessed December 13, 2001).

128. *Wall Street Journal*, May 9, 2001.

129. *Wall Street Journal*, November 9, 2000.

130. www.autonewseurope.com (accessed July 2000).

131. *Wall Street Journal*, February 27, 2001.

Chapter Four

1. Timothy Bresnahan, "Competition and Collusion in the American Automobile Oligopoly," *Journal of Industrial Economics* 35, no. 4 (1987): 457–62.

2. Robert C. Feenstra, "Automobile Prices and Protection: The United States–Japan Trade Restraint," in *The New Protectionist Threat to World Welfare*, ed. Dominick Salvatore (New York: North Holland, 1987), 333–51.

3. The European Union recently moved to curtail European producers from enforcing market segmentation that allowed them to charge widely differing prices in different European countries.

4. Daimler-Chrysler was a participant in the original bidding process in which the Korean Development Bank picked Ford (in 2000) and subsequently GM (in 2002) when Ford retracted its bid.

5. F. M. Scherer, *Industry Strategy, Structure and Public Policy* (New York: Harper-Collins, 1996), 299, and *Industrial Market Structure and Economic Performance*, 3rd ed. (Boston: Houghton Mifflin, 1990), 254–55.

6. For a discussion of how vigorous rivalry may be present with a small number of producers, see Michael Porter, *The Competitive Advantage of Nations* (New York: Free Press, 1990), 117–24.

7. Both the chain store and the prisoners' dilemma are explained in Ken Binmore, *Fun and Games: A Text on Game Theory* (Lexington, Mass.: D.C. Heath, 1992).

8. Porter, *The Competitive Advantage of Nations*, 116–22. Porter is well known for disagreeing with the popular stereotype of Japanese industries as collusive oligopolies managed by the Japanese government; he fears that Americans will draw the wrong lessons from this misconception (that is the need for economic planning in the United States).

9. Scherer, *Industry Strategy, Structure and Public Policy*, 289.

10. J. Womack, D. Jones, and D. Roos, *The Machine That Changed the World* (New York: Simon & Schuster, 1990), 61.

11. A. Altschuler, M. Anderson, D. Jones, D. Roos, and J. Womack, *The Future of the Automobile: The Report of MIT's International Automobile Program* (Cambridge, Mass.: MIT Press, 1984), 148.

12. www.autonews.com (accessed July 5, 2000).

13. *BusinessWeek* (January 13, 2003) commented disapprovingly on Toyota's financial aid to several unprofitable members of its *keiretsu*.

14. www.just-auto.com (accessed February 11, 2002).

15. www.auto.com (accessed July 11, 2000); *Financial Times*, July 3, 2001; www.autonewseurope.com (accessed August 18, 2000); www.autonews.com (accessed March 22, 2002).

16. *Financial Times*, April 19, 2002.

17. www.auto.com (accessed February 12, 2002).

18. *Wall Street Journal*, January 9, 2001. The after-market activities of Magneti Marelli were sold in March 2002; see *Wall Street Journal*, March 7, 2002. *Financial Times* (May 16, 2002) notes the sale of Comau.

19. PricewaterhouseCoopers, *The Second Automotive Century* (Bloomfield Hills, Mich.: PricewaterhouseCoopers, 2000).

20. See Lance Ealey and Luis Troyano-Berm/Dez, "Are Automobiles the Next Commodity?," *McKinsey Quarterly* 4 (1996): 62–75.

21. www.just-auto.com (accessed May 8, 2002).

22. www.just-auto.com (accessed February 12, 2002) on Inchape; www.just-auto.com (accessed May 22, 2002) on Spanish distribution; www.just-auto.com (accessed June 25, 2002) on Toyota South Africa.

23. www.automotivenewseurope.com (accessed June 3, 2002).

24. *Wall Street Journal*, May 31 and June 24, 2002.

25. www.autonews.com (accessed March 27, 2002).

26. *Financial Times*, August 28, 2000; www.autonewseurope (accessed July 14, 2000); *Wall Street Journal* (February 22, 2000.

27. www.just-auto.com (accessed April 10, 2001).

28. *Wall Street Journal*, May 8, 2000.

29. *Financial Times*, September 6, 2001.

30. *Wall Street Journal*, January 22, 2002.

31. *BusinessWeek*, December 31, 2001.

32. *Financial Times*, March 25, 2002.

33. www.just-auto.com (accessed April 23, 2001).

34. www.autonewseurope (accessed June 4 and August 27, 2000).

35. www.auto.com (accessed November 10, 2000); www.just-auto.com.com (accessed November 9, 2000).

36. www.auto.com (accessed May 9, 2002).

37. www.just-auto.com (accessed February 25, 2002).

38. www.autonewseurope.com (accessed February 11, 2002); *Financial Times*, December 27, 2001.

39. europe.autonews.com (accessed November 25, 2002).

40. *Wall Street Journal*, February 21, 2000.

41. *Wall Street Journal*, January 10, 2002.

42. www.automotivenewseurope.com (accessed March 11, 2002).

43. Association des Constructeurs Européens d'Automobiles (European Automobile Manufacturers Association), *ACEA Observations on the European Commission's Proposal for Regulation on the Application of Article 81(3) of the Treaty to Categories of Vertical Agreements and Concerted Practices in the Motor Vehicle Industry* (Brussels: Association des Constructeurs Européens d'Automobiles, 2002), 5.

44. www.autonews.com (accessed February 18, 2002).

45. Porter, *The Competitive Advantage of Nations*, 149.

46. For one person's misanthropic account of working on a vehicle assembly line in an area of Michigan with few alternative employment opportunities, see Ben Hamper, *Rivethead: Tales from the Assembly Line* (New York: Warner, 1992).

47. www.just-auto.com (accessed January 30, 2001).

48. P. Dunnett, *The Decline of the British Motor Industry: The Effects of Government Policy, 1943–1979* (London: Croom Helm, 1980), 109.

49. G. Maxcy, *The Multinational Automobile Industry* (New York: St. Martin's, 1981), 182.

50. *Financial Times*, August 20, 2001.

51. *Financial Times*, February 17, 2000.

52. www.just-auto.com (accessed February 20, 2002).

53. Chris Brady and Andrew Lorenz, *End of the Road: BMW and Rover, a Brand Too Far* (London: Financial Times and Prentice Hall, 2001), 36.

54. *Wall Street Journal*, March 20, 2000.

55. M. Fitzgerald, "Longbridge Rover Activist Speaks Out," interviewed November 3, 1998, www.socialist.net (accessed October 8, 1999).

56. *Financial Times*, March 5, 2002.

57. *London Times*, March 16, 2002.

58. *Financial Times*, June 26, 2001.

59. *Wall Street Journal*, January 9, 2002.

60. www.autonews.com (accessed November 13, 2002).

61. *Wall Street Journal*, October 4, 2001.

62. See John Conybeare, Hayes McCarthy, and Mark Zinkula, "NAFTA and the Strange Coalition of Environmentalists and Protectionists," *International Executive* 37, no. 3 (1995): 211–24, and John Conybeare and Mark Zinkula, "Who Voted for NAFTA? Trade Unions v. Free Trade," *World Economy* 19, no. 1 (1996): 1–12.

63. *Wall Street Journal*, May 23, 2001.

64. www.autonews.com (accessed July 23, 2001).

65. europe.autonews.com (accessed October 3, 2002); *Wall Street Journal*, December 17, 2002.

66. *Financial Times*, July 12, 2000; *Wall Street Journal*, January 11, 2000.

67. *Wall Street Journal*, September 26, 2000.

68. www.autonews.com (accessed July 23, 2001).

69. *Wall Street Journal*, March 14, 2001.

70. www.auto.com (accessed January 10, 2002).

71. www.auto.com (accessed March 11, 2002).

72. www.just-auto.com (accessed October 19, 2001).

73. *Financial Times*, April 1, 2002.

74. See, for example, www.just-auto.com (accessed May 29, 2002).

75. www.autonews.com (accessed October 7, 2002); *Wall Street Journal*, January 6, 2003.

76. Brady and Lorenz, *End of the Road*, 54.

77. www.auto.com (accessed June 27, 2002). When Kansei Paint resisted price cuts, Nissan stopped buying its paint and sold its shares in Kansei; *Financial Times*, July 17, 2002.

78. *BusinessWeek*, April 4, 2001.

79. *Wall Street Journal*, July 11, 2001.

80. www.auto.com (accessed May 31, 2002).

81. www.just-auto.com (accessed March 12, 2001).

82. www.autonews.com (accessed January 28, 2002).

83. www.just-auto.com (accessed October 11, 2002).

84. The study was done by the Automotive Consulting Group of Ann Arbor and reported in www.just-auto.com (accessed July 6, 2002).

85. www.just-auto.com (accessed March 16, 2000).

86. www.autonews.com (accessed March 4, 2002).

87. Northrop took over TRW in July 2002 and sold TRW's automotive business to the Blackstone Group; www.autonews.com (accessed November 13, 2002).

88. PricewaterhouseCoopers, *Automotive Sector Insights* (Bloomfield Hills, Mich.: PricewaterhouseCoopers, 2000), 26; PricewaterhouseCoopers, *The Second Automotive Century*, 2; PricewaterhouseCoopers, *Global Automotive Deal Survey, 1998* (Bloomfield Hills, Mich.: PricewaterhouseCoopers, 1999), 13.

89. www.autonewseurope.com (accessed March 19, 2001).

90. *Financial Times*, March 13, 2001.

91. *Financial Times*, July 12, 2000.

92. www.autonewseurope.com (accessed November 27, 2000).

93. *Financial Times*, April 17, 2000.

94. *Wall Street Journal*, April 2, 2001.

95. *Wall Street Journal*, August 15, 2002.

96. *Financial Times*, January 22, 2001.

97. *Financial Times*, June 6, 2000.

98. www.autonews.com (accessed March 27, 2001).

99. It is for such reasons that suppliers often resist automakers' demands to cluster around vehicle plants in "supplier parks" in which the component makers provide facilities to serve a single vehicle manufacturer. Suppliers have very little bargaining power once they have sunk cost into a local facility to supply an assembly plant of one vehicle maker. Suppliers will almost invariably like to supply vehicle makers from large factories that can allocate their output to more than one vehicle maker. See *Financial Times*, July 10, 2001.

100. www.autonews.com (accessed May 16, 2001).

101. www.just-auto.com (accessed April 20, 2001).

102. *Wall Street Journal*, April 22, 2002.

103. Quoted in *Financial Times*, July 5, 2002.

104. Ronald Coase, "The Nature of the Firm," *Economica* 4 (1937): 386–405.

105. The ECM typically consists of a motherboard with computer chips. It monitors and adjusts all engine and some transmission functions and may also yield fault codes. BMW and Porsche have been using the Motronic system since the early 1980s (in the case of Porsche, starting with the 1984 911 Carrera), and many other makers have followed.

106. www.just-auto.com (accessed March 14, 2002).

107. www.auto.com (accessed March 15, 2002).

108. I am grateful to Glenn Mercer of McKinsey & Company for this insightful observation.

109. www.auto.com (accessed June 27, 2002).

110. www.autonews.com (accessed June 28, 2002).

111. Data for 1987, from Scherer, *Industrial Market Structure and Economic Performance* (1990), 518. Since the share of the motor vehicle industry in U.S. national income has remained constant from the 1980s to 2000, the current share of steel output going to the motor vehicle sector should still be close to 15 percent, though perhaps somewhat lower because of substitution of plastics for steel in auto construction. The glass industry sold 18.5 percent of its output to the auto sector in 1987.

112. *Wall Street Journal*, November 18, 2002; www.autonews.com (accessed January 28, 2003).

113. *Financial Times*, April 13, 2000; *Wall Street Journal*, March 9, 2001.

114. www.autonews.com (accessed July 31, 2001).

115. www.autonews.com (accessed June 7, 2000); www.nj.com (accessed June 21, 2000).

116. Grässlin's biography of Daimler executive Jürgen Schrempp offers a critical analysis of these acquisitions from the perspective of a representative of the Organization of Critical Shareholders of Daimler-Benz; Jürgen Grässlin, *Jürgen Schrempp and the Making of an Auto Dynasty* (New York: McGraw-Hill, 2000).

117. www.autonews.com (accessed January 24, 2002).

118. *Business Week*, December 31, 2001.

119. www.autonews.com (accessed July 5, 2002).

120. Much to the horror of Porsche 911 owners.

121. *Financial Times*, April 19, 2001.

122. *Financial Times*, April 2, 2002.

123. www.auto.com (accessed January 19, 2001).

124. *Wall Street Journal*, March 28, 2000. In 2002, VW's new chief executive officer, Bernd Pischetsrieder, announced that VW would sell its stake in Scania because VW would not remain in the truck business unless it could be Europe's largest or second-largest producer, a target it could not reach through ownership of Scania; www.autonews.com (accessed February 1, 2002).

125. www.just-auto.com (accessed March 25, 2002).

126. *Financial Times*, December 19, 2001.

Chapter Five

1. If debt is not being serviced, the corporation is insolvent, and the debt holders in effect become the owners and are entitled to any residual stream of earnings, displacing the shareholders, whose entitlement to earnings falls behind that of debt holders.

2. Surveys of the range of corporate governance issues may be found in Oliver E. Williamson, *The Economic Institutions of Capitalism: Firms, Markets, Relational*

Contracting (New York: Free Press, 1985), and Gary Miller, *Managerial Dilemmas: The Political Economy of Hierarchy* (Cambridge, U.K.: Cambridge University Press, 1992).

3. *Wall Street Journal*, September 1, 2000.

4. *Financial Times*, January 30, 2001.

5. www.just-auto.com (accessed January 8 and 15, 2001); *Financial Times*, June 26, 2000, and February 5, 2001.

6. *Financial Times*, January 30, 2001.

7. *Wall Street Journal* (1 September 2000).

8. www.auto.com (accessed March 8, 2001).

9. *Financial Times*, September 21, 2000.

10. *Wall Street Journal*, June 6, 2001, and February 27, 2002.

11. *Wall Street Journal*, February 18, 2002.

12. *Wall Street Journal*, January 7, 2003.

13. *Wall Street Journal*, March 15, 2000.

14. www.just-auto.com (accessed March 27, 2000).

15. *Financial Times*, September 5, 2000.

16. *Wall Street Journal*, February 29, 2000.

17. www.just-auto.com (accessed August 17, 2000).

18. *Wall Street Journal*, July 27, 2001.

19. www.auto.com (accessed September 6, 2000). Note that the European Union's policy on mergers affects the ability of firms to vertically integrate as well as horizontally merge.

20. *Wall Street Journal*, September 20, 2000.

21. www.just-auto.com (accessed December 6, 2000).

22. www.autonews.com (accessed January 10, 2002); *Financial Times*, February 5, 2002.

23. www.autonewseurope.com (accessed February 11, 2002).

24. www.just-auto.com (accessed May 22, 2002); www.autonews.com (accessed June 27, 2002).

25. *Wall Street Journal*, May 30, 2002.

26. www.autonews.com (accessed June 27, 2002).

27. The collusive pricing in the U.S. auto industry during the 1950s was probably unique to the period before significant import penetration, beginning in the late 1950s; Timothy Bresnahan, "Competition and Collusion in the American Automobile Oligopoly," *Journal of Industrial Economics* 35, no. 4 (1987): 457–62.

28. Maryann Keller, *Rude Awakening: The Rise, Fall and Struggle for Recovery of General Motors* (New York: Morrow, 1989), 91.

29. U.S. Department of Justice, International Competition Policy Advisory Committee, *Final Report*, www.usdoj.gov/atr/icpac/finalreport.htm (2000) (accessed October 24, 2001).

30. *Wall Street Journal*, May 8, 2002.

31. *Wall Street Journal*, December 19, 2002.

32. www.autonewsinternational.com (accessed July 12, 2000).

33. www.just-auto.com (accessed August 15, 2002).

34. *Financial Times*, August 1, 2000.

35. www.auto.com (accessed September 21, 2000).

36. *Guardian*, February 2, 2001.

37. *Wall Street Journal*, December 16, 1999.

38. www.autonews.com (accessed May 21, 2002).

39. *Wall Street Journal*, December 20, 2001. The European Union ruled that Hungary was a credible, lower-cost alternative but that the amount of the aid was excessive.

40. www.just-auto.com (accessed May 8, 2002); *Wall Street Journal*, May 22, 2002.

41. *Wall Street Journal*, April 4, 2002. The European Union ultimately approved $366 million in aid to BMW's Leipzig plant in December 2002.

42. www.just-auto.com (accessed June 5, 2002).

43. *Wall Street Journal*, October 30, 2001.

44. *Financial Times*, April 2, 2002.

45. www.autonews.com (accessed January 7, 2002).

46. Chris Brady and Andrew Lorenz, *End of the Road: BMW and Rover, a Brand Too Far* (London: Financial Times and Prentice Hall, 2001), 172.

47. *Financial Times*, May 3, 2000.

48. P. Dunnett, *The Decline of the British Motor Industry: The Effects of Government Policy, 1943–1979* (London: Croom Helm, 1980), 136.

49. Dunnett, *The Decline of the British Motor Industry*, 163.

50. Glenn Mercer, "Case Studies of Automobile M&A" (paper presented at GERPISA Conference, Paris, June 7–9, 2001).

51. *Wall Street Journal*, January 2, 2003.

52. *Wall Street Journal*, June 19, 2001.

53. *Financial Times*, February 15, 2000, and January 18, 2002.

54. www.auto.com (accessed March 20, 2002).

55. A. Altschuler, M. Anderson, D. Jones, D. Roos, and J. Womack, *The Future of the Automobile: The Report of MIT's International Automobile Program* (Cambridge, Mass.: MIT Press, 1984), 232.

56. www.auto.com (accessed March 20, 2002).

57. *Wall Street Journal*, July 10, 2001. In 1996, the ASEAN group agreed to reduce auto tariffs to 5 percent by 2005, though it now appears unlikely to meet that goal.

58. In May 2002, the Chinese government invoked safety issues to suspend imports of a Daimler minibus; *Wall Street Journal*, May 28, 2002. Australia has long had a policy of specifying auto safety standards that are sufficiently different from international norms as to significantly raise the cost of exporting to Australia.

59. *Wall Street Journal*, December 18, 2001.

60. *Financial Times*, January 12, 2000.

61. Altschuler, *Future of the Automobile*, 33, 231.

62. Altschuler, *Future of the Automobile*, 17.

63. G. Maxcy, *The Multinational Automobile Industry* (New York: St. Martin's, 1981), 107.

64. www.autonewsinternational.com (accessed July 12, 2000).

65. Though auto agreements can be found among developed countries, one example being the U.S.–Canada free trade in autos agreement that preceded the North American Free Trade Agreement.

66. www.auto.com (accessed April 8, 2002).

67. *Wall Street Journal*, April 1, 2002. The Malaysian government announced in December 2002 that by 2005 it might reduce import tariffs on autos to 20 percent; www.just-auto.com (accessed December 17, 2002).

68. *Wall Street Journal*, February 16, 2000. This is another illustration of the political popularity of bilateral trade balancing despite its lack of an economic logic.

69. *Financial Times*, April 12, 2000.

70. *Wall Street Journal*, May 18, 2000.

71. Both have free trade within the group. Customs unions share a common external tariff, while members of free trade areas retain their own external trade barriers.

72. See, for example, Robert Gilpin, *War and Change in World Politics* (Cambridge, U.K.: Cambridge University Press, 1981).

73. Thucydides, author of *The Peloponnesian War* (Harmondsworth, U.K.: Penguin, 1954), an incomplete history of the war (431–404 b.c.),was born between 460 and 455 B.C. and died about 400 B.C. He is perhaps the first social scientist to believe that one could observe a phenomenon of organizational overexpansion and subsequent collapse. Like many observers who followed him, he attributed this to a boundless drive for power.

74. Paradoxically, though Chamberlain worried about the overextension of the empire, his primary prescription for the "Weary Titan" was more centralized management of the empire, a policy that was at the time implemented with respect to the Afrikaner republics.

75. Edward Luttwak, *The Grand Strategy of the Roman Empire* (Baltimore: The Johns Hopkins University Press, 1981).

76. Peter Liberman, *Does Conquest Pay? The Exploitation of Occupied Industrial Societies* (Princeton, N.J.: Princeton University Press, 1996).

77. For example, R. Davis and R. Huttenback's study of the British Empire (*Mammon and the Pursuit of Empire: The Political Economy of British Imperialism, 1860–1912* [London: Cambridge University Press, 1986]) revealed a pattern of subsidies from taxpayers to investors in the empire, implying that the British Empire as a whole was a loss-making venture for Britain, though parts of it may well have been profitable.

78. It was suggested by A. Berle and G. Means, *The Modern Corporation and Private Property* (New York: Macmillan, 1932), in their classic study of the modern corporation.

79. References to these studies may be found in D. W. Carleton and J. M. Perloff, *Modern Industrial Organization*, 3rd ed. (Reading, Mass.: Addison-Wesley, 1999), 27; D. Waldman and E. Jensen, *Industrial Organization* (Reading, Mass.: Addison-Wesley, 1996), 513–15; and Dennis C. Mueller, "Mergers: Theory and Evidence," in *Mergers, Markets and Public Policy*, ed. G. Musati (Amsterdam: Kluwer, 1995), 9–43.

80. Cited in Mark L. Sirower, *The Synergy Trap* (New York: Free Press, 1997), 6.

81. Dennis C. Mueller, "A Cross-National Comparison of Determinants and Effects of Mergers," in *The Modern Corporation: Profits, Power, Growth and Performance*, ed. Dennis C. Mueller (Brighton, U.K.: Wheatsheaf Books, 1986), 186.

82. F. M. Scherer, *Industrial Market Structure and Economic Performance*, 3rd ed. (Boston: Houghton Mifflin, 1990), 172–73.

83. F. M. Scherer, *Industrial Market Structure and Economic Performance* (Chicago: Rand McNally, 1970), 112, 120.

84. Mathias Bekier, Anna Bogardus, and Tim Oldham, "Why Mergers Fail," *McKinsey Quarterly* 4 (2001): 1–4.

85. Scherer, *Industrial Market Structure and Economic Performance* (1990), 172–74; see also discussions in Scherer, *Industrial Market Structure and Economic Performance* (Chicago: Rand McNally, 1970), 120–22.

86. Scherer, *Industrial Market Structure and Economic Performance* (1970), 112.

87. Milton Friedman, *Essays in Positive Economics* (Chicago: University of Chicago Press, 1953). Friedman went on to suggest that it is therefore reasonable to construct economic theories of the firm based on the assumption that firms behave "as if" they are profit maximizers (even if they are not) because in the long run only those that do maximize profits will survive, regardless of whether they are deliberately or accidentally maximizing profits.

88. Scherer, *Industrial Market Structure and Economic Performance* (1970), 103.

89. *BusinessWeek*, January 25, 1999.

90. www.just-auto.com (accessed December 12, 2000).

91. Graham Allison, *Essence of Decision* (Boston: Little, Brown, 1971).

92. William Niskanen, *Bureaucracy and Representative Government* (Chicago: Aldine, 1971). For a critical review of the limitations of the budget-maximizing model of bureaucratic behavior, see John Conybeare, "Bureaucracy, Monopoly and Competition: A Critical Analysis of the Budget-Maximizing Model of Bureaucracy," *American Journal of Political Science* 28, no. 3 (1984): 479–502.

93. Stern Stewart Research, "M&A: Why Most Winners Lose," *Evaluation* 3, no. 4 (2001): 10. See also George Foster, *Financial Statement Analysis*, 2nd ed. (Englewood Cliffs, N.J.: Prentice Hall, 1986), 461.

94. G. Meeks, *Disappointing Marriage: A Study of the Gains from Merger* (Cambridge, U.K.: Cambridge University Press, 1977); Anthony Downs, *Inside Bureaucracy* (Boston: Little, Brown, 1967).

95. For general surveys of these issues, see Miller, *Managerial Dilemmas*, and Williamson, *The Economic Institutions of Capitalism*.

96. Voiced unsuccessfully at the April 2001 annual shareholders' meeting; *Wall Street Journal*, April 12, 2001.

97. www.autonews.com (accessed February 27, 2002).

98. Scherer, *Industrial Market Structure and Economic Performance* (1970), 112; see quotation from Scherer cited in note 86.

99. B. Burrough, *Barbarians at the Gate* (New York: Harper & Row, 1990).

100. Stern Stewart Research, "M&A," 10.

101. *Wall Street Journal*, January 27, 2000. Schrempp also tried unsuccessfully to arrange a merger with British Aerospace in 1998; Jürgen Grässlin, *Jürgen Schrempp and the Making of an Auto Dynasty* (New York: McGraw-Hill, 2000), 108.

102. *Financial Times*, December 6, 2000, printed the full transcript of the interview with Schrempp. The admission prompted a law suit by financier Kirk Kerkorian claiming that Chrysler shareholders had been denied their rightful acquisition premium; see www.autonews.com (accessed March 25, 2002).

103. Robert Sobel, *Car Wars: The Untold Story* (New York: Dutton, 1984), 311.

104. Lee Iacocca, with Sonny Kleinfield, *Talking Straight* (New York: Bantam, 1989), 310.

105. www.autonews.com (accessed April 15, 2002).

106. *Wall Street Journal*, October 3, 2001.

107. www.autonews.com (accessed January 18, 2001).

108. www.just-auto.com (accessed May 24, 2002); George Kacher, "Last Reitzle," *Automobile*, August 2002, 67–68.

109. www.auto.com (accessed January 23, 2002).

110. *Wall Street Journal*, February 27, 2002.

111. *Wall Street Journal*, January 9, 2001.

112. *Wall Street Journal*, February 23, 2001.

113. Goldman Sachs, *Global Automobiles and Auto Parts* (New York: Goldman Sachs, 2003), 19.

Chapter Six

1. MG Rover announced in December 2002 that it would produce a rebadged version of an auto designed by the India Tata company; www.just-auto.com (accessed December 23, 2002).

2. See Ronald Coase, "The Nature of the Firm," *Economica* 4 (1937): 386–405, and Richard E. Caves, *Multinational Enterprise and Economic Analysis* (Cambridge, U.K.: Cambridge University Press, 1972).

3. Consider the parallel with the following: When testing for the role of ideology in determining the votes of legislators, it is common practice to regress votes on measurable variables such as campaign contributions and label the error term a measure of the influence of ideology.

4. Bill Vlasic and Bradley Stertz, *Taken for a Ride: How Daimler Drove Off with Chrysler* (New York: Morrow, 2000), document the almost contemptuous skepticism of many Chrysler executives with regard to Daimler's claims of the new markets and products that would ensue from a Daimler-Chrysler merger.

5. As R. Davis and R. Huttenback, *Mammon and the Pursuit of Empire: The Political Economy of British Imperialism, 1860–1912* (London: Cambridge University Press, 1986), and others have noted, the empires acquired during the nineteenth century were net drains on the wealth of the home countries. Similarly, it may be the for-

merly distressed Chrysler that is exploiting the resources of Daimler rather than the reverse.

6. See F. M. Scherer, *Industrial Market Structure and Economic Performance*, 3rd ed. (Boston: Houghton Mifflin, 1990), 141–46.

7. A. Altschuler, M. Anderson, D. Jones, D. Roos, and J. Womack, *The Future of the Automobile: The Report of MIT's International Automobile Program* (Cambridge, Mass.: MIT Press, 1984), 194, went on to predict that "most of today's 'household names' in the auto industry will be in business 20 years hence . . . [and] . . . few if any new names will be added."

8. Given the controlling share ownership of the Quandt family and BMW's profitability, a Ford takeover is unlikely unless BMW is beset by some future financial disaster.

9. www.just-auto.com (accessed March 7, 2003).

10. VW is reorganizing itself into two groups, one traditional (VW, Skoda, and Bentley) and one with a more sporting image (Audi, Seat, and Lamborghini); www.autonewseurope.com (accessed April 29, 2002).

11. www.just-auto.com (accessed December 18, 2001).

Bibliography

World Wide Web

www.ai-online.com
www.auto.com
www.autonews.com
www.autonewseurope.com
www.autonewsinternational.com
www.just-auto.com

Newspapers

The following newspapers were consulted through their websites:
BusinessWeek: www.businessweek.com
The Economist: www.economist.com
Financial Times: news.ft.com
Guardian: www.guardian.co.uk
London Times: www.the-times.co.uk
Wall Street Journal: online.wsj.com
Washington Post: www.washingtonpost.com

Books and Articles

Adarkar, Ashwin, Asif Adil, David Ernst, and Paresh Vaish. "Emerging Market Alliances." *McKinsey Quarterly* 4 (1997): 120–37.

Aizcorbe, A., C. Winston, and A. Friedlander. "Cost Competitiveness of the U.S. Automobile Industry." In *Blind Intersection? Policy and the Automobile Industry*, edited by C. Winston and Associates. Washington, D.C.: Brookings Institution, 1987, 6–35.

Allison, Graham. *Essence of Decision*. Boston: Little, Brown, 1971.

Altschuler, A., M. Anderson, D. Jones, D. Roos, and J. Womack. *The Future of the Automobile: The Report of MIT's International Automobile Program*. Cambridge, Mass.: MIT Press, 1984.

Association des Constructeurs Européens d'Automobiles (European Automobile Manufacturers Association). *ACEA Observations on the European Commission's Proposal for Regulation on the Application of Article 81(3) of the Treaty to Categories of Vertical Agreements and Concerted Practices in the Motor Vehicle Industry*. Brussels: Association des Constructeurs Européens d'Automobiles, 2002.

Barnet, Richard J., and Ronald E. Müller. *Global Reach: The Power of the Multinational Corporations*. New York: Simon & Schuster, 1974.

Bekier, Mathias, Anna Bogardus, and Tim Oldham. "Why Mergers Fail." *McKinsey Quarterly* 4 (2001): 1–4.

Berle, A., and G. Means. *The Modern Corporation and Private Property*. New York: Macmillan, 1932.

Binmore, Ken. *Fun and Games: A Text on Game Theory*. Lexington, Mass.: D. C. Heath, 1992.

Bloomfield, G. *The World Automotive Industry*. Newton Abbot, U.K.: David and Charles, 1978.

———. "The World Automotive Industry in Transition." In *Restructuring the Global Automobile Industry: National and Regional Impacts*, edited by Christopher M. Law. London: Routledge, 1991, 19–60.

Bouvard, F., M. Cesar, H. Corlay, and W. Sfeir. *Assessing the Impact of Platform Strategy on Technical Economies of Scale: A Quantitative Simulation Tool*. Paris: McKinsey & Company, 1999.

Brady, Chris, and Andrew Lorenz. *End of the Road: BMW and Rover, a Brand Too Far*. London: Financial Times and Prentice Hall, 2001.

Bresnahan, Timothy. "Competition and Collusion in the American Automobile Oligopoly." *Journal of Industrial Economics* 35, no. 4 (1987): 457–62.

Brooks, R., and L. Catão. "The New Economy and Global Stock Returns." IMF Working Paper, no. 216 (December 2000).

Bueno de Mesquita, Bruce. *The War Trap*. New Haven, Conn.: Yale University Press, 1981.

Burrough, B. *Barbarians at the Gate*. New York: Harper & Row, 1990.

Carleton, D. W., and J. M. Perloff. *Modern Industrial Organization*. 3rd ed. Reading, Mass.: Addison-Wesley, 1999.

Caves, Richard E. *Multinational Enterprise and Economic Analysis*. Cambridge, U.K.: Cambridge University Press, 1972.

Clark, Kim B., and Takahiro Fujimoto. *Product Development and Performance: Strategy, Organization, and the Management of the World Auto Industry.* Cambridge Mass.: Harvard Business School Press, 1991.

Coase, Ronald. "The Nature of the Firm." *Economica* 4 (1937): 386–405.

Cohen, Robert B. "The Prospects for Trade and Protectionism in the Auto Industry." In *Trade Policy in the 1980s*, edited by William R. Cline. Washington, D.C.: Institute for International Economics, 1983, 527–73.

Conybeare, John. "Bureaucracy, Monopoly and Competition: A Critical Analysis of the Budget-Maximizing Model of Bureaucracy." *American Journal of Political Science* 28, no. 3 (1984): 479–502.

Conybeare, John, Hayes McCarthy, and Mark Zinkula. "NAFTA and the Strange Coalition of Environmentalists and Protectionists." *International Executive* 37, no. 3 (1995): 211–24.

Conybeare, John, and Mark Zinkula. "Who Voted for NAFTA? Trade Unions v. Free Trade." *World Economy* 19, no. 1 (1996): 1–12.

Cott, J., and T. Piper. *Nissan Motor Company.* Case 9-200-067. Boston: Harvard Business School Cases, 2000.

Davis, R., and R. Huttenback. *Mammon and the Pursuit of Empire: The Political Economy of British Imperialism, 1860–1912.* London: Cambridge University Press, 1986.

Downs, Anthony. *Inside Bureaucracy.* Boston: Little, Brown, 1967.

Dunn, James A. "Automobiles in International Trade: Regime Change or Persistence." *International Organization* 41, no. 2 (1987): 225–52.

Dunnett, P. *The Decline of the British Motor Industry: The Effects of Government Policy, 1943–1979.* London: Croom Helm, 1980.

Ealey, Lance, and Luis Troyano-Berm/Dez. "Are Automobiles the Next Commodity?" *McKinsey Quarterly* 4 (1996): 62–75.

Ernst, David, and Tammy Halevy. "When to Think Alliance." *McKinsey Quarterly* 4 (2000): 47–55.

Faiz, A., et al. *Air Pollution from Motor Vehicles.* World Bank, 1997, www.worldbank.org/wbi/cleanair (accessed April 17, 2001).

Feenstra, Robert C. "Automobile Prices and Protection: The United States–Japan Trade Restraint." In *The New Protectionist Threat to World Welfare*, edited by Dominick Salvatore. New York: North Holland, 1987, 333–51.

Fitzgerald, M. "Longbridge Rover Activist Speaks Out." Interviewed November 3, 1998, www.socialist.net (accessed October 8, 1999).

Flynn, Michael S., Sean P. McAlinden, Kim Hill, Kara F. Alkire, and Morgan H. Edwards. *Cars, Capacity and Competition in the 21st Century.* Ann Arbor: University of Michigan Transportation Research Institute, 2000.

Foster, George. *Financial Statement Analysis.* 2nd ed. Englewood Cliffs, N.J.: Prentice Hall, 1986.

Friedman, Milton. *Essays in Positive Economics.* Chicago: University of Chicago Press, 1953.

Gao, Paul. *Passenger Car OEMs in China: At a Crossroads between Capturing Massive Value and Facing Immense Value Destruction* (McKinsey & Company, internal publication, 2002).

———. "A Tune-Up for China's Auto Industry." *McKinsey Quarterly* 1 (2002): 1–3.

Gillis, Jack. *The Ultimate Car Book, 2002.* New York: HarperCollins, 2002.

Gilpin, Robert. *War and Change in World Politics.* Cambridge, U.K.: Cambridge University Press, 1981.

Goldman Sachs. *Global Automobiles and Auto Parts.* New York: Goldman Sachs, 2003.

———. *Volkswagen Automobiles.* London: Goldman Sachs, 2002.

Grässlin, Jürgen. *Jürgen Schrempp and the Making of an Auto Dynasty.* New York: McGraw-Hill, 2000.

Hamper, Ben. *Rivethead: Tales from the Assembly Line.* New York: Warner, 1992.

Hardt, M., and A. Negri. *Empire.* Cambridge, Mass.: Harvard University Press, 2000.

Iacocca, Lee, with Sonny Kleinfield. *Talking Straight.* New York: Bantam, 1989.

Institute of Labor and Industrial Relations. *Contributions of the Automotive Industry to the US Economy in 1998.* Ann Arbor: University of Michigan, 2001.

International Organization of Motor Vehicle Manufacturers. *OICA Statistics 2001,* 2002, www.oica.net (accessed September 1, 2002).

Kacher, George. "German Occupation." *Automobile,* November 2001, 73–75.

———. "Last Reitzle." *Automobile,* August 2002, 67–68.

Kaplan, Robert S. *Porsche AG.* Case 9-193-071. Boston: Harvard Business School Cases, 1992.

Keller, Maryann. *Collision: GM, Toyota, Volkswagen and the Race to Own the 21st Century.* New York: Doubleday, 1993.

———. *Rude Awakening: The Rise, Fall and Struggle for Recovery of General Motors.* New York: Morrow, 1989.

Kiley, David. *Getting the Bugs Out: The Rise, Fall, and Comeback of Volkswagen in America.* New York: Wiley, 2002.

Laux, J. *The European Automobile Industry.* New York: Twayne, 1992.

Law, Christopher, ed. *Restructuring the Global Automobile Industry.* New York: Routledge, 1991.

Lawrence, Paul R., and Jay W. Lorsch. *Organization and Environment: Managing Differentiation and Integration.* Boston: Harvard Business School Press, 1967.

Lewis, William, Hans Gersbach, Tom Jansen, and Koji Sakate. "The Secret to Competitiveness—Competition," *McKinsey Quarterly* 4 (1993): 29–43.

Liberman, Peter. *Does Conquest Pay? The Exploitation of Occupied Industrial Societies.* Princeton, N.J.: Princeton University Press, 1996.

Luttwak, Edward. *The Grand Strategy of the Roman Empire.* Baltimore: The Johns Hopkins University Press, 1981.

Maxcy, G. *The Multinational Automobile Industry.* New York: St. Martin's, 1981.

Maxton, Graeme. "Global Car Forecasts to 2005—The Outlook for World Car Sales." 2002, www.just-auto.com (accessed August 1, 2002).

Maxton, G., and J. Wormald. *Driving over a Cliff: Business Lessons from the World's Car Industry.* Wokingham, U.K.: Addison-Wesley, 1994.

Maynard, M. "Amid the Turmoil, a Core Success." January 2001, http://web.lexis-nexis.com (accessed February 1, 2001).

McKinsey Global Institute. *Reaching Higher Productivity Growth in France and Germany, Sector Case: Automobiles.* Düsseldorf: McKinsey & Company, 1999.

Meeks, G. *Disappointing Marriage: A Study of the Gains from Merger.* Cambridge, U.K.: Cambridge University Press, 1977.

Mercer, Glenn. "Case Studies of Automobile M&A." Paper presented to the GERPISA Conference, Paris, June 7–9, 2001.

Milgrom, P., and J. Roberts. *Economics, Organization and Management.* Englewood Cliffs, N.J.: Prentice Hall, 1992.

Miller, Gary J. *Managerial Dilemmas: The Political Economy of Hierarchy.* Cambridge, U.K.: Cambridge University Press, 1992.

Mitani, Sam. "Mazda Cosmo Sport." *Road and Track,* April 2002, 78–84.

Motor Vehicle Manufacturers Association. *World Motor Vehicle Data, 1979.* Detroit: Motor Vehicle Manufacturers Association, 1980.

Mueller, Dennis C. "A Cross-National Comparison of Determinants and Effects of Mergers." In *The Modern Corporation: Profits, Power, Growth and Performance,* edited by Dennis C. Mueller. Brighton, U.K.: Wheatsheaf Books, 1986, 170–86.

———. "Mergers: Theory and Evidence." In *Mergers, Markets and Public Policy,* edited by G. Musati. Amsterdam: Kluwer, 1995, 9–43.

Niskanen, William. *Bureaucracy and Representative Government.* Chicago: Aldine, 1971.

Olson, Mancur. *The Rise and Decline of Nations.* New Haven, Conn.: Yale University Press, 1982.

Pal, N. *The New Beetle.* Case 9-501-023. Boston: Harvard Business School Cases, 2000.

Porter, Michael. *The Competitive Advantage of Nations.* New York: Free Press, 1990.

PricewaterhouseCoopers. *Global Automotive Deal Survey, 1998.* Bloomfield Hills, Mich.: PricewaterhouseCoopers, 1999.

———. *Automotive Sector Insights.* Bloomfield Hills, Mich.: PricewaterhouseCoopers, 2000.

———. *The Second Automotive Century.* Bloomfield Hills, Mich.: PricewaterhouseCoopers, 2000.

Purrington, C. *Chrysler and BMW: Tritec Engine Joint Venture.* Case 9-600-004. Boston: Harvard Business School Cases, 2001.

Scherer, F. M. *Industrial Market Structure and Economic Performance.* Chicago: Rand McNally, 1970.

———. *Industrial Market Structure and Economic Performance.* 3rd ed. Boston: Houghton Mifflin, 1990.

———. *Industry Strategy, Structure and Public Policy.* New York: HarperCollins, 1996.

Schumpeter, J. *Imperialism and Social Classes.* New York: Kell, 1951.

Servan-Schreiber, Jacques. *The American Challenge*. New York: Atheneum, 1968.

Sirower, Mark L. *The Synergy Trap*. New York: Free Press, 1997.

Sobel, Robert. *Car Wars: The Untold Story*. New York: Dutton, 1984.

Stern Stewart Research. *Best of Times, Worst of Times*. New York: Stern Stewart Research, 2001.

———. "M&A: Why Most Winners Lose." *Evaluation* 3, no. 4 (2001): 1–12.

St. George, A. *Mercedes-Benz in Alabama*. Case 9-199-026. Boston: Harvard Business School Cases, 1999.

Telser, Lester. *Economic Theory and the Core*. Chicago: University of Chicago Press, 1978.

Thucydides. *The Peloponnesian War*. Harmondsworth, U.K.: Penguin, 1954.

Transportation Research Institute. *The Contribution of the International Auto Sector to the US Economy*. Ann Arbor: University of Michigan, 1998.

Tsurumi, Y. *The Japanese Are Coming: A Multinational Spread of Japanese Firms*. Cambridge, Mass.: Ballinger, 1976.

U.S. Department of Commerce, Bureau of Economic Analysis. *GDP by Industry*, 2002, www.bea.doc.gov/bea/dn2/gpo.htm (accessed March 3, 2002).

U.S. Department of Justice, International Competition Policy Advisory Committee. *Final Report*, 2000, www.usdoj.gov/atr/icpac/finalreport.htm (accessed October 24, 2001).

Vernon, Raymond. *Sovereignty at Bay: The Multinational Spread of US Enterprises*. New York: Basic, 1971.

Vlasic, Bill, and Bradley Stertz. *Taken for a Ride: How Daimler Drove Off with Chrysler*. New York: Morrow, 2000.

Waldman, D., and E. Jensen. *Industrial Organization*. Reading, Mass.: Addison-Wesley, 1996.

Waller, David. *Wheels on Fire: The Amazing Inside Story of the Daimler-Chrysler Merger*. London: Hodder & Stoughton, 2000.

Williamson, Oliver E. *The Economic Institutions of Capitalism: Firms, Markets, Relational Contracting*. New York: Free Press, 1985.

Womack, J., D. Jones, and D. Roos. *The Machine That Changed the World*. New York: Simon & Schuster, 1990.

Wood, J. *Wheels of Misfortune: The Rise and Fall of the British Motor Industry*. London: Sidgewick & Jackson, 1988.

World Bank. *World Development Indicators*, 2002, www.worldbank.org/data (accessed September 1, 2002).

Index

Africa, 75–76
American Motors (AMC), 38–39. *See also* Chrysler; Renault
antitrust. *See* competition policy
Asia, 66–71
Asia Pacific Economic Cooperation (APEC), 71
Association of Southeast Asian Nations (ASEAN), 70–71, 119
Audi, 8, 53
Auto Union, 8, 53

Block Exemption, 88–89, 111–12. *See also* European Union; vertical integration
BMW, 8, 13, 53, 56, 58–59, 91
British Leyland, 7. *See also* Rover

capacity utilization, 37–40
cash reserves, 19, 123–25
chain store paradox, 82
China, 63, 66–71, 116–17
Chrysler, 13–14, 23, 39–40, 54, 58, 60–61, 94, 124–25. *See also* Daimler

Citroën. *See* Peugeot-Citroën (PSA)
collusion. *See* competition policy; monopoly; monopsony
commercial vehicles, 103–4
comparative advantage, 40–46, 68, 151n87
competition policy, 80–83, 88–89, 109–12
components makers, 84–85, 93–102, 137
cost sharing, 31–32, 35–37, 136
Covisint, 98–99. *See also* electronic markets
customs union, 74, 119–20. *See also* trade policy

Daewoo, 10–13, 55, 61, 71
Daimler, 1, 8, 13–14, 23, 36, 47–49, 56–61, 90, 124–28. *See also* Chrysler
developing countries, 11, 45–46, 61–76, 100–101, 119, 141–42
diseconomies of scale, 24, 33
distribution and sales, 32–34, 86–89

eastern Europe, 71–74
economies of scale, 24–35, 86–89, 135–36; in engine production, 30–31; pecuniary, 89
electronic markets, 96–99
European Union, 88–89, 104, 108, 110–15, 118

factor endowment, 41, 45–46
Fiat, 9, 12, 14–16, 55. *See also* General Motors (GM); Peugeot-Citroën (PSA)
Ford, 1, 7, 12, 54, 58, 71, 94
France, 9, 114
free trade area, 74, 119–20. *See also* trade policy
fuel cell technology, 36–37

General Agreement on Tariffs and Trade (GATT). *See* World Trade Organization (WTO)
General Motors (GM), 1, 5, 7, 11–13, 49, 51, 55, 62, 94. *See also* Daewoo; Fiat
Germany, 8, 83, 110–11, 114
government equity in auto companies, 114–17

Herfindahl index, 17
Honda, 10, 16
hubris, as merger motive, 127–29

imperialism, 121–22, 127–28
income, effect on auto demand, 65–66
infant industry, 62, 74, 118. *See also* trade policy
Internet, 96–99
Italy, 9, 115

Jaguar, 54
Japan, 9–10, 42–45, 76, 83, 117–18

keiretsu, 84–85. *See also* vertical integration

Latin America, 74–75, 119–20
labor unions, 39, 90–93
lean production, 42, 57. *See also* productivity

macroeconomic policy, 108–9
Mazda, 31, 49, 54
mercantilism, 3, 143n7
Mercedes-Benz. *See* Daimler
mergers: of components makers, 96–97; definitions of, 5; history of, 6–17; profitability of, 5, 59, 122–23
modular construction, 28–30, 36, 38, 99–100
monopoly, 80–83
monopsony, 89–102

national income, 4, 143–44n8
natural selection, 123–24
Nissan, 10, 48

oligopoly, 8, 83, 136, 143n1
organizational integration, 33–34
outsourcing, 28–30, 99–100

Peugeot-Citroën (PSA), 1, 9, 12
Porsche, 8, 30–31
portfolio diversification, 46–47, 102–4
power trains, 30–31
prisoners' dilemma game, 82
production, annual data, 2–3, *18–19*, 65–66
productivity, *27*, 41–45, 64
products, acquisition of as merger motive, 52–60
profitability of auto companies, 129–30, 140–41

Renault, 9, 38–39, 48, 71, 114
research and development (R&D), 35–37
robotic technology, 26

Rover, 7, 13, 39, 56, 59, 91–92, 115. *See also* BMW
Russia, 60, 71–74

Saab, 5, 25–26, 54–55
size maximization as merger motive, 121–31, 138
South Korea, 10–11, 61, 93, 109, 115–16
subsidies, by governments, 112–14
synergy, 58–60, 133–34

tariffs. *See* trade policy
technology, merger to acquire, 52–58
Toyota, 1, 10, 16, 57
trade policy, 69, 72–76, 81, 101–2, 117–20

unbundling, 134–36
United Kingdom, 6–8, 11–12, 91–92, 108–9, 115
United States, 7, 42–45, 76–77, 80–82, 92–93, 101–2, 112–13, 117–18
urbanization, effect on auto demand, 65–66

vertical integration, 83–89
Volkswagen (VW), 1, 8, 13, 53, 73, 114
Volvo, 54, 147n2

world car concept, 62
World Trade Organization (WTO), 4, 63, 67–70, 72–73, 116–17, 137

About the Author

John A. C. Conybeare is professor of political science at the University of Iowa, where he specializes in international politics and political economy. He has previously held faculty positions at Columbia University and the Australian Graduate School of Management. His book *Trade Wars* (1987) applied concepts of trade theory, bargaining games, and interest group lobbying to the explanation of a variety of trade conflicts from classical Greece to the present day. He has published in professional journals on a variety of subjects, including military alliances, war cycles, piracy, terrorism, tariff policy, bureaucratic budgeting, and global environmental issues.